A

CONCISE

HISTORY OF EDUCATION

TO 1900 A.D.

by

E.H. GWYNNE-THOMAS

School of Education
University of Missouri, Kansas City

UNIVERSITY
PRESS OF
AMERICA

LANHAM • NEW YORK • LONDON

Copyright © 1981 by

University Press of America,™ Inc.

4720 Boston Way
Lanham, MD 20706

3 Henrietta Street
London WC2E 8LU England

Library of Congress Cataloging in Publication Data

Gwynne-Thomas, E. H.
    A concise history of education to 1900 A.D.

    Bibliography: p.
    Includes index.
    1. Education—History. I. Title.
LA91.G94   370'.9   81-40315
ISBN 0-8191-1659-9   AACR2
ISBN 0-8191-1660-2 (pbk.)

PREFACE

This work is intended as an introductory survey of the more significant events in educational thought and institutional practice over the period extending from approximately 500 B.C. to A.D. 1900. It is intended that consideration of developments in the twentieth century be the subject of a subsequent publication.

Education represents merely one component of activity within the complex of any society, and, since no society can ever exist in splendid isolation either from its inherited past or from association with its immediate geographic contacts, it is appropriate that reference be made to apposite political, economic and cultural developments within the particular period being studied with respect to its educational developments. Hence, each chapter in this work is prefaced with a brief historical background, which the reader may readily supplement by reference to standard works of authority.

A major objective of the current project is to stimulate the reader into an analysis of existing educational systems, not merely with the view to the better comprehension of their status and function within the historical continuum, but also to provide such insight and perspective as will lead to a recognition of those desirable elements and concepts out of the past which should be preserved and applied to ensure further advance in the education of the future generation. It is hoped that the ample bibliography will encourage further research and study; since this is by no means exhaustive, reference should also be made to articles in encyclopedias and scholarly journals.

I wish to express my gratitude to Mrs. Sibyl Storm for her painstaking labors in typing and retyping the manuscript until it attained its final format.

E.H. GWYNNE-THOMAS

CONTENTS

CHAPTER ONE

GREEK EDUCATION

Introduction

A study of the cultures of the Ancient world reveals the inescapable fact that the Greeks were a unique people—that in almost every major dimension of human activity they made a distinct contribution towards the advancement of civilization. However, the intriguing mystery remains as to how and why so much was achieved by so few in so short a time.

Politically, the Greeks were unique since, not only did they never succeed in developing an empire, but they even failed to unify themselves into a consolidated national state under one ruler. Other peoples bordering the Mediterranean Sea—Egyptians, Assyrians, Babylonians, Medes, Persians, Romans—all created significant and centrally-governed empires, whereas the Greeks appear to have preferred the status of splendid isolation until the emergence of Macedonia, a formidable land power to the north, overwhelmed them militarily, an event which ultimately proved to be the catalyst whereby Greek culture came to be disseminated throughout almost the entire area of the Middle East. In the process, Alexandria was destined to displace Athens as the center of Greek culture.

The character of the physical configuration of the territory now known as Greece provides a substantial answer to the question as to why the

1

Greek peoples were never unified. Greece con-
sists of two mountainous peninsulas, the one
in the north, (so-called "mainland Greece")
rising to almost 10,000 feet (Mt. Olympus, 9700
feet; Mt. Parnassus, 8000 feet,) which is separated by the Gulf of Corinth from the smaller
peninsula in the south, (Peloponnesus or Morea)
of lesser elevation but still rugged. Settlements in both regions remain confined either to
small isolated plains along the coast, or to the
many islands which encompass the country. Consequently, hundreds of small city-states developed,
with economic and cultural contact one between
the other primarily established and maintained
by maritime intercourse.

Between the mid-eighth and mid-sixth centuries B.C., many of the city-states, possibly
by reason of pressure of acute over-population
upon the limited land resources, embarked upon
a remarkable program of overseas colonization
which eventually was to extend from beyond
Massilia (Marseilles) in the Western Mediterranean to Colchis at the eastern end of the
Black Sea, a distance of well over two thousand
miles. These activities brought the Greeks in
contact with a variety of different peoples and
must have appreciably contributed to the cosmo-
politan outlook of certain of the major cities,
notably Athens. Receptivity to new ideas, if
not encouraged, was certainly tolerated under
the flexible provisions of Greek religion, which
again were unique in the Ancient World.

Greek religion has been classified as being
a type of "anthropomorphic polytheism," which
may be translated as being a religion wherein its
communicants recognized a plethora of gods who
assumed normal human appearance. Presumably,
every conceivable aspect of mankind's activities
on earth was supervised by some god or other and

his innumerable progeny (the Heroes).[1] The gods in fact appeared to be human beings, very frail in all human frailties, exhibiting the vices of anger, jealousy, lust, deceit, lying, fickleness, and aggressiveness, but they were immortal and they did possess superior strength and wisdom and were, above all virtues, capable of intervening, either positively or negatively, in earthly affairs, and for that simple but overwhelming reason, they had to be placated by mortal beings. Unlike all other states in the Ancient World the Greeks had neither a centrally organized established church nor any formidable hierarchy of priests. In Athens there was even an "Altar to the Unknown God," a circumstance which enabled the apostle Paul on his proselytizing visit to that city to claim that he was the exclusive representative of that deity.

Despite the decentralized and disunified tenor of their existence, the Greeks, (and posterity), were still able to recognize a "Greek tradition" characterized by the use of a common written language, a common written literature, and a common acceptance of a traditional, legendary, heroic-type religion, which came to be reinforced by the pan-Hellenic "National" Olympic games (instituted in 776 B.C. and held in honor of Zeus) as well as the Pythian games (held in honor of Apollo at Delphi and initiated around 582 B.C.).

By 500 B.C. two rival major city-states had emerged to claim precedence and allegiance with-

---

1. Among the more prominent deities were:

Time:	CHRONOS	Agriculture:	DEMETER
War:	MARS	Wine:	DIONYSUS
Love:	APHRODITE	Heaven:	ZEUS

in the Greek-speaking lands. These were Athens
and Sparta, and they represented the ultimate
polarities in political (and consequently educational) experiment, with Athens having progressed
sequentially through monarchy, oligarchy, tyran-
ny to democracy, while Sparta deviated little
from a long established rigid, tyrannical, dual
monarchy. The two city-states pursued their
respective political experiments without undue
external interference until their isolation and
independence were rudely interrupted in 499 B.C.
by the rebellion of the Greek colonists in Ionia
against the new empire of Persia, which, after
the defeat of Croesus, King of Lydia, (in 546
B.C.) had come to occupy the entire territory
of Asia Minor.

Uncertain as to the degree of their direct
concern and involvement, the city states had
sent only meager aid to their Ionian kinsmen
who were defeated in 494 B.C., but even this
token assistance was regarded by the Persians
as ample excuse for a major invasion of Greece
itself. To their credit, the city states
responded in unison to this critical situation,
and for the one and only time in their entire
history they presented a united front against
the aggressor upon whom they inflicted major
defeats in the battles of Marathon (490 B.C.),
Salamis (480 B.C.) and Plataea (479 B.C.).

Regrettably, this unity did not endure, and
within a comparatively short time Athens and
Sparta became engaged in an exhausting long-
drawn out conflict, the Peloponnesian Wars (461-
404 B.C.), which proved disastrous to both.
First, Athens fell to Sparta (404 B.C.) and then,
in 371 B.C. at the battle of Leuctra, Sparta fell
to Thebes, and tragically, as a result of a century of internecine wars, the whole of Greece
fell to Persian domination with hardly the loss
of a single Persian soldier.

4

The final humiliation and disarray of the Greeks came with the invasion of their country by their northern neighbor, Macedonia. The Greek armies were defeated by the forces of Philip at the battle of Chaeronea in 338 B.C. Following Philip's assassination two years later, his son and heir, Alexander, mentored by Aristotle, developed an empire on his own, which, though partitioned after his death (323 B.C.) provided both Egypt (under the Ptolemies) and Syria-Palestine (under the Seleucids) with a substantial veneer of Greek culture for a further three centuries until the advent of the Romans.

Education

All the peoples of the Ancient World must each have possessed an educational system of some sort. The building of massive pyramids, temples, palaces, and irrigation systems, the emergence of hieroglyphic, cuneiform, and other varieties of written expression, the need for trained bureaucrats, lawyers, and priests to maintain empires—all these dimensions of normal living necessitated instruction and training of no mean caliber. While reasonable conjecture allows us to ascertain a broad outline of the content and form of these early experiments in education, in no single instance (prior to the emergence of the great city-states of Greece), was there ever an attempt to specify and clarify the precise nature of the particular philosophy which determined the objectives of education, nor is there extant any document which purports to provide curricular guidelines for the respective levels of instruction.[2]

What impelled the Greeks in general and the Athenians in particular to be so different will remain the great mystery of all time. But different they were, and within the incredibly brief period of less than two hundred years, commentaries were written, published, and circulated relevant to virtually every single domain of life —politics, economics, philosophy, medicine, mathematics, art, music, literature and education. As at all times prior to (and since)

---

2. The Old Testament of the Hebrews, and the Book of the Dead of the Egyptians provide aphorisms and axioms relating to the rearing of children, but neither set of writings can be remotely considered as an educational treatise.

6

this remarkable literary effulgence, education itself was implicitly a reflection of the societal structure either of a particular city state or of one or other of the idealised utopian republics formulated by some of the great Greek writers.

ATHENS

Athenian political society had been in turmoil during the sixth century B.C. A great impetus to the development of democracy had been provided in 594 B.C. by the constitution of the lawgiver and statesman, Solon, whereby propertied commoners as well as hereditary aristocrats were granted citizenship and the right to vote. The lower classes benefited still further from the actions of the tyrant Peisistratus (in power from 546 to 527 B.C.) since he distributed state lands among them, but the crowning achievement of the century was the constitution of Cleisthenes which, in 502 B.C. established direct democracy in Athens by granting all citizens the right to vote in the Assembly.[3] The Persian War then intervened, but with final victory ensured (by 479 B.C.) the Athenians felt free to occupy themselves in domestic affairs by debate and discussion both within and without the Assembly.

It was at this juncture that the Sophists appeared. Obscure in origin but presumably from Ionia, they were itinerant teachers who came to

---

3. Women and slaves were excluded from citizenship, and in practice probably less than one per cent of the Athenian population participated in the deliberations of the Assembly.

Athens and other cities professing to answer
the basic question in education, "What knowledge
is of most worth?" Their response was: "Knowledge of the art of presenting viewpoints in
public," obviously a very desirable acquisition
for, and of great appeal to, all Athenians attending the Assembly.

This art of Rhetoric, as it came to be
known, was well developed by the Sophists who,
on the one hand, guaranteed for a fee, to instruct the individual but inarticulate Athenian
in the preparation and presentation of a particular address or oration—but who also, on the
other hand, had no regard or scruple for the
particular merits of the actual content of the
speech. As far as the Sophists were concerned
the presentation could be a complete pack of lies,
half-truths, or pure propaganda. Their sole and
ultimate interest lay in masterful, demagogic,
public oratory, which, if, in their view, was
received with acclamation, was ample justification for their existence.

It was to this Sophist opportunist approach
that Socrates (c. 470-399 B.C.) strongly objected.
As the self-labeled "Gadfly of Athens" he insisted that his basic maxim, "Know Thyself,"
implied that the individual Athenian should not
only meticulously analyze arguments with respect
to their authenticity, as verified by all the
available facts and evidence, but that he should
also, with like care, scrutinize the legitimacy
of his personal motives and objectives in pursuing his particular standpoint. The Sophists
maintained that "Man is the measure of all things,"
an apothegm which Socrates considered to be
nothing less than undisciplined individualism,
and which he countered by advocating that Truth
was the ultimate measure, and that only by the
systematic, unending search for Truth by the use
of Reason (the Dialectic method) could a harmoni-
ous society ever develop.

Despite the plausible and superficial nature of their approach the Sophists did render a notable service by helping to break through traditional, stereotyped beliefs and ways of thinking, thus facilitating the emergence of the great original philosophers. It would appear, however, that Athenian society of the late fifth century was not prepared for such exposure of its frailties, imperfections, and prejudices as acclaimed by Socrates, in consequence of which he was eventually obliged to pay the ultimate penalty.

All that is known of Socrates is recorded in the writings of his pupil, Plato, (c. 429-347 B.C.), who likewise occupied himself with the investigation of the fundamental and basic question as to how Society could best be organized so that citizens could pursue goodness and truth and achieve happiness. To Plato the State was a positive institution which, if governed by reasonable and wise men, could and should ensure that its citizens contribute to the general welfare to the best of their abilities, and in so doing would come to enjoy the good life.

Since, in Plato's view, the State is the "individual writ large," then, just as the "soul" of each individual was considered by him to consist of three parts, so then did the State:

First, the rational part, was represented by the rulers, the philosopher-statesman, whose virtue was wisdom;

The second, the emotional or spirited part was represented by the warriors, whose virtue was courage;

The third, the desiring part, consisting of chaotic, uninhibited appetites was represented by the workers and producers, whose virtue was temperance and moderation.

9

Convinced that the foregoing classification
represented the ideal political arrangement,
Plato, in his Republic and other writings, (as
well as in his teaching at his 'school', the
Academy) elaborated upon the means and methods
whereby his ultimate objective was to be achieved.
The most potent instrument to be employed in this
process was that of Education, and it is Plato
who in history first formulated a detailed curriculum which literally extended from "the womb
to the tomb." Justification lay in his precept
"Virtue is Knowledge" and therefore could be
taught, but certain virtues were inferior to
others: Courage and temperance, based on "right
beliefs," were demonstratably low in the hierarchy whose acme was the virtue of wisdom, based
on reason. Only a minority of citizens were
capable of attaining the supreme virtue so that
yet another political precept was advanced:
that of "Wisdom for the few, and Justice for the
many."

While Plato's ideal "Republic" was most
certainly a class society, its apex was not a
hereditary aristocracy, as was typical of many
Greek city-states, but rather an aristocracy of
talent, identified through his carefully devised
scheme of education, which at well-defined inter-
vals incorporated a process of selection whereby
the less capable were systematically eliminated.
Plato's "aristocracy" was literally defined as
"rule by the best," i.e. those most capable of
assuming power and directing the entire affairs
of the State by the use of Reason.

In the Athens of his day, the education of
children was considered to be the private concern
of the individual family. Different categories
of schools [4] existed: the palaestra, which

4. The word 'school' originated with the Greek,
    "skole" - a place of leisure (for learning.)

10

focused upon physical education, (including proficiency in the events of the pan-hellenic games, such as running, jumping, wrestling, javelin and discus-throwing); the music school, where the student might have the opportunity to learn to play an instrument, as well as to dance; and the school of the grammatist, who provided instruction in the three R's. It was customary for a young child to be accompanied to school by a slave, who might well have been a well-educated prisoner of war awaiting ransom, and who could therefore, in his own right, function as a capable tutor. Be that as it may, the modern term "pedagogue" (for a teacher or educator) is precisely the term employed by the Greeks for a slave who performed the foregoing duties, and the unfortunate pejorative association between 'slave' and 'teacher' has bedeviled the latter's status ever since.

Plato was not satisfied with this casual and arbitrary system of education. Instead he advocated that the State take an active role in promoting and supervising a life-long planned course of instruction which, he envisaged, could be divided into distinct stages:

Stage 1: The Infant Stage: from birth to the age of 6 years, Plato laid stress upon the family as being the foremost educational agency in the upbringing of a young child. Learning at this stage was to be entirely informal with emphasis upon the inculcation of good health and social habits, and Plato provided ample advice to all persons desirous of becoming model parents. To such persons he first of all offered his own definition of education:

> Now I mean by education that training which is given by suitable habits to the first instincts of virtue in children, when the right pleasures and

11

pains, likes and dislikes are implanted in souls not yet capable
of understanding the nature of
them and who find them, after
they have attained reason, to be
in harmony with her.

Parents were to recognize that the young
child was a chaotic mass of uncontrolled impulses, desires, and instincts, all of which
needed to be reduced to order:

We do not allow children to be
free until we have set up a constitution in them...until by
nourishing the best in them, we
have provided a guardian to bear
rule within them....then we give
them their liberty.... The beginning is always the most critical
part of education....for in infancy,
more than at any time, the character
is implanted through habit.

Stage 2: Boyhood through Adolescence: 6
to 18 years. While the more formal subjects of
instruction were to be introduced during this
period, the main thrust of schooling was to be
placed upon character education. Since the
ultimate objective of all existence was to be
the Good Life, Plato insisted that if students
were expected to grow up to appreciate the good,
the beautiful, the virtuous, then the School
(and home) environment should be one which emphasized these attributes—in other words, the best
in education was "caught" rather than "taught."
In this, Plato fully recognized the natural im-
pulse of all students to imitate, and was fully
prepared to implement the foregoing principles
by nothing less than a state program of censorship. He was acutely aware of the power of
suggestion:

Without question, man's ultimate aim
should be to order all his affairs
from the lowest to the highest in
the cold clear light of reason. But
life cannot be suspended until that
ideal has been realized; and by suggestion the people obtain meanwhile
at least the partial vision without
which in literal truth they would
perish.

Plato expressed concern about many of the
unedifying episodes recorded in the Greek myths
and legends involving the Gods and Heroes. It
was not, in his view, at all appropriate that
students should be exposed to the reading and
study of the very questionable actions of the
deities, and for that reason, careful selection
of suitable passages in literature was mandatory.
Moreover,

The poets must be told to speak well
of that other world.... The first
principle to which all must conform
in speech and writing is that heaven
is not responsible for everything,
but only for what is good.

Plato approved of Music[5] as a subject in

---

5. In its broadest sense, Music signified any
    art presided over by one of the nine Muses,
    the daughters of Mnemosyne (the Goddess of
    Memory) and Zeus. These were:

CALLIOPE - Epic Poetry;   POLYHYMNIA - Singing
CLIO   - History;   TERPSICHORE- Dancing
ERATO   - Lyric Poetry   THALIA   - Comedy
           and mime: URANIA   - Astronomy
EUTERPE - Lyric Poetry
           and Music:
MELPOMENE- Tragedy;

the curriculum, but, again, with certain reserva-
tion. Music, he asserted, had an incalculable
influence upon the emotions: martial music could
rapidly arouse aggressive impulses, while sooth-
ing melodies could help relax and soften tension.
Obviously, then, there was always the danger
that subversive opinions accompanied by the
"wrong" type of music could quickly wreak havoc
and even imperil the very existence of the State.
Regulation was imperative, and Music was to be
judged according to the effect it tended to produce on character as well as to the amount of
pleasure derived by listening.

Plato concerned himself not merely with the
content of education, but also with the manner
of instruction, regarding which he tersely
commented:

> Knowledge which is acquired under
> compulsion obtains no hold on the
> mind. So do not use compulsion,
> but let early education be a sort
> of amusement.

Stage 3: Military Training, 18 to 20 years
of age.

Since the survival of the city-state depended upon adequate defense, conscription of its
young men, now endowed with appropriate moral
character and physical prowess, was necessary.

Stage 4: Higher Education, 20 to 30 years
of age.

This represented the period when, according
to Plato, serious academic studies should be embarked upon with a view to selection of those
citizens competent to direct or to assist in the
direction of the affairs of the State. In his
famous Allegory of the Cave he made very evident

14

the ultimate objective of education: prior to
being educated (in accordance with Plato's
principles) men could be envisioned as being imprisoned in a cave with their backs toward the
entrance (whence came the "Light") so that the
sum total of their experience lay in staring at
thickening shadows on the wall. Education could
therefore be interpreted as the process whereby
individuals in the cave could gradually be turned
around towards the entrance, so that the intellect
("soul") could be directed towards the "Light",
i.e., of Reality and Truth.[6]

Plato's conception of an adequate academic
curriculum was tripartite:

1) <u>Mathematics</u> — divisible into the
several components of Arithmetic,
Geometry, Astronomy, and the Elements of Musical Harmony.

2) <u>Dialectic</u> — the application of Reason
in argument for the purpose of eluci-
dating the nature of Truth.

3) <u>Philosophy</u> — the direct search for
"Wisdom," i.e. the guiding principles for the organization and
administration of the Good Society.

A selection examination at the age of thirty
decided which of those students should proceed
still further in academic pursuits, and which of

----

6. Probably at no time during the last two thousand years has Plato's Allegory of the Cave
been more applicable to a society than that
of the late Twentieth Century, when teachers
of the principles of the Light or Truth have
been so confronted, confused, and compromised
by the flickering shadows of unreality on the
television screen.

those students should terminate their studies and be delegated to the routine but yet essential duties of bureaucracy as civil servants.

Stage 5: <u>Advanced Education</u>: 30 to 35 years of age.

The most capable candidates were now to advance to their final academic period of studies during which they were to focus exclusively upon the acme of all disciplines: Philosophy—the nature of pure Knowledge, Truth, and Reality.

Stage 6: <u>The Elder Statesman</u>: 50 years of age and beyond.

By this time Plato considered that a sound balance had been achieved between theory and practice, and that the rulers were now eminently capable of making decisions entirely according to the dictates of Reason and not to any arbitrary personal whim or prejudice. Reluctant as they might be to assume power the Elder Statesmen (the so-called "Philosopher Kings") were each in turn to accept the responsibilities of government but without remuneration.

In formulating this comprehensive scheme, Plato recognized the intimate relationship between politics and education, and since he regarded it as an essential duty of the State to promote morality, he considered it imperative to put into operation an educational system which would ensure the emergence of altruistic and competent leaders.

His life-long plan placed emphasis in the earlier stages upon the family as a formative and stabilizing institution, upon which, the State could proceed to reinforce the building of character, and only when this was ensured could an intellectually rigorous program be instituted. Moreover, balance was to be sought between the academic, physical, and aesthetic dimensions of life so that the ultimate objective of education should be the development of the complete or "whole" human being.

Yet, commendable as were his ideas, their negative implications are apparent and cannot be ignored. Plato's ideal Republic was a class society in which probably at least ninety per cent of the citizens had no voice in the political, economic, or social decision-making processes which directly or indirectly concerned their welfare. It was also a society predicated upon the existence of a worker-slave class whose function it was to produce all the essential commodities; on-the-job vocational training was to be provided by craftsmen and trades-people, and not by the State.

Aristotle (384-322 B.C.), shared with Plato (whose student he was) the latter's views on many aspects of education. He firmly believed in the positive functions of the State as an institution ensuring the good life and happiness of its citizens, so that:

> Since the State...has but one aim, it is evident that the political education of all the citizens ought to be the same, and that this is a matter for the State to attend to, and not one to be left to individual caprice, as is now almost universally done, when every parent attends to the education of his own children and gives them whatever schooling suits his own fancy.

Aristotle advocated that the State determine what persons be permitted to marry,[7] the number of children they be allowed to rear, and whether defective children be exposed to die. Healthy children were to be taught to face hardship as early as possible:

> Children, on account of their high natural warmth are the proper subjects for inurement to cold.

But he was opposed to violent physical exercise and stated that:

> there are not more than two or three examples on record of persons having been victorious at the Olympic Games both as boys and men. The explanation of this is, that the others were robbed of their strength in their boyhood by the training they had to undergo.

Aristotle, in general, accepted the normal school curriculum of his day but although, like Plato, he advocated that some degree of censorship be imposed upon the use of improper language, stories, gestures, or pictures, he appeared to be in favor of allowing students to witness the great Greek dramas, whether comedy or tragedy, by reason of their cathartic influence upon the emotions which, in this way, could be trained to be subordinate to Reason.

Aristotle made the distinction between 'liberal' and 'illiberal' pursuits:

> it is manifest that only such knowledge as does not make the learner mechanical (vulgar) should form part of "liberal" education.

---

7. Aristotle considered that the ideal age of marriage for a man was 37, and for a woman, 18.

This was a viewpoint shared by all Greek
intellectuals, although Aristotle elaborated
upon this in his writings more so than did his
contemporaries. Commenting upon Music, for
example, as a school subject, he first of all
justified its inclusion even to the extent of
agreeing that students should be taught to play
certain of the instruments:

> ....Since people must, to some extent,
> learn things themselves in order to
> form a correct judgment about them,
> they ought to learn the practice of
> them while they are young, so that
> when they grow up, they may be able
> to dispense with it, and yet, through
> their early studies, be able to judge
> them correctly and take the proper
> delight in them.

He deplored any extension of instruction
which would tend to train the student to become
a "professional" musician:

> "professional" we call all instruction
> that looks toward public exhibitions
> (and) we hold that such practice is
> not proper for free men, but savors
> of meniality and handicraft. The
> aim, indeed, for which they under-
> take this task is an ignoble one,
> for audiences, being vulgar, are wont
> to change their music, and so react
> upon the character of the professionals
> who cater to their tastes, and this
> again has its influence upon their
> bodies, on account of the motions
> which they are obliged to go through.

Whether or not one concurs with Aristotle's
views on education, the fact remains that his

encylopaedic knowledge and interests were monumental and remain legendary:

> Aristotle is the Father of the Inductive
> Method and he is so for two reasons:
> First, he theoretically recognized its
> essential principles with a clearness,
> and exhibited them with a conviction,
> which strike the modern man with
> amazement; and then he made the first
> comprehensive attempt to apply them
> to all the science of the Greeks.
> (Wilhelm Oncken).

In his school, the Lyceum, he instructed his
students in the principles of the scientific classification of knowledge, and he later incorporated
his philosophic doctrines concerning the nature
of reality, truth, reason, and the divine, in his
famous books Metaphysics, Ethics, Politics, and
Logic, books which during the almost one thousand
years which elapsed between the fall of the Roman
Empire and the close of the Renaissance were the
most influential textbooks in the Western World.[8]

SPARTA

Sparta has represented the apotheosis of the
military state both during the period of Ancient
Greece as well as ever since. It was a city which
lived in constant fear, fear on the part of the
citizens lest the subject peoples (Helots) rebelled, and fear on the part of the latter lest
they be massacred. The proportion of citizens

---

8. The application of Aristotle's principles of
   logic to theology formed the basis of Scholasticism, associated with the period of the
   rise of the universities.

to slaves was only 1 to 20, and in this situation
which was one of ruthless suppression, rebellion
and massacre represented a way of life.

The education system reflected this tense
and grievous state of affairs. Sick children
were exposed to die soon after birth, while
healthy children were indoctrinated from an early
age that they existed only to serve the State in
whatsoever capacity it dictated. At the age of 7,
boys were removed from their families to boarding
schools, where austerity and rigorous discipline
were practised, and where unquestioning obedience
and loyalty were at all times demanded. Intellectual, creative, and aesthetic attainments were
placed at the lower end of the spectrum of educational priorities, since these were not essential
to survival.

At the age of 20, young men were conscripted
for ten years of active military service, after
which the honor of citizenship was conferred upon
them and they were expected to marry.

Girls in Sparta were likewise trained at
home or by the State to be subservient to the
demands of the Polis. Apart from their normal
domestic duties they were organized into groups
or packs for quasi-military training designed
to produce the patriotic, healthy mothers of the
future.

CHAPTER TWO

ROMAN EDUCATION

Introduction

753 B.C. is the traditional, legendary date of the founding of Rome. For the next half millenium the city was engaged first in throwing off its subjugation to the Etruscans, and then in the slow process of subduing its neighbor recalcitrant tribes. A major landmark was attained in the year 287 B.C. with the inception of a public Assembly, the Comitia Tributa, which gave equal rights to plebeians as well as patricians. Thus ensured of reasonable political stability at home, Rome could proceed with a program of expansion which was ultimately to make it the imperial capital of the Western World.

In the year 146 B.C. yet another landmark was passed not only with the complete destruction of its major rival, Carthage, but also with the reduction of Corinth, the last Greek city state to resist military domination. From this date onwards Rome proceeded to expand until the year 116 A.D. when the empire reached its ultimate limits: Northern England (eventually Hadrian's Wall), in the northwest, and the Gulf of Arabia in the southeast, representing a territory spanning almost half the known world at that time.

The translation in status of Rome from provincial city to imperial capital, responsible for the administration of an empire, lineally extending a distance of over 4,000 miles, placed incredible pressure and tension upon the decision-

making processes of a committee-like Assembly.
It was Julius Caesar whose assassination best ex-
emplifies the dilemma. Murdered in 44 B.C.[1]
having been accused of aspiring to an imperial
throne, he was ironically succeeded only 17 years
later by his avenger, Octavius, who assumed the
title of Augustus as well as that of Emperor.

Continuity in the imperial succession (though
not necessarily by heredity) was maintained until
the fall of Rome in 476 A.D., but by that date a
consolidated Roman Empire had long ceased to exist.
Faced by the ever-increasing problems of adminis-
tering such diverse territories from a single
center, Constantine decided in 330 A.D. to establish his city of Constantinople at a site nearer
to the disturbed areas of the empire. A little
earlier, in 313 A.D., he had been instrumental in
promoting the Edict of Milan which had accorded
toleration of worship to Christians throughout
the empire. This was a political gesture osten-
sibly designed to provide support for the regime
by religious dissidents, but the Christians themselves were so fragmented by "heresy" that the
intended marriage of church and state did not
evolve as envisioned.

Moreover, the division of the empire itself,
with its two major capitals, came to be more than

----

1. Five years earlier, following the conquest of
    Gaul, Caesar and his army had returned to
    Northern Italy but had then crossed the
    Rubicon River, (the frontier between Cisalpine
    Gaul and the directly Roman-administered ter-
    ritory of Italy), contrary to the mandate of
    the Roman Senate. He had occupied Rome and
    had then pursued his arch-enemy Pompey who was
    eventually defeated and killed in Egypt (48
    B.C.) leaving Julius Caesar as supreme com-
    mander in the Empire.

a mere territorial partition of administrative
and strategic convenience. Two entirely different
cultures were involved: that based on Rome disseminated Latin language, literature and tradition
throughout Western Europe, while that based on
Constantinople helped to evoke and revive the
Greek (Hellenistic) language, literature, and
tradition throughout the entire area bordering
the Eastern Mediterranean Sea. The twain never
met, and time merely served to exacerbate their
differences until the ultimate rift occurred
between the Roman Catholic and the Greek Orthodox
Churches with the Great Schism of 1053 A.D.

Aggressive "barbarian" attacks against the
Empire had begun during the latter half of the
third century A.D. but, for the most part, they
had been successfully resisted. In 376 A.D.,
however, permission was granted to the Visigoths
(under pressure from the Huns), to settle within
Roman-held territory. For the Western Empire,
this was the beginning of the end, since wave
after wave of migrant hordes from Eastern Europe
gradually overwhelmed the imperial domains.
After the elapse of precisely one hundred years
from this date, the last Western Roman Emperor,
Romulus Augustulus, was deposed, a relatively
minor episode in the history of the Roman Empire
since, in 476 A.D., Italy was under the control
of the Ostrogoths, Spain was ruled by the Visigoths, North Africa had fallen to the Vandals,
while Gaul was being invaded by the Franks. The
"Dark Ages" had begun.

Education

Preoccupied by problems of survival and
security for at least five hundred years after
its legendary foundation, Rome had nothing to
offer by way of literacy, aesthetic, or creative
written production at the end of that period, with
one major exception: The Laws of the Twelve
Tables, published about 450 B.C. gave ample evidence of the existence of acute, legalistic, and
rational intellects at work. This publication
remained virtually the sole school text for the
next two centuries or so, providing Roman youth
from a very early age with a firm grasp of the
state constitution and of its own civic and
domestic responsibilities, in conjunction with
the teaching of the rudiments of reading and
writing.

In the process of territorial expansion the
Romans had come into contact not only with a variety of primitive Latin tribes, but also with a
culture far superior to their own. Small yet substantial Greek colonies had been established in
the Western Mediterranean Basin earlier than 700
B.C. as at Massilia (Marseilles) in Southern
France, Naxos in Sicily, and Cumae, mother-city
of Neapolis (Naples), in Central Italy. In fact,
the greater the expansion of Rome, the more inevitable became the increasing contact and intercourse with Greek culture, so that when, in 241
B.C., (following the defeat of Carthage in the
first Punic War) Rome acquired its first province,
Sicily, it did, in effect acquire an island with
Greek architectural monuments of such advanced
design and noble proportions as to have excited
the Romans with unsuppressible emotions of aston-
ishment and wonder.[2]

----
2. It is true that most likely the Romans on
    their way south from Rome would have passed
    the three magnificent Doric temples at
    Paestum (near Salerno) constructed by Greek
    settlers from Sybaris.

It was to be expected that Greek prisoners of war would be employed as slaves, and the more educated would find service as teachers (precisely as had happened at an earlier date in Athens). It is on record that at the time of the Roman acquisition of Sicily, the <u>Odyssey</u> had already been translated into Latin by a slave named Livius Andronicus from the Greek city of Tarentum (captured in 272 B.C.). Other texts soon followed so that young Romans, taught by Greek teachers using the Greek classics, came to know and possibly appreciate far more of Hellenistic culture, history and tradition than they did of their own. Since the Greek language had become the lingua franca of the Eastern Mediterranean, it was also of no little advantage to the Romans, as they expanded their empire, to gain skill in speaking that language so that they could better communicate with, as well as better administer the territories of, the subject peoples.

There remained one further significant contribution of the Greeks to Roman culture. Since, as in Athens, the Romans had established a citizen Assembly, it was imperative that participants in discussion and debate of major political issues be competent in the arts of articulation, presentation, and persuasion, so that their respective points of view could be understood and appreciated by their colleagues. Thus Rhetoric[3] became as important a subject in Roman schools as it had been during the Golden Age of Athenian hegemony in the Greek world.

Of all early Roman Rhetoricians by far the best remembered is Cato (234-149 B.C.) whose incessant hysterical fulminations against Carthage were concisely summarized in his terse but for-

----

3. Well defined as "the art of thinking on one's feet."

ever memorable refrain: <u>Delenda est Carthago</u>
("Carthage must be destroyed"). He died only
three years before his proclaimed objective was
achieved. In the year of his death, Cato had
published a history of Rome called <u>Origenes</u>, a
major landmark, since it was the first Roman historical treatise to be written in Latin and not
Greek.

Cicero (106-43 B.C.), who had traveled and
studied in Greece and the Middle East, was a
gifted and versatile speaker and writer. He was
an uncompromising proponent of honesty in government and public affairs, and he risked his life
in the unrelenting pursuit and exposure of corruption and self-profit on the part of certain
Roman politicians and administrators. He is possibly best remembered for his essays on such
topics as old age (De Senectate), friendship (De
Amicitia), public duties (De Officiis) and on
the functions of the orator (De Oratore). This
last work, published in 55 B.C., is assumed to
be a compendium of advice for his own son, Marcus,
and its general theme is the necessity for a
broad and well-rounded education in the liberal
arts to provide the basic knowledge for a scholarly, instructive speaker seeking to advance the
interest of the public domain rather than that
of his personal, self-motivated ambitions. His
writings gained such prominence as to be subject
of a famed Latin axiom for students: <u>ut quisque
erit Ciceroni simillimus</u> (study other authors
only in so far as they resemble Cicero).

By far the most outstanding of Roman teachers
was Quintilian (35-97 A.D.). Born in Spain, but
educated in Rome, he became an instructor of
Rhetoric and was among the first recipients of
state remuneration for teachers, a policy initiated by the emperor Vespasian. <u>His most seminal
publication was his Institutio Oratoria</u> (The
<u>Institutes of Oratory</u>), the first significant
practical treatise on education in the West.

Quintilian asserted that the good orator should
also be a person of good character, so that his
gifts and talents as an influential persuasive
speaker should not be misdirected and lead to
the corruption of, and false reasoning by, his
audience.

Quintilian formulated a set of guidelines
of instruction designed to achieve the foregoing
objective, with character education emphasized
throughout. From ages one to seven years, the
growing child was most in need of responsible
parents, competent tutors, and sociable companions. Particular attention at this stage should
be given to the attributes of correct speech
since harmful or undesirable dialect and language
assimilated during infancy were most difficult
if not impossible to eradicate in later years.

Formal schooling was recommended from the
age of seven, and, as a practicing teacher of
long experience, Quintilian recognized the advantage of small classes so that individual abilities, interests, and needs might be better identified, and more appropriate instruction thereby
provided for each member of the class. The
teacher at the elementary school stage, (the ludi
magister), was exhorted to keep his students
actively learning by encouragement and praise,
and by making his lessons interesting so far as
was possible, and not by resort to corporal
punishment.[4] Moreover,

> If a boy's composition were so faulty
> as not to admit of correction, I have
> found him benefited whenever I told
> him to write on the same subject again,
> after it had received fresh treatment
> from me, observing that 'he could do

---

4. "No man should be allowed too much authority
   over an age so weak and so unable to resist
   ill treatment."

still better,' since study is cheered
by nothing more than hope....above
all, a 'dry' master is to be avoided,
not less than a dry soil for plants
that are still tender.

A child's health was important so that play
and gymnastic training should form an integral
part of the school day.

Quintilian advocated the teaching of both
Greek and Latin, and stressed the value of the
memorization of appropriate passages of poetry
or literature to serve as models of correct,
apposite, and beautiful language.

At secondary school level, and taught by the
"grammaticus," the student was now to develop his
reasoning powers to the utmost of his ability.
Literary exposition, analysis, and criticism were
to be introduced, along with a wider range of
subjects, to include history, philosophy, astronomy, geometry, and music.

At the time when Quintilian wrote, Rome had
developed a substantial literature of its own.
In the field of history there were the writings
of Caesar, Livy, Sallust, Tacitus, and Pliny.
The greatest of all Latin poets, Virgil, had died
in 19 B.C. and his famous epic, the Aeneid, was
already a classic, as were the Odes of Horace,
his contemporary, while the prolific writings of
Cicero provided students of prose and speech with
ample material for intellectual digestion.

At the age of sixteen or seventeen, young
men who had demonstrated competency could enter
the school of the rhetor to be trained as orators.
The subject disciplines were to be extended to
incorporate law, logic, and ethics:

It is the perfect orator that we are
training and he cannot even exist

unless he is a good man. We therefore demand in him not only excep-
tional powers of eloquence but also
every mental excellence.

Such a trained person would be fitted:

....to take his share in the management of public and private affairs,
able to govern cities by his wise
counsels, to establish them upon a
sure foundation of good laws, and
to improve them by the administration of impartial justice.

Apart from the spread of schools of Rhetoric
in Rome two other developments of significance
occurred in due course. In the first place, concern for, and patronage of, education by the
emperors (subsequent to Vespasian), had led to an
increase in control, such that by the reign of
Theodosius (379-385 A.D.) virtual complete state
monopoly and supervision were imposed. Secondly,
two types of professional schools slowly came
into being, those of medicine and law, respectively.

The medical profession still accords to the
Greek physician, Hippocrates of Cos, a place of
honor in its annals. Hippocrates, a contemporary
of Socrates, taught at the shrine of Asclepius,
and according to the writings of his disciples,
laid the firm foundation in the principles of
clinical procedures. The Greeks also developed
a form of public health service, so that a substantial basis of studies in the field of
medicine was available to Rome when those interested in the profession came to take up
practice. Galen (130-200 A.D.), a Greek from
Pergamum, but settled in Rome, appreciably
advanced the cause of medicine by his research
in anatomy, while Dioscorides, a Greek army
surgeon in Nero's army wrote a <u>Materia Medica</u>

which justifiably allows claim to his being the
Father of Pharmacy.

Just as the Greeks of antiquity made a notable and enduring contribution in the field of
philosophy, so did the Romans in the domain of
law. Almost a thousand years were to elapse
between the publication of the <u>Laws of the Twelve
Tables</u> (c. 450 B.C.) and the <u>Institutes</u> and <u>Digest</u>
of Justinian (529-534 A.D.), and during this
period a substantial corpus of written materials
by way of laws, constitutions, case studies, court
rules and procedures, texts and commentaries had
become available in libraries and archives for
all persons bent on a legal and/or political
career.

As the Roman Empire had expanded, so had contact with "barbarians"—the Celts and Germanic
peoples in the west, the Greeks, Hebrews, Persians
and Egyptians to the east—all with their own
traditional laws and customs, many of which con-
flicted diametrically with those which had been
formulated by their conquerors. Accommodation
and compromise became imperative, a situation
recognized by the Romans in the initial two-fold
categories of Law, the <u>ius</u> <u>civile</u>, which was to
apply to Roman citizens, and the <u>ius</u> <u>gentium</u>, to
all others.

While there were no schools of law as such,
it may be accepted that competent practitioners
in the field would attract a congerie of prospective apprentices, to whom the master jurist
would assign research in case study and precedent
and who would, at the same time, expect intellectual familiarity with the writings of some of
the famed Roman legal commentators, including
Cicero, Gaius, and Ulpianus.

That so much in Western European legal tradition is based upon Roman law remains as the
lasting tribute to the monumental achievement of
the Romans in this complicated and exacting dimension of imperial administration.

CHAPTER THREE

EARLY CHRISTIAN EDUCATION

Introduction

The city founded by Constantine as his eastern
capital of the empire was to endure almost a thousand years after the political demise of Rome in
476 A.D. until it ultimately fell to the Turks in
1453 A.D. But it was a bulwark of Greek rather
than of Roman civilization, and its very existence
served to emphasize the unresolved conflict and
persistent rivalries between East and West until
its civilization was obliterated by the Ottoman
hordes.

Justinian (527-565 A.D.) had attempted to re-
create the Roman Empire, and, in sequence, he
successfully destroyed the Vandal Empire in North
Africa, forced the Ostrogoths out of Italy, and
had siezed Southern Spain from the Visigoths.
His successors were, however, unequal to the task
of consolidating and extending these conquests,
particularly when, within a hundred years of his
death, two major waves of invasion threatened to
overwhelm the Eastern Empire.

The first was that of the Slavs who slowly
and relentlessly were moving westwards out of
Asia into the Danube Valley and the Balkan Peninsula, much of which they came to occupy permanen-
tly, so that in due course the entire region of
Central Europe was to emerge as the great zone of
disputed territory between the Teutonic peoples
in the west and the Slavs in the east. The second
wave was that of the Arab Moslems who, after the

death of Mohammed in 632 A.D., proceeded to destroy the Persian Empire in the east and then turned west along North Africa, whence they moved northwards into Spain and France where they were defeated by the Franks in 732 A.D. Forced back into Spain, they were not finally subdued until the fall of Granada in 1492.

The (Byzantine) Empire in the east was therefore fully occupied in a struggle for survival throughout its entire existence after the death of Justinian, so that it little involved itself in the affairs of the West. The latter, in contrast, after the convulsive turmoil of the fifth and sixth centuries A.D. proceeded to restore comparative order out of chaos, the dominating agents in this process being the Teutonic Franks. Clovis, their initial aggressive leader, established Paris as a major city (508 A.D.), while less than three hundred years later, Charlemagne was to rule an empire extending from the Elbe to the Ebro. It was unfortunate for the subsequent peace of Western Europe that upon the breakup of this empire (under the terms of the Treaty of Verdun, 843 A.D.) the separate territories now known as France and Germany came into existence, along with an indeterminate intervening zone between them, labeled Lotharingia,[1] which owed allegiance to neither, and was subsequently claimed by both, resulting in discord and conflict which were to endure for more than a thousand years.

France emerged as the first great nation-state in Western Europe although not until centuries later were its rulers able to consolidate into one domain all the territory now

----

1. Lotharingia extended from the North Sea southwards along the Rhine and Rhone Valleys into central Italy.

recognized as being French. Viking invasions had
ravaged the entire coastland areas bordering the
Atlantic Ocean, and one formidable group of
Northmen had forced the French Kings to cede the
lower Seine Valley to them, thus creating the
province of Normandy, whence, in 1066, they invaded England, and there they proceeded to create
a powerful island state.

In Spain, the long and arduous task of evic-
ting the Moslems led to the founding of separate
regional kingdoms whose refractory attitudes
delayed unification until the late fifteenth century. In Italy, the creation of the Papacy as a
temporal power extending from Rome to Ravenna (in
consequence of the famous Donation of Pepin in
756 A.D.) led to the division of the country into three parts, (each with a different, separate,
though interrelated history), which resisted
merger in a united kingdom until 1870.

Separatism was also a characteristic feature
of the German States, whose rulers appear to have
lacked the determination and tenacity required to
force national unity upon the large disparate
territory which lay between the Rhine and the
Elbe. Bestowal of the title, (Holy) Roman
Emperor, by Pope Leo III upon Charlemagne in 800
A.D. did little for his German successors elected
by their peers, who frequently chose the weakest
among themselves to avoid domination. In time,
the strongest states came to be those on the
eastern border since they were perpetually menaced
by aggressive Magyars and Slavs, and were obliged
to set up their military defenses accordingly.

During these centuries of political disturb-
ances the one institution which retained its
power and prestige was the Christian Church
centered in Rome. Despite the collapse of the
political Roman Empire, the Church had not only
maintained its extensive organization and hierarchical structure, but was progressively

gaining converts among the heathen conquerors, although it was disturbed by the extent to which heresies (particularly Arianism[2]) appeared to prevail.

A major political issue which rent the Christian world was the question of the status of the Pope in Rome as compared with the leaders of the great churches in the East, notably those of Constantinople, Antioch, Jerusalem, and Alexandria, all of whom claimed parity with Rome, a claim strongly resisted and resented by the Papacy.[3]

The latter suffered from the disadvantage of having no strong power in the West as sponsor and patron comparable to the support given to the Patriarchs of Constantinople by the Byzantine Emperors, and there is little doubt that it was this state of affairs which Pope Leo III intended to remedy when he crowned Charlemagne as the (Western) Roman Emperor. This action obviously served to exacerbate rather than reconcile the contending parties, to the extent that in 1053, the year of the Great Schism, Europe came to be divided into Western Roman Catholic Christians and Eastern Greek Orthodox Christians. In less than twenty-five years following this event Jerusalem had fallen to the Seljuk Turks (1077 A.D.). The Crusades which followed represented

----

2. The term Arianism derives from Arius, a presbyter (church elder) of Alexandria who held that Christ was not God. Arianism was declared a heresy at the Council of Nicaea, 325 A.D.

3. Valentinian III gave recognition to the Bishop of Rome as supreme in the West in 445 A.D. He was then called Pope (Papa=Father). The Papacy made its first claim to primacy in the entire Christian world c. 490 A.D.

in essence a deplorable sequence of episodes in which Western Christians literally did their damnedst to wreak havoc among their Eastern co-believers in Christ, and they performed this objective so successfully that in 1453 Constaninople fell irretrievably to Turkish Moslems, while Jerusalem almost a thousand years later, remains not in any way a "Christian" city, but rather a location destined for perpetual dispute between Arab and Jew.

Education

As indicated in the foregoing section, by 476 A.D., the date of the final dissolution of the Western Roman Empire, the Christian Church was a well-established territorial institution with a recognized hierarchy in both Italy and France. Consequently, during the succeeding centuries of political turmoil and turbulence, it stood out as the sole, effective institution sustaining the elements of learning and culture upon which subsist any semblence of civilization. In the task of achieving this formidable objective two dimensions may be distinguished:

The first was composed of the churches themselves where the priests undertook the task of instructing prospective members of the congregation in catechumenical schools. In time, demand for more advanced instruction in Christian thought and doctrine led to the development of catechetical schools, some of which in the East became prestigious centers of learning associated with the great early Christian period scholars, including Origen (Alexandria), Chrysostom (Antioch), Eusebius (Caesarea) and Nestorius (Edessa). The second dimension, originating from the ascetic desert traditions of the Middle East, was that of monasticism. Communities of persons wishing to withdraw from society in order to devote their time to religious contemplation became common first in Egypt where St. Anthony and Pachomius initiated the movement during the fourth century A.D. St. Basil extended it to Greece, while in the west, this new type of institution gradually became established as a result of the work and energy of St. Athanasius in Rome, John Cassianus at Marseilles, St. Honoratus on the island of Lerins in Southern France and St. Martin at Tours. By far the most influential personality was the Italian monk, Benedict of Nursia who (traditionally) founded in 529 A.D. a monastery at Monte

Cassino, which became the parent institution of the Benedictine Order. The Rule of St. Benedict required that each monk should work and pray, as well as observe mandates relating to chastity, poverty, and obedience. It was further recommended that each monk read the Bible daily.

Great uncertainty prevailed among the early Christians as to the extent to which classical literature should be studied. Many of their leaders, including Origen, Jerome, and Augustine, had themselves been educated in "pagan" schools and were thoroughly familiar with the works of the great Greek and Latin authors. At first, after making some attempt to reconcile pagan and Christian literature and philosophy, the Christian fathers ultimately rejected the classical authors. The Fourth Council of Carthage (398 A.D.) expressly prohibited the reading of secular material but this edict was obviously not universally observed since two centuries later Pope Gregory the Great found it necessary to declare that liberal studies encouraged dissent and heresy and again decreed that classical works be banned.

Long before this pronouncement, however, there had been wide-spread fear among Christian and pagan alike, that the barbaric invasions would destroy all culture,[4] and appreciable efforts appear to have been made to publish and make available a considerable number of new writings designed to preserve knowledge as well as to advence it.

----

4. That these fears were not entirely without substance may perhaps be confirmed by the lamentation of Gregory of Tours (who wrote a History of the Franks, c 591 A.D.) complaining that he could find no one in Gaul capable of reading, writing, or understanding Latin.

During the fourth century, Aelius Donatus, a Rhetoric teacher in Rome, published a Latin Grammar (the Ars Minor) which served as a basic text for centuries, as did the Institutio de Arte Grammatica of Priscian (c. 526 A.D.). Some authors favored the extensive compilation of all learning, and in successive centuries (the fifth, sixth, and seventh, respectively), "encyclopaedias" were sequentially published by Martiannus Capella, Cassiodorus, and Isidore of Seville.

It was Martiannus Capella, who, in a book entitled the Marriage of Philology and Mercury, formalized the seven-fold concept of the Trivium and Quadrivium dimensions of the classical and mediaeval curriculum, a concept which Cassiodorus, a century later, found to be in accordance with a Biblical reference: Proverbs (IX, 1): "Wisdom builded her house; she has hewn out her seven pillars." As noted earlier, the classical Seven Pillars were grammar, rhetoric, dialectic, music, arithmetic, geometry, and astronomy. During the (so-called) Dark Ages, the Trivium gained precedence over the Quadrivium except that, in the first place, there was found little need for rhetoric, and (Latin) grammar came to be progressively taught as a foreign language; secondly, Music was accorded an unexpected amount of study with emphasis upon singing and hymnology, notably advanced by the "discovery" in the eighth and ninth centuries of melodious harmony arise out of part-singing techniques. Astronomy was ignored, while arithmetic and geometry, virtually incomprehensible under Roman numeration, awaited the introduction in later centuries of the Arabic method of computation.[5]

----

5.   Augustine of Hippo declared that, while he could add and subtract using Roman numerals, he found it impossible to multiply and divide.

Cassiodorus (c. 480-575 A.D.) served as
secretary at the court of Theodoric, King of the
Ostrogoths in Italy. A Christian, he founded a
monastery in southern Italy, where he set aside
a scriptorium, a room in which manuscripts were
copied and bound, and it was due to his initiative
in this respect that monasteries subsequently
founded came to be the repositories of most
learning during the Dark Ages.

His colleague, Boethius (c. 480-524 A.D.),
minister to Theodoric, conceived the virtually
impossible idea, for one person, of translating
the entire works of Plato and Aristotle into
Latin. Unfortunately, he fell out of favor and
was accused of (and later executed for) treasonable activities, but, yet, during his short lifetime, he did produce translations and commentaries
of considerable value to scholars of a later age.

Jerome (c. 340-420 A.D.), was born of
Christian parents in Dalmatia. He went to Rome
and was a student of Donatus. He then traveled
widely in Gaul and the Eastern Mediterranean
lands where he produced the Vulgate, his famed
Latin translation of the entire Bible.

Augustine (c. 354-430 A.D.) was a native of
North Africa who lived the normal, epicurean,
life of a young man of his day and age. He
became a teacher of rhetoric at Rome, being
strongly influenced by the works of Plato and
Aristotle, but following a visit to Milan he
fell under the sway of the great Bishop Ambrose,
and for some time afterwards was torn between
the demands of the flesh and spirit, typfied in
his plea: "O Lord, give me chastity, but not
yet." In the year 387 A.D. he was baptised into the Christian Church by Ambrose and he returned to North Africa eventually to become
Bishop of Hippo. Like St. Paul, he was a
prolific writer and no fewer than two hundred
of his letters alone have been preserved. In

410 A.D. Rome was sacked by Alaric the Visigoth,
and it was this tragic event which apparently
prompted and inspired Augustine to write the
twenty-two books which make up his monumental
work, De Civitate Dei (The City of God), in which
he compared the status of mankind on earth with
that in the eternal City of Heaven. Concerning
himself intimately with the problem of Reason
versus Faith, he concluded that the need for
Faith was uppermost, and that when firm belief
had been established, understanding followed
and came naturally. Consequently, the entire
goal of education should be to strengthen Faith.

Another Christian contemporary, John
Chrysostom (c. 347-404 A.D.) emphasized in his
work, Concerning the Education of Children, the
importance of the home and family in the inculcation of good moral precepts in the child which
should in time serve it well in the choice of
an eligible mate and lead to a happy Christian
marriage.

The Visigoth sack of Rome in 410 A.D. had
momentous consequences upon the north-western
outpost of the Empire, Britain. The island had
been visited by Caesar in 55 and 54 B.C. but had,
thereafter, been ignored by the Romans for almost a century until in 43 A.D., Claudius
initiated its systematic conquest. In due course,
the Celtic-Britons had become Roman-Britons,
although only in England and Wales, since the
Romans failed to conquer Scotland (setting up
their boundary at Hadrian's Wall, constructed
c. 125 A.D.) and also never even set foot in
Ireland. It is uncertain as to how and when
the Christian religion was introduced into
Britain, but it is on record that a Conference
at Arles (314 A.D.), summoned by Constantine,
was attended by three bishops from the island,
those of London, York, and Lincoln (or possibly
Colchester).

Roman legions were withdrawn after 410 A.D.
leaving the inhabitants of Britain entirely to
their own military resources, so that the island
became the target of invasion by the northern
Germanic tribes of the continent, commencing with
the Saxons, the Jutes, and the Angles (who subsequently were to bestow their name upon the
country as Angle-land = England).

The remarkable fact remains that, despite the
turmoil, the Christian faith survived, although
the Papacy had soon good reason to become concerned with certain unorthodox practices and
beliefs which had manifested themselves in the
course of the political isolation of the islands.
A Celtic monk and scholar, Pelagius, having
visited Rome in 400 A.D., had been so shocked by
the corruption and immorality of Christians in
the city that he set up a reform movement and a
body of teaching which was contrary to the accepted beliefs of the Roman Church. Pelagius denied
the concept of original sin, the necessity for
the baptism of infants, and he raised again the
religious controversy of Grace versus Free Will.

The Roman Church became alarmed at the
spread of this "heresy" and it is believed that
St. Patrick (c. 389-461 A.D.) was dispatched from
Gaul (or Britain) to Ireland in 432 A.D. for the
purpose of disseminating the "true faith." The
absence of large towns in Ireland encouraged the
development of monastic communities, and for
centuries later the island was isolated. Yet
its monks produced one of the finest mediaeval
illuminated manuscripts in existence: the first
four books of the New Testament, known as the
Book of Kells.

In South Wales, the small but vigorous Celtic
Church set up "colleges" associated with the names
of St. Padarn, St. Cadoc, and St. David (the
patron saint of Wales),[6] where young Christians
----
6. The term "saint" at this period indicated not
    merely a "holy man" but also a man of learning.

42

were trained to become priests and missionaries.

In Northwest England, St. Columba set up a famed monastic community on the island of Iona, and its influence spread to the equally famed monastic establishments in Northumbria, at Jarrow and the island of Landisfarne, respectively. It was at the latter named monastery that another priceless illuminated manuscript, the Gospel Book of Landisfarne was produced (c. 700 A.D.).

Pope Gregory the Great (594-604 A.D.), concerned with the isolation of Britain from the mainstream of the Catholic world, decided to send Augustine to the island, and it was the latter who, in the year 597 A.D., established the mother institution of the Christian faith in England, the church (as well as school) of Canterbury, in (the modern county of) Kent. For the next half century debate and controversy raged between the Celtic and the Roman Churches, regarding the respective merits of their rituals and practices, a conflict more or less resolved at the Synod of Whitby (663 A.D.) which concluded with the overall acceptance by the Christians in Britain of the orthodox ordinances of the Roman Church.

Much of our knowledge of the events of this period is due to the research of one man, the Venerable Bede (c. 673-735 A.D.), who wrote the Ecclestiastical History of the English Nation. Born near the Benedictine monasteries of Wearmouth and Jarrow he became a student at the age of seven, and developed as a good scholar with a particular interest in history, noting that:

> If history relates good things of good
> men the attentive hearer is excited to
> imitate that which is good, or if it
> mentions ill things of wicked persons,
> nevertheless the religious and pious
> hearer or reader, shunning that which
> is hurtful or perverse, is the more

43

excited to perform those things which
he knows to be good, and worthy of God.

Bede wrote commentaries on the works of
Augustine and Jerome, he surveyed the lives of the
Christian saints, and published a Chronology of
World Events, as well as several texts on grammar.
It was one of his students, Archbishop Egbert, who
founded the cathedral school at York, attended by
another great educator of the period, Alcuin (735-
804 A.D.), whose name is ever associated with that
of Charlemagne.

The western Franks under Clovis had already
found it expedient to accept the Christian faith
but those in the east remained pagan and it was to
them that in 719 A.D. Pope Gregory II sent an
English Benedictine priest, Wilfred, (later known
as Boniface). He accomplished prodigious work
such that he reformed the entire Frankish Church
by organizing bishoprics and councils and was himself appointed as Archbishop of Mainz in 748 A.D.
Gradually the Frankish Kings came to appreciate
the political as well as the cultural advantages
of a well organized Christian Church within their
realms so that when Charlemagne, aware of the need
for competent administrators,[7] met Alcuin in Rome

----

7.   In a Capitulary of 787, Charlemagne stated:

....there has arisen in our minds the
fear lest, if the skill to write rightly were
thus lacking, so too would the power of rightly
comprehending the Sacred Scriptures be far less
than was fitting, and we all know that though
verbal errors be dangerous, errors of the
understanding are yet more so. We exhort you
therefore not only not to neglect the study of
letters, but to apply yourselves thereto with
perserverence and with that humility which is
well pleasing to God so that you may be able
to penetrate with greater ease and certainty
the mysteries of the Holy Scriptures.

he siezed upon the opportunity to offer him a
position at the royal court at Aachen, an invi-
tation which Alcuin accepted. He proved himself
an excellent teacher at the palace school, preparing Latin texts, popularizing script writing,
and further developing a manuscript library in
which Charlemagne had shown considerable interest.
At a later date Alcuin became abbot of the monastery of Saint Martin at Tours, where he also set
up a school.

The monastic institutions gradually withdrew
from the task of education, and the Council of
Aachen in 817 expressly prohibited monastery
schools other than for oblates, that is, those
serious in their intent to devote their lives as
monks. The role of the organized church therefore commensurately increased, and in 826 the
General Council of Pope Eugenius demanded that:

> All bishops shall bestow all care
> and diligence both for their subjects
> and for other places in which it shall
> be found necessary, to establish mas-
> ters and teachers who shall assiduously
> teach grammar schools and the principles
> of the liberal arts, because in these
> chiefly the commandments of God are
> manifested and declared.

The Council of Rome of 853 advocated that
every parish should set up a school for the
teaching of religion and that every cathedral
should establish a school for the teaching of the
liberal arts, making it very evident that by this
date, the Church was coming to recognize that
there was in existence a valid corpus of knowledge, with which its men of learning should be
familiar and should take into account in their
reading of the Scriptures and their propagation
of the Christian faith. Although yet a few centuries ahead, the vision of the development of

major centers of learning, the universities, was now just a little beyond the horizon. The delay was occasioned by the collapse of Charlemagne's empire, and not until relative political stability could be restored were conditions once more favorable and conducive to the furtherance of intellectual objectives.

CHAPTER FOUR

THE RISE OF THE UNIVERSITIES

Introduction

In the year 1200 A.D. the University of Paris
obtained its charter, the first academic school to
be so elevated in Western civilization. The two
hundred years which span each side of this significant date represents a fascinating period of
study for the historian engaged in research into
the origins of the many concepts and institutions
considered as being typical and representative of
the period, including those of feudalism, chivalry,
guilds, banking, capitalism, heresy, academic freedom, scientific inquiry, as well as all the terms
associated with the development of the university
itself.

The feudal period which followed the demise
of Charlemagne's Empire was marked by the co-
existence of two seemingly contradictory components,
those of chaos and stability, respectively. Chaos
appeared inevitable in the absence of firm centralized government, and a host of petty kings, princes,
dukes, and barons vied somewhat ineffectively for
power for centuries. The more dominant aspirants
were prepared, in the event of victory, to make
promises and offer concessions, usually by way of
substantial grants of territory, in exchange for
military assistance from vacillating supporters.
The latter, often owing allegiance to none, would
seek the highest bidder, and it was not unknown
for armies to change sides on the very field of
battle, following bargaining sessions with the rival

contenders. So long as such a situation existed, countries became incessantly ravaged by war, with their inhabitants subjected to recurring famine and pestilence, both of which were recognized characteristics of the age.

Yet it was also a period when the major political convulsions which had accompanied and succeeded the fall of the Roman Empire were showing every evidence of gradual subsidence. The Germanic peoples were no longer on the move, but instead had been consolidating and fortifying themselves against the onslaughts and incursions of three contrasting groups of invaders, the Slavs in the east, the Moslems in the south and the Vikings in the north. While all three groups were still capable of menacing the west, by the year 1000 A.D. they were not only being contained, but were progressively being harassed in the regions they had once sought to dominate. This was especially true of central Europe, Spain, and Southern Italy.

Thus, despite the fact that conflict and war appeared to be integral features of the natural predestined order for mankind there slowly emerged a more predictable and more secure way of life. The ruling landed princes and barons, despite their predilection for military adventures, did, within their own domains, provide reasonable protection for their subjects who, while obligated to serve their masters without question, now could and did produce regular crops and harvests.[1] Given favorable weather conditions surplus food became available, so that exchange of products

----

1. The many monasteries in Western Europe practised good husbandry, and were the essential agents whereby better farming practices, (including the three-field system, the use of horses and heavier ploughs) were disseminated.

took place at convenient centers, or markets. It was to the advantage of the lord of the manor to provide facilities and security under charter, which, while defining his obligations, also guaranteed him a substantial source of income from tolls and taxes.

Consequently, all over Western Europe there was a marked increase in the number of new townships, along with a commensurate expansion of existing urban communities. This process led to a great demand for craftsmen, particularly masons and carpenters, who set up guilds not only to ensure mutual aid and protection, but also to preserve standards of performance—legitimate goals which were eventually to produce the magnificent cathedrals of the Middle Ages.

As markets developed, there also emerged the new class of wealthy merchants, impatient with feudal restrictions, and who, becoming more aware of their power vis-a-vis both the landed aristocracy as well as the Church, established municipal councils for better representation and bargaining power. These secular authorities demanded independence, and their insistence led to the creation of the new phenomenon in Western Europe, the city-states of Northern Italy, as well as of Flanders in north-west Europe.

At this very juncture in time the Turks appeared in the Middle East[2] and in due course the Crusades were set in motion, the first in 1096 and the last almost two hundred years later.[3] Osten-

----

2. They occupied Bagdad in 1055 A.D. and made it their capital.

3. The final major Crusade was that of the Eighth in 1270, in which Louis IX (St. Louis) of France participated and succumbed of fever. The fall of Acre to the Turks in 1291 left the West with no foothold in the Holy Land.

sibly originating from a religious motive (to free Jerusalem), they gradually relapsed into the undisguised political objective of dismembering the Eastern Byzantine Empire for the benefit of enriching the new and aggressive city and nation-states of Western Europe, most of whom immeasurably profited financially from the undertaking. Initially, also the Church of Rome gained prestige, but in so doing it came into conflict with the temporal ambitions of the new hereditary dynasties which were being founded in Germany, France and England, the nadir of its fortunes being reached in the Babylonian Captivity[4] of 1309-1378, and in the succeeding period of the schism, 1378-1417, when there were, at one time, not merely two rival popes but three.

The three great powers of northern Europe, after successfully emerging from the Dark Ages, almost destroyed themselves by the intemperate ambitions of their respective rulers. This was certainly true of Germany which, having once more achieved a substantial semblance of unity, began to interfere in the affairs of Italy, presumably in furtherance of substantiating its claim to a Holy Roman Empire. The actions of the German (Hohenstaufen) rulers so infuriated the Papacy that the obsessive objective of the latter came to be the destruction of the Dynasty, a goal so thoroughly achieved in 1268, that German unity was irreparably destroyed over the period of the next six hundred years.[5]

Following their successful invasion of England in 1066 the Normans proceeded to subdue the country so rapidly and effectively that

----

4.   So labelled by Petrarch.

5.   Until 1870.

50

William (the Conqueror) was, in 1086, able to
initiate a complete land survey (for the purpose
of eventual taxation assessment) known, with probably good reason, as the Domesday Book. Secure
in their island fortress, several of William's
equally aggressive successors set about expanding
their possessions in France moving outwards from
their base in Normandy. By intrigue, marriage,
or by force of arms, England soon acquired the
entire Atlantic coast, and Henry II (d. 1189)
owned more of France than did the French King himself. However, Philip (Augustus) II of France,
taking advantage of the inept rule of King John of
England, soon restored the balance and forced the
latter to cede substantial portions of English-
held France by 1204. Philip's great victory
over John and Otto (Germany) at the Battle of
Bouvines (1214), began a new era in the history of
France, by forcing his political neighbors to
recognize the country as a major political power
to be reckoned with.

English pretensions to French territory did
not subside, and just over a century later, both
states became involved in the devastating, pro-
tracted conflict known as the Hundred Years War
(1337-1453), which ended in a complete victory
for France and in the elimination of all English-
held territory.[6]

At the time of the Middle East Crusades
there were in progress in Europe, two other, less
publicized but yet significant, crusades in progress. In Spain, the retreat to the south of the
Arab Moslems (following upon their decisive
defeat in France in 732 A.D. by Charles Martel),
had permitted the rise of Christian Kingdoms,

----

6. Except for the city of Calais, which England
    finally ceded in 1558.

51

including Leon, Castile, Navarre, and Aragon.
Toledo was captured in 1085 and Cordoba in 1236,
but disunity and discord among the Christians
delayed the capture of the last Moslem (Moorish)
stronghold, Granada, until 1492.

German participants during the Third Crusade
(1189 A.D.) had collaborated to establish a
fraternity hospital which in 1198 was militarized
to form an Order of Knights. After returning
home, the new Teutonic Order was redirected to a
program of the expansion of Christianity eastwards from Germany into Slavic territory. Thus
was initiated the geopolitic concept of the
German "Drang Nach Osten" (the Drive to the East).
Within a hundred years the Knights had moved eastwards along the south coast of the Baltic Sea to
occupy the territory eventually identified as
Prussia. Conquest was followed by settlement,
and a sequence of German-occupied cities was
eventually established throughout the entire area.
The significance of this development lies in the
fact that the state of Prussia which emerged as a
political power five hundred years later and which
became the nucleus of the German Empire had its
origins in the Northern Crusade of the Teutonic
Knights.

Education.

    Throughout the period under consideration
the Catholic Church retained and, in many respects,
even enhanced its status as the one single, dominant, and unifying institution in the Western
World. Its progress was uneven, particularly in
the political arena, but nevertheless as a uni-
tary state it succeeded in developing agencies
which were to function as correctives and stabi-
lizers for a sometimes overburdened, overcentral-
ized and unimaginative bureaucrat church government.

    Already, for four centuries, the many
Benedictine monasteries had performed miracles
by keeping alight the candleglow of culture
during the endless gloom of the so-called Dark
Ages. The transformation of the glow into a
beacon began when the Abbey of Cluny (founded c.
910 A.D.) in south-east France inaugurated a new
era in organizational technique. Hitherto, all
Benedictine abbeys had developed as isolated
units, separate and independent, one from the
other. In contrast, Cluny emerged as the headquarters of a prodigious network of over 200
satellite monasteries throughout Northwestern
Europe. In this supportive role the individual
monasteries gained confidence and inspiration,
while the monks became recognized for their
discipline and dedication to the Church.

    The ferment led to the founding of other
monastic orders including those of the
Carthusians,[7] the Premonstratensians,[8] and
especially the Cistercians. The latter Order,
----

7. Founded by St. Bruno of Cologne in 1084 in
    the valley of Chartreuse near Grenoble.

8. Founded by St. Norbert in 1119 in the valley
    of Premontre near Laon.

originating at Citeaux (Latin, Cisternium) near
Dijon in 1098, gradually replaced the Benedictines
in prestige, and the vigor and energy of its
adherents led to the establishment of no fewer
than 700 Houses within its first two hundred
years of existence. Its most famous member was
St. Bernard, Abbot of Clairvaux (1090-1153), who
almost singlehanded, successfully preached for the
Second Crusade (1146).

Everywhere, monasteries were nucleii of culture and civilization in an uncultured and unciv-
ilized world. They observed an uncomplicated set
of Christian beliefs along with a work ethic
which served as practical ideals for the lay pop-
ulace. Nevertheless, for the most part, monasteries remained as rural institutions, and the
rapid growth of urban communities during the
eleventh and twelfth centuries demanded innovation
on the part of the religious hierarchy. The
Catholic Church to some degree kept pace with
developments, but it was left to a completely
new movement, that of the mendicant friars, to
supply the Christian missionary zeal and fervor
commensurate to the secular energy and vigor displayed by the citizens of the expanding commercial
centers.

The four original orders of mendicant friars,
the Dominicans, Franciscans, Carmelites, and
Augustinians, were founded not so much as a response to the needs of growing towns and cities
but rather as counter-movements in part against
inadequacies within the established church, and
in part against heretical beliefs and practices
which had sprung up in the wake of the explosion
of 'pagan' (classical) knowledge. The Dominican
Order (the Black Friars) was specifically founded
(c. 1216) by St. Dominic, a Spaniard, to counteract the spread of the Albigensian heresy[9] in south-
----
9.   Named after the town of Albi. The 'heresy'
     was a puritanical reform movement, based on
     the teachings of Mani a Persian of the third
     century A.D. who advocated extreme asceticism.

west France. At a later date the Dominicans were
made responsible by the Pope for the conduct of
the Inquisition established to root out heresy,
but essentially they were well educated teachers
and disciplined preachers who operated within
society, and not apart from it, as did most members of the monastic orders.

The first intellectual renaissance, that of
the tenth, eleventh, and twelfth centuries, emanated from Spain. Scholars in Baghdad had, as
early as the ninth century, translated into
Arabic the works of many Greek writers, including
those of Aristotle, and had then concerned themselves with the problems of reconciling the concepts propounded by the Greek philosophers with
the traditional tenets of the Moslem faith. The
translations and commentaries, together with the
inevitable controversies, had passed from the
Arab Middle East to Arab Spain, and it was thence
that the greatest scholar in the West, Gerbert
of Aurillac (in southern France), went for the
purpose of familiarizing himself with Arab and
Greek erudition. He was particularly interested
in Arabic mathematics and science, and it is he
who is credited with the introduction into
Western Europe of Arabic numerals, as well as
the abacus.[10] Upon his return, Gerbert embarked
upon a remarkable career during which he was

----

10. "Arabic" numeration is presumed to have
    entered the Middle East from India during
    the eighth century A.D. Al-Kowarizmi was
    reputed to have written (c. 825) a mono-
    graph on the subject eventually translated
    into Latin by Adelard of Bath (England) in
    1120, under the title Liber Algorismi De
    Numero Indorum. The earliest known European
    manuscript containing Arabic numerals is
    dated 976 and was published in Spain.

tutor to two Holy Roman Emperors, Otto II and
Otto III of Germany, as well as to the son of
Hugh Capet, the future King Robert of France.
It was Otto III who eventually elevated Gerbert
to the Papacy as Sylvester II (999-1003).

Gerbert was literally the Renaissance Man
of his age. He was not only a man of science,
he was also an accomplished musician, and applied
his genius to the construction of music organs.
He was fascinated by the scholarship of the great
classical authors, regarding whose contributions
in the field of literature and rhetoric he wrote:

> I have always added the fondness of
> speaking well to the fondness for
> living well, although by itself it
> may be more excellent to live well
> than to speak well, and if one be
> freed from the cares of governing,
> the former is enough without the
> latter. But to us, busied in the
> affairs of State, both are necessary.
> For speaking effectively to persuade,
> and restraining the minds of angry
> persons from violence are both of the
> greatest usefulness.

In Spain itself, Averroes (1126-1198), the
greatest of all Arab philosophers in the West,
wrote extensively upon a wide variety of topics
relating to Moslem theology and Greek philosophy.
In time, his works were translated into Latin,
and Greek scholarship again became available to
the Western world, albeit often in such poor translation[11] that the Pope was led to proscribe the
work of Aristotle because of its confusing and

----

11. In the 1150's the work of translating the
writings of Aristotle into Latin was undertaken by Raymund, Bishop of Toledo, who
established a school of translators in the
city.

perplexing effect upon the religious community. Eventually William of Brabant (or Moerbeke) a Dominican monk and scholar, was commissioned to provide an accurate translation of Aristotle directly from the original Greek into Latin. His task was completed in 1267.

Long before this date, faithful members of the Catholic Church had become perturbed with the autocratic and authoritarian approach of the hierarchy which permitted little or no discussion on issues with which scholars were directly concerned and upon which there was no general agreement. Circumventing a possible charge of heresy, Peter Abelard (1079-1142), a canon at the Cathedral of Notre Dame in Paris, subtly presented, in a work entitled <u>Sic Et Non</u> (Yes and No), a well structured symposium of 158 theological propositions,[12] and, without comment, he juxtaposed negative and positive statements and viewpoints relative to each proposition. Thereby, he conclusively demonstrated that the presumed established authorities were themselves in conflict, and that reform was urgently needed.

It was Abelard who may be said to have initiated what came to be known as the Scholastic approach in theology. In the Prologue to his work Abelard stated:

> Constant questioning is the first key to wisdom. For through doubt we are led to inquiry, and by inquiring we discern the truth.

----

12. The propositions were presented in the form of questions such as:

> Is God omnipotent?
> Has God freewill?
> Is it worse to sin openly than in secret?

He suffered considerable persecution at the
instigation of St. Bernard of Clairvaux, who vigorously opposed Abelard's contentions that rational
explanations could be provided for many assumed
theological 'mysteries'. Despite such opposition,
Abelard's contentions were not to be easily set
aside, and one of his students, Peter Lombard
(1100-1164),[13] was to write a universally-used
monumental textbook entitled Sententiae (Opinions)
in which he sought to conciliate the opposing viewpoints in orthodox dogma exposed by Abelard.

Within a century of Abelard's death, and
despite the interdictions of the Papacy, theological scholars had become increasing aware of, and
involved in, discussion concerning the ramifica-
tions of Aristotelian philosophy.[14] Divisions
subsequently arose within the ranks of intellectual
Christians who resolved themselves into two
schools of thought: Realists, led by Anselm
(d. 1109)[15] Archbishop of Canterbury, and Nominalists, led by Roscellinus (d. 1121) of France.
To the Realists, ultimate concepts such as God,
goodness, truth, the Trinity, actually existed
outside the human mind, and to this degree their
viewpoint represented that of the established
Church.

The Nominalists held that reality did not
exist outside the human mind, so that there could

----

13. later elected Bishop of Paris.

14. Jewish scholars were just as concerned at the
     implications for their particular faith, and
     Moses Maimonides (1135-1204) of Spain, wrote
     for them his Guide for the Perplexed.

15. Anselm had no difficulty with the problem of
     Reason versus Belief, stating that "A sure
     belief must precede any theory of belief,"
     and, "I believe in order that I might under-
     stand."

be no universal spiritual entities. By maintaining these ideas the adherents of Nominalism
bordered close upon being labelled as heretics,
although for the most part they succeeded in
avoiding physical persecution. Their major importance lay in the stimulating climate of analytical criticism which they engendered, and
which resulted in the study of theology becoming
the dominant academic discipline in northern
Europe.

It was to the foregoing problems of Realism
versus Nominalism, and Faith versus Reason, that
the greatest intellect of the Middle Ages, Thomas
Aquinas (1225-74), diligently applied himself.
Born in Italy and enrolled at the Benedictine
Abbey of Monte Cassino at the age of five,
Aquinas later studied at Naples, Rome, and Paris.
Ordained as a Dominican priest, he eventually
qualified as a teacher of theology at the University of Paris. In 1272 he published his Summa
Theologica, in which he presented his synthesis
of Christian Faith and Aristotelian Reason:
according to Aquinas, since all truth emanates
from God, there can be no conflict as to whether
truth is based on faith or reason; however, the
powers of human reason are circumscribed and
limited, and therefore mankind must ultimately
and of necessity depend upon faith.

His conclusions proved acceptable to the
Catholic hierarchy, which at this date could not
have been expected to anticipate the Pandora's
Box which Aquinas had opened when he declared
that, since God had given mankind the power to
reason, it was legitimate to employ that power
towards the solution of intellectual problems.
He maintained that scholars should be permitted
to undertake objective search for truth by investigation into the sources of facts and knowledge,
to be followed by the orderly presentation and
publication of their findings. It was Aquinas
who developed the disputation as a method of

teaching in the classroom, whereby confusion in
the minds of the students might be resolved by
the systematic exposition of two (or more) presumably authoritative viewpoints, publicly expressed, and immediately subjected to discussion
and inquiry. If nothing else, the approach
demanded the rigid and accurate definition of
concepts. Only one further step remained until
mankind was poised on the threshold of possibly
the first New World -- the application of inquiry
into phenomena of the physical world, i.e. the
realm of science.[16]

The stimulating events of the period demanded an equally stimulating institution wherein animated intellects might convene, contend,
and converse. The monastic and cathedral schools
which had provided such admirable service to
civilization during its darkest hours were now
no longer adequate to cope with the strong pul-
sating movements of secular enterprises which
were beginning to dominate the political, social,
and economic life of the western world.

The new institution which was to develop was
that of the university, and initially its beginnings were modest. An eminent teacher would
attract a clientele of students from beyond the
confines of the local city or region, and so
establish a "studium generale:" a place of study
open to all without restriction. The instructors
might or might not be attached to already existing cathedral schools, but there would be no
recognized teaching qualifications neither would

----

16. Already, during the age of Aquinas, an English
     Franciscan friar, Roger Bacon (c. 1220-92),
     a teacher at the universities of Paris and
     Oxford, had engaged himself in experimental
     studies in alchemy, astronomy and optics,
     and had later been imprisoned for his sus-
     pect, innovative research.

the students be awarded diplomas or degrees.
As the thirst for knowledge increased, so would
the number of students and teachers who, in time,
would find it to their mutual benefit and protection to form societies or associations, along
the lines of the already formidable craft guilds.
These societies were known as "universitas",
and some gained recognition by civic as well as
religious authorities. Students would also find
it to their financial advantage to set up inexpensive accommodation in residential halls,
termed 'colleges', which were often the recipients of grants and endowments by wealthy patrons.[17]

   The first renaissance of learning (of the
eleventh and twelfth centuries) occurred in Southern Europe, more specifically in Italy, and its
format was rather different from that which took
place in the north, since it was a distinctly
secular and non-clerical professional movement.
The first great Studium was undoubtedly that at
Salerno, a city which acknowledged the suzerainty
of the Byzantine Empire, and as such its teachers
had become acquainted with Greek (as well as Arab)
scholarship, particularly in the field of medicine.
Salerno possessed mineral springs which made it
a natural center for the healing arts, and while
it never rose to the status of a university, it
did eventually receive (c. 1230) a charter as a
school of medicine from Frederick II conferring
upon the faculty the right of examining those
students wishing to practise medicine in the
Kingdom of Sicily. The Greek writings of
Hippocrates and Galen, and the works of the great

----

17. At Oxford and Cambridge Universities in
     England, the individual colleges have re-
     tained their unique status, independence,
     and prestige extending into the modern era
     due to their wealth.

Persian physician, Avicenna, (979-1103 A.D.)[18]
were here translated into Latin, and these became the basic texts for all the medical schools
of Western Europe during the Middle Ages.

In northern Italy, the great revival of trade
and consequently of city life had created a major
political and economic problem relating to the
degree of authority, (in terms of the imposition
of regulations and taxation), to be exercised by
the Catholic Church and/or by the Holy Roman
Emperor over the territorially expanding and com-
mercially prosperous municipalities. The latter
in their own defense sought recourse in Law and
thereby pioneered a revival of the study of the
works of the ancient Roman Jurists, and in particular the code of Justinian: the Corpus Juris
Civile. Schools of law were instituted at Pavia
and Ravenna, but by far the most notable establishment became that of Bologna which received a
charter of special privileges from Frederick I
Barbarossa in 1158. Bologna was unique in that
the students, an older and more mature body than
elsewhere, gained almost complete control over
the entire operations of the institution. They
arranged for the election of the rector, head of
the university, and they possessed the power to
engage, dismiss, and determine the payment of
the instructors, whose activities they regulated
to a minute degree.[19] Since the enrollment of
students numbered several thousands, they were
also able to exact appreciable concessions by

----

18. Including his Book of Healing and the
    Medical Encyclopedia.

19. The students specified the length and pace
    of the lectures (since note taking was im-
    perative in the absence of readily-avail-
    able texts), and could dispense with un-
    popular instructors who failed to attract
    more than five students to their classes.

way of food and lodging rates from the citizens,
simply by threatening to move the institution to
some other town offering more favorable terms.

Two famous scholars gave Bologna unchal-
lenged precedence in the field of law. Irnerius
(c. 1050-1130), by his detailed commentaries on
the Justinian Code, was responsible for establishing the study of civil law as an academic discipline, while Gratian (c. 1080-1150), a monk,
directed his energies towards resolving contra-
dictions in canon law, and c. 1140 published his
famous work entitled, The Harmony of Discordant
Decrees (The Decretum).

The law school at Padua[20] was founded (c.
1222) from Bologna, and in 1245 Pope Innocent IV
created the "University of the Roman Court" in
Rome to provide instruction and training in both
civil and canon law. In Naples (c. 1224) Frederick
II established a school initially designed to
train bureaucrats for the better administration of
the Holy Roman Empire; in due course this institution gradually absorbed the faculties and
activities of Salerno.

In contrast to Italy, where political and
economic changes and conditions had conjoined to
erode the influence of the Catholic Church, the
latter remained the dominant establishment in
Northern Europe. But, that it was yet responsive
to the climate of the period, is clearly indicated by the decree of the Lateran Council in 1179
requiring that every cathedral (or bishop's
church) maintain a school to educate priests and
clerics. Theology, therefore, rather than law
and medicine, was to emerge as the dominant discipline, with the University of Paris (chartered

----

20. Made famous by Shakespeare, since Portia of
     "The Merchant of Venice" was a graduate of
     this school.

c. 1200 by Philip Augustus) as the model institution. It appeared to have been created by the
merger of three extant schools: the school of
the collegiate church of Ste. Genevieve, the
school of the canons of St. Victor, and the
cathedral school of Notre Dame (where both
William of Champeau and Peter Abelard had been
head teachers). In the midst of the doctrinal
turmoil of the thirteenth and fourteenth centuries
Paris tended to function as the center of orthodox teaching. Stress was laid upon dialectic and
logic, debate and disputation, for the specific
objective of demonstrating, clarifying, and integrating established viewpoints, rather than for
the purpose of initiating and projecting possible
reforms. The instructors were priests, friars,
and members of the clergy and a high proportion
of the students were in training for the same
profession, although in due course faculties of
(canon) law and medicine were developed. A
liberal arts curriculum comprising grammar, philosophy, logic, mathematics, metaphysics, and
rhetoric, served as the prerequisite to a professional course of studies.

Initially, it was the Chancellor of the
Cathedral School who issued the "licentia docendi",
the certificate to teach, but the masters at the
University gradually insisted that this prerogative
was theirs, and, following an appeal to Pope
Innocent III, they succeeded (1212 A.D.) in obtaining the right to select and forward the names of
qualified candidates to the Chancellor, who thence-
forward, was automatically obliged to confer upon
them the requested appropriate degrees.[21] At
----
21. During the thirteenth century, the teaching
certificate, the licentia docendi, of an individual university was extended, by application to the Pope, into a more universal teaching certificate, the jus ubique docendi,
which permitted its holder to teach at any
university in Western Europe.

64

first, the basic degree was that of the Master;
extended studies could lead to the doctorate,
while at the lower level an intermediate stage
in the master's course came to be accepted as
the baccalaureate degree.

Within less than two centuries following
the charter granted to the University of Paris,[22]
universities were established in France at
Toulouse, Montpellier, Orleans, Angers, Avignon,
Cahors, Grenoble, Orange, Perpignan, Chartres,
Laon, Reims and Liege.

As a result of a political dispute between
Henry II of England and Louis VII of France,
theological students from England were either
withdrawn or expelled (c. 1167-8) from the schools
in Paris, and many of the returning scholars domiciled at Oxford. Following disagreements a group
of masters and students migrated to Cambridge
(c. 1209). The two institutions as developed
were to remain the only universities in England
and Wales for the next six hundred years.[23]
While some discrepencies exist concerning precise dates, both universities progressed along
identical lines, with residential halls or
colleges emerging as influential, semi-autonomous,
endowed units within the university organization.

----

22. c. 1256 Robert de Sorbon endowed a dormitory
     for 16 students as a "college." This devel-
     oped as the Sorbonne, the liberal arts
     department of the University of Paris.

23. until 1828, when University College, London,
     was opened. It was founded by Nonconform-
     ists for members of their persuasion, since
     Oxford and Cambridge remained closed insti-
     tutions to all non-communicants of the
     Church of England until 1858.

At Oxford, the first three colleges to gain recognition were University College (1249), Balliol (1263), and Merton (1264), and at Cambridge, they were Peterhouse (1284), Michaelhouse (1323), and King's Hall (1326).[24]

The unstable political situation did not favor interest in higher education in Scotland until the fifteenth century, when universities were established at St. Andrews (1411), Glasgow (1453), and Aberdeen (1494).[25]

Elsewhere in Europe, a surge of enthusiasm for advanced studies spread outwards from France and Italy. Salamanca (1243) and Seville (1254) were the first universities in Spain, to be followed by Valladolid founded in 1346.

The earliest university in Central Europe was that of Prague (1347). Others established during the fourteenth century included Cracow (1364), Vienna (1364), Erfurt (1379), Heidelburg (1386), and Cologne (1388).[26]

By the year 1500, it has been estimated that there were almost eighty universities flourishing in Western Europe, and it was inevitable, with the political, economic, and social changes which were occurring, that the rigid and formal sectarian approach of theoretical scholasticism would, in due course, become outmoded, and be replaced by a more pragmatic concern with the contemporary

----

24. Michaelhouse and King's Hall were merged to form Trinity College two centuries later.

25. Edinburgh University came a century later, in 1582.

26. Dates in all the foregoing instances are proximate only.

problems of the age. This next phase came to be
known as classical humanism, characteristic of
the great period of the Renaissance.

CHAPTER FIVE

THE RENAISSANCE

Introduction

The Renaissance may be regarded as a cultural efflorescence arising out of a series of events spread over several centuries. It had its immediate origin in the intellectual curiosity manifested by scholars from the twelfth century onwards, a curiosity vastly stimulated by the opportunities for academic discussion, disputation and inquiry afforded by the establishment and spread of universities all over Western Europe. The consequence was the slow but inexorable erosion of traditional religious authority and orthodoxy.

The period under consideration was one when the mediaeval city states and provinces were reaching a zenith of prosperity, creativity, and independence. It was also one which witnessed the rise of nation-states, the first of which[1] was in effect that of the Papacy itself, whose territory, the Papal States, extended across Central Italy from Rome to Ravenna. Perhaps Italy's tragedy has always been that, while the Papal States represented a powerful political bloc, it was usually, by reason of support from outside forces, enmeshed in a balance-of-power situation.

----

1. following the demise of the Second (or Holy) Roman Empire with the fall of the Hohenstaufen Dynasty in 1254.

That support was limited, since never at any time did any European power even consider, let alone sanction, the possibility of the creation of a united Italy with the Pope at its helm. Consequently, the city-states of Northern Italy enjoyed unprecedented affluence seemingly unaffected by temporary setbacks, whether economic or political. Wealthy aristocrats and merchants provided lavish patronage for the creators of beauty and excellence in the arts of painting, sculpture, architecture, and literature. Hence it was here that the Renaissance emerged and attained its finest aesthetic achievements.

Elsewhere in Western Europe the situation was very different. England, after centuries of exhausting wars with France, followed by a civil war (The Wars of the Roses), finally achieved relative peace and unity with the accession of the Tudor monarchy (1485), which inaugurated a new era of aggressive nationalism. In France, likewise, the expulsion of the English at the conclusion of the Hundred Years' War (1453) had permitted the French kings to undertake the territorial unification and consolidation of the country. This objective was achieved so rapidly and thoroughly that in 1494 Charles VIII was able to undertake a military invasion of Italy which thereafter became the convenient battlefield of rival continental powers.

Spain, disunited for centuries, was suddenly affected by a series of unrelated accidents of time and place. The aggravation of the presence of Moorish Moslems on Spanish soil ended in January 1492 with the fall of Granada. By October of the same year, Columbus had discovered a New World, which removed Spain forever from the disadvantage of being located on the outermost edge of the Old World. The marriage of Isabella and Ferdinand provided the country with a unified monarchy ready to exploit the new situation, a monarchy which was yet to be further enhanced by

the later accession of the Hapsburg, Charles V,
who inherited not only the New World but also substantial sections of the Old, including Spain,
Sardinia, Sicily, the Netherlands, and Austria.
But within half a century of the discovery of the
New World, the Mediterranean region, for millenia
the focal region of western civilization, had
declined to the level of an economic backwater.
Already, the capture of Constantinople by the
Turks in 1453 had severely curtailed the trading
opportunities of most of the Northern Italian
city-states. The sudden expansion of the horizon
westwards across the Atlantic Ocean accompanied
by the rise of the powerful nation states bordering the same ocean led inevitably to the economic
demise of the city-states and with it the intellectual demise of the Renaissance in Southern
Europe.

There was however another Renaissance -
that of Northern Europe, of a more intellectual
and austere character, reflecting the climate,
perhaps, but more a product of the growing political irritation with and rejection of the Catholic
Church as the ultimate arbiter of all matters
relating to doctrine, destiny, and action. Papal
prestige had reached a nadir when the French king,
Philip IV, arrested Boniface VIII in 1303, and
later forced the election of a Frenchman as Pope
Clement V, whom he virtually imprisoned at
Avignon, thus initiating the Babylonian Captivity
(1309-77). This was followed by the Papal Schism,
with again two, sometimes three contending rivals
for the papal throne, and not until 1417 did one
elected Pope again prove acceptable to the whole
of Western Christendom. It was during this century of turmoil, that traditional loyalties began
to waver. It became easier to support the resolute ruler of a state or duchy, than to court
confusion by offering homage to an uncertain
Pope. Release from rigid papal restraint gave
rise to more apperceptive and rational analyses

of philosophical and theological writings, which
in turn made it easier to focus attention upon
the shortcomings of the Catholic Church. Hence,
the Renaissance of the North proved to be the
precursor of the Reformation of the North. There
was no Reformation in Southern Europe.

Education

The dawn of the Renaissance was heralded by
the writings of three great Italians, all natives
of Florence: Dante, Petrarch, and Boccaccio, all
of whom revelled in a hitherto unheard-of freedom of literary expression, often secular if not
directly pagan in content, yet sensitive to the
underlying mysticism and wonder of Christian
faith.

Alighieri Dante (1265-1321), while well
versed in the classics was the first great
writer in Italian literature,[2] thereby providing
in the vernacular a major text, albeit in manuscript format, for any teacher who might have
required such a work as an alternative to the
many readily available books by Latin authors,
whether classical or Christian. His Divine
Comedy was essentially a poetic allegory (written
in terza rima: rhyming three line stanzas)
wherein Dante's soul was conducted, first by the
Latin poet Virgil through Hell (where incredibly
they found a recently deceased Pope: Nicholas
III, who had died in 1281), thence through Purga-
tory, to Paradise, where Dante's mentor was
Beatrice, whom apparently he had loved, but from
afar, in real life.

Petrarch (1304-74), also infatuated with a
pedestalled beauty, Laura,[3] was initially qualified in both law and theology. A gifted scholar,

----

2. The Scriptures were not translated into
    Italian until the thirteenth century and
    even then only in segments. The first com-
    plete Italian Bible (in Venetian dialect,
    and translated by Niccolo Malerbi) became
    available in 1471.

3. to whom he dedicated his renowned Sonnets.

he was imbued by a love of learning and antiquity, and during his extensive travels in Western Europe he proceeded to amass an impressive collection of classical manuscripts which he arranged to have carefully copied and thereafter made available to kindred spirits.

Among the most illustrious of Petrarch's students was Giovanni Boccaccio (1313-75), whose Decameron is considered to be the first modern novel. Written in Italian and superficially bawdy, it offered an incomparable satirical commentary on the mores of the period, and as such, together with its non-religious theme, it was clear evidence of a new and native concept of literary freedom.[4]

Subsequently, however, creative impulses in Italy found their major outlet less in literature than in painting, sculpture, and architecture, possibly by reason of lack of the ready patronage which was made available to skilled practitioners of the fine arts by the Church.

Nevertheless, certain of the universities continued to innovate, with the encouragement of the ruling aristocracies, as, for example, at Florence, where in 1396 Emanuel Chrysoloras, a scholar from Constantinople was persuaded to pursue his studies in Greek.[5]

4. Boccaccio, a great admirer of pagan (Greek) culture was instrumental in securing the appointment of Leontium Pilatus, a Greek of Southern Italy, to the University of Florence as the first professor of Greek in Western Europe.

5. Greek studies in the West received appreciable impetus following the Council of Florence (1438-9), where representatives of the Papacy and of the Greek Orthodox Church made a last final effort to restore unity before Constaninople was overwhelmed by the Turks (1453).

One of his students, Pietro Paolo Vergario, (Vergerius),[6] having already issued a tract on Quintilian's Institutio Oratoria: The Education of an Orator, published in 1404 what may be considered as the first formal Renaissance exposition on education, entitled On the Manners of a Gentleman and on Liberal Studies. The work was apparently compiled as a set of guiding precepts for the upbringing of the son of the lord of Padua. It reiterated many of the principles propounded by Quintilian, including emphasis upon the family as the basic educational institution, and upon the primacy of moral education over that of mere content learning. Its methodology was as sound as that of the much-revered Roman, with its insistence upon the pedagogic recognition that the teacher should adapt his approach to the age and intellectual capacity of the student; that he should employ systematic review to promote retention; and that he should consider himself to be a friendly mentor and counselor with whom the student could discuss his problems and difficulties without fear of insult and embarrassment. Vergerius' definition of liberal studies is worthy of quotation without comment:

> "We call those studies liberal which are worthy of a free man; those studies by which we attain and practice virtue and wisdom; that education which calls forth, trains and develops, those highest gifts of body and mind which ennoble man and which are rightly judged to rank next in dignity to virtue only."

Guarino da Verona (1370-1460), son-in-law of Manuel Chrysoloras, the first major Greek propagandist in the West, spent five years in Constantinople mastering Greek before returning to Italy as a professor of the language at various univer-

---

6. Later a professor of logic at the University of Padua.

sities including Venice and Ferrara.[7] Aided by
the lords of Ferrara he made the university a
center of scholarship, and he established at the
ducal residence a court school possibly without
rival in terms of its unique influence upon the
rulers of any city.[8]

Guarino's son, Battista, wrote of his father's
approach to teaching in a work entitled, Upon the
Method of Teaching and of Reading the Classical
Authors (1459). Guarino placed great emphasis on
scholarship to be achieved by systematic reading,
interpretation, discussion, and possibly memorization of significant literary passages, along with
analyses of grammar and syntax.

A great and influential teacher, yet Guarino
was surpassed in fame by one of his students at
Venice, Vittorino da Feltre (1378-1446) considered
by posterity to be justly rated as the first of
modern schoolmasters. Born at Padua, he learned
Greek under Guarino, and later returned as a

----

7. Where, it is said, he spent many enjoyable
   hours with students indulging in "fave e
   favole" (beans and conversation).

8. It was Niccolo III d'Este who in 1429 engaged
   Guarino to teach his three sons at the court
   school, each of whom succeeded in turn as
   ruler of the duchy of Ferrara: Leonello (1441-
   50), Borso (1450-71) and Ercole (1471-1505).
   All were enlightened patrons of the arts, as
   were also Ercole's two famous daughters,
   Isabella and Beatrice. Isabella married the
   duke of Mantua, and Beatrice married the
   (later) duke of Milan. Both were lavish host-
   esses of the famous artists and writers of the
   day, including Leonardo da Vinci, Raphael,
   Titian, Bramante, and Castiglione.

professor of Latin and mathematics at the University of Padua where he taught for twenty-five years. Some time later he was invited by Gianfrancesco Gonzaga, lord of Mantua, to set up a school at his court for the purpose of educating his children. Vittorino accepted, and established La Giocosa (The House of Joy) where he spent over twenty congenial years teaching not only the sons and daughters of the noble families of Mantua, but also poor gifted children whom he considered to be capable of benefitting from the education he provided.

Vittorino took advantage of the very agreeable and attractive environment of the school, and he made every effort to implement the Latin aphorism, MENS SANA IN CORPORE SANO, by placing emphasis upon physical fitness and health with appropriate outdoor activities such as participation in games, walking, and climbing.

Like other classical scholars of his day, Vittorino received substantial inspiration from the writings of two of the ancient Latin authors, Cicero and Quintilian, but he earnestly advanced a synthesis and harmony of classical and Christian values. He clearly recognized his unique and onerous responsibility of providing for the education of future rulers of the city-state, and consequently he laid stress upon the moral aspects of education emanating from the noble works of antiquity, in which he urged his students to take great interest and pride.

Such was his admiration of the classical authors that Latin, and not the vernacular language, was the medium of instruction at the school, an approach in common with all other humanistic teachers of the period, who considered that a universal culture in Western Europe, based on Christian Catholic principles, could only be communicated through the medium of a universal language, that of Latin.

The basis of the curriculum was classical literature and language, involving the study of original writings.[9] Included also in the courses for study were mathematics, science, history, geography and ethics. As a gifted teacher, Vittorino stressed the importance of self-motivated learning through interest, personal pride, and praise for achievement rather than through harsh punishments and sanctions. He insisted upon quality in assignments but recognized the imperative need to relate work loads to the age and capacity of the individual student. Thus for the younger pupils, he devised letter games in language, while for the older children he required the memorization of appropriate passages of literature, along with training for competency in composition. Cognizant of his personal role as mentor of future statesmen, Vittorino instituted a system of school self-government in the form of student councils, whereby he hoped that his proteges would become less imperious as autocratic rulers and more sensitive of their social obligations so as to respond more readily to the needs of their subjects.

Among the most renowned of Vittorino's students was Federigo Di Montefeltre, future ruler of Urbino (1444-82).[10] His court attracted countless intellectuals, while at his library, foremost

----

9. By Vittorino's time, there had become available complete texts of the works of Quintilian on education, and of Cicero's three great tracts on rhetoric.

10. Situated in Northern Italy between Rimini and Loreto.

in Italy outside the Vatican, Federigo employed
at least thirty copyists solely for the repro-
duction of invaluable manuscripts eventually to
be made available to scholars of the Western
World.

It was this court which Baldessare Castiglione
(1478-1529) attended and from which he derived
inspiration for his Book of the Courtier (Il
Cortegiano) written in 1516 (though not published
until 1528). In it Castiglione provides a comprehensive curriculum for his concept of the ideal
ruler: a man gifted in intelligence and wit,
adept in the military arts as well as the social
graces, a versatile conversationist in the classical languages as well as in the vernacular, and
a person of temperate passion, responsive to the
welfare and well-being of the state and its
citizens.

In direct contrast to the high moral precepts
propounded in the foregoing treatise, there was
published in 1513 the more famous but also more
notorious discourse entitled The Prince (Il Principe)
by Niccolo Machiavelli (1469-1527). The latter
was a talented diplomat in the service of the
city-state of Florence at a time when its fortunes
drifted and gusted "like the sand on a tray."
Pragmatic and energetic, he longed for stability,
yet, having been an eye-witness observer of so
much deceit, treachery, and cunning in politics,
he asserted that only a leader possessed of these
and other vices could hope to conquer and retain
his lands. He sought and found the personifica-
tion of his ideal in Cesare Borgia (son of
Pope Alexander VI), a resolute, ruthless, and
cruel commander who succeeded in carving out for
himself a substantial domain in central Italy.
Although Borgia was subsequently deposed,
Machiavelli still maintained that he had amply
demonstrated the practical assets necessary to
succeed in the demoralizing and depraved arena of
power politics.

In Northern Europe, the Renaissance was so
much a prelude to the Reformation, the "reform"
of the Catholic Church, that it is better designated simply as the Pre-Reformation period (i.e.
prior to 1517). Certainly absent was the aesthetic exuberance of the craftsmen of Italy revel-
ling in the light and color of luminous southern
landscapes and in the malleable, responsive
qualities of the natural stone of the country.
Instead, there was every evidence of dedicated,
almost obsessive, concern with the ponderous
problems affecting men of great intellect wrestling with what were, by this time, considered to
be the unduly restrictive bonds of the established
Church in the face of new secular knowledge, new
economic horizons, and new political institutions.

While they had not, as yet, succeeded in
finally evolving new national identities, the
northern countries were conscious of a new urge
for political independence,[11] and it is therefore
within this very different frame of reference
that educational developments must be considered.

The towering giant of the northern Renaissance
was Erasmus (1466-1536), but he,himself, was a
theoretician rather than a practitioner in the
domain of education (although he was for a time a
university professor). As a youth he attended
----

11. Even in the University of Paris, with Latin
    as the universal medium of instruction and
    communication, there were the four "nations"
    of instructors and students: the French,
    Norman, Picard (the Netherlands) and English
    (including Germans and Scandinavians),
    respectively.

one of the schools of the Brethren of the Common
Life, a remarkable religious order initially
founded for socially charitable involvement by
Geert Groot of Deventer in 1376. Its members
were laymen although they were dedicated religious persons who placed priority upon moral
education. The Brethren established a well-
developed system of schools in the Netherlands
and Western Germany, and Erasmus attended the
school at Deventer when it had as its headteacher,
Alexander Hegius,[12] an enthusiastic pedagogue who
successfully coped with no less than two thousand
students, and with only a limited number of teachers
at his disposal, he employed what, in the nineteenth century became popularised as the monitorial
system. The two thousand students were divided
first into eight age groupings, which were in turn
divided into groups of ten, each in the care of
an older student. A carefully devised curriculum
ensured a sequence of studies over the span of
eight years, commencing with grammar and reading,
progressing into the classics (with attention to
literature, rhetoric, law, and philosophy), and
culminating in the final year with theology.

Erasmus himself was not impressed by the
discipline and instruction he had received at
Deventer and later complained he had had to waste
much time either on laborious Latin grammar exercises or in the composition and analysis of Latin
verses, based, on what were, to him, irrelevant

----

12.   Another Dutchman, Rudolf Huysman (latinized
      as Agricola) a contemporary of Hegius, was a
      scholar who travelled and studied in Italy,
      became a university professor at Heidelberg,
      and was a gifted musician, artist, and lin-
      guist. He wrote a tract on education, De
      Formando Studio, which gave priority to
      studies in religion, philosophy, and history,
      and as a man of learning he was much admired
      by Erasmus.

themes. Yet, having mastered the language he considered it to be the great unifying and universal medium of communication of Christendom. He wrote nothing in his native Dutch vernacular, which he once contemptuously described as "those unlovely letters for which I was not born." Later ordained as an Augustinian monk,[13] he eventually studied in Paris and on several occasions visited England where he met and was very much impressed by Sir Thomas More,[14] (Chancellor under Henry VIII, but executed by him in 1535), and John Colet, professor of theology at Oxford University and sponsor of the famous St. Paul's School, London.

It was in England that Erasmus wrote his best known work, In Praise of Folly (Encomium Moriae), a scathing satirical commentary[15] on all the foibles and weaknesses of mankind in general but of certain professional species in particular:

 a) theologians, embroiled in endless, inconsequential, miniscule deliberations on rites and rituals at the expense of considering essential and basic questions concerning Man's relationship with Man and with God;

----

13. He disliked life in the monastery, in part because of the amount of fish consumed by the monks. Years afterwards, he was to state that while his heart was Catholic, his stomach was Lutheran.

14. It was Erasmus who designated More as "A Man for all Seasons," (title of the twentieth century play by Robert Bolt.)

15. Illustrated by amusing marginal pen drawings by Hans Holbein, the famous Dutch artist, when he was only 18.

b) philosophers, who likewise in-
dulged themselves in abstruse
speculation, and contributed nothing to the solution of the imperative and immediate problems of the
day;

c) grammarians, imbued with antiquated
scholastic traditions whose main
impact had occurred several centuries previously, and whose thinking and research had fossilized,
and had not advanced one iota beyond that period.

Mindful of the unpleasant memories of his
own school days, Erasmus composed several tracts
relating to education including, On the Right
Method of Instruction (De Ratione Studii) and
On the Liberal Education of Boys from the Beginning (De Pueris Statim Ac Liberaliter Instituendis).
To Erasmus:

The first and most important function
of education is to ensure that the
youthful spirit may be given the seeds
of piety; the next, that it may live
and learn the liberal studies; the
third, that it may be prepared for the
duties of life; and fourth, that it may,
from earliest childhood, become habitu-
ated in good manners.

He insisted that all instruction be given
in Latin as soon as possible, but he deplored
the formal scholastic emphasis on laborious
grammar exercises:

For it is not by learning rules that
we acquire the power of speaking a
language, but by daily intercourse with
those accustomed to express themselves
with exactness and refinement, and by
the copious reading of the best authors.

Furthermore, he offered a set of simple, sound principles for the classroom practitioner:

> First, do not hurry, for learning comes easily when the proper stage is reached. Second, avoid a difficulty which can be safely ignored, or at least postponed. Third, when the difficulty must be handled, make the boy's approach to it as gradual and as interesting as you can.

Erasmus recognized that effective learning could only be achieved when studies were related to the intellectual capacity of the individual student. His basic maxim was "Understand, arrange, repeat," and he was firmly of the opinion that only by kindness, gentleness, and praise is a boy "quickened to excel in all he does." Moreover:

> Where the method is sound, where teaching and practice go hand in hand, any discipline may ordinarily be acquired by the flexible intellect of man.

Erasmus was fully cognizant of the deplorable conditions under which schools and teachers of his day were forced to operate. He stressed the paramount role of the family as the primary institution in the upbringing and education of the child, but he recognized that the family was unable to accomplish everything; neither, in his view could the Church schools, by reason of their narrow minded, circumscribed approach to reform and the development of receptive, open-minded intellectual students. Erasmus came to the inevitable conclusion that an adequately organized school system with well-trained, well-paid teachers could only be implemented by a secular state system prepared to promote the dual virtues of excellence and citizenship. With these ends in view he wrote yet another treatise,

<u>The Education of a Christian Prince</u> (Institutio
Principis Christiani), wherein he formulated and
expanded upon many of the precepts basic to the
development of the ideal state which he had
advanced in his work, <u>In Praise of Folly</u>. In
the latter book he had already made public his
abhorrence of violence and brutality:

> Of all the ills that destroy the life
> of man, the most odious and the most
> harmful is war. ......The majority of
> the people hate war and desire peace.
> A minority, whose wretched good for-
> tune always depends on the misery of
> the people, wants war: must their
> humanity outweigh the will of so many
> good people? ...... Wars lead to
> other wars; revenge provokes revenge;
> indulgence generates indulgence; ben-
> evolence calls forth benevolence, and
> the highest esteem will be reserved
> for those who give up something of
> their rights.

The proposals of Erasmus relative to the
education of a ruler radically contrast with
those of Machiavelli.[16] Erasmus sought the cosmo-
politan goal of universal harmony among peoples,
a goal to be achieved not by the ruthless sav-
agery of an aggressive warmonger, without conscience or principle, but rather by the understanding tolerance and readiness for compromise
by altruistic leaders with the welfare of their
citizens always foremost in their hearts. Erasmus
was an internationalist, eager for the establishment of a universal Christian society under the
leadership of a wise and benevolent Papacy. But
the Papacy of his day and age was a travesty of
everything which Erasmus was advocating and ex-
pecting of it. Nevertheless, loyal to, yet
----
16. Machiavelli's <u>Prince</u> was published in 1513.
Erasmus' work was published in 1516.

ignored by the Establishment, he remains the intellectual colussus of the Renaissance.

In France, three of the foremost humanists of that country were to publish educational commentaries: Guillaume Bude (1468-1540), who wrote On the Education of a Prince, and expressed sentiments echoing those of Erasmus and Da Feltre; Michel de Montaigne (1533-92), whose Essays, On Pedantry, and On the Education of Children, embodied his distress with the poor teaching methods of his day, an opinion shared by Francois Rabelais (1495-1553), who, in outlining a ridiculously detailed curriculum for Gargantua (son of Pantagruel sought to satirize the deplorable learning standards of the period.

The best known English humanist educator was not English: he was Juan Luis Vives (1492-1540), who came to England under the patronage of Catherine of Aragon to whom he dedicated his work, On the Education of a Christian Woman. He served as tutor to Catherine's daughter, Mary, for whom he wrote On the Right Method of Instruction for Girls. A later work, De Anima et Vita, is often ranked as being the first modern work in psychology.

Roger Ascham (1515-68) served as instructor to the future Queen Elizabeth, and eventually wrote The Scholemaster, while Sir Thomas Elyot, in The Boke named the Gouvernor, concerned himself with the education of prospective rulers. Finally, Richard Mulcaster (1530-1611) incorporated his more than twenty years experience as a teacher in two treatises, Positions, and The Elementarie, respectively, within which sound practical advice is offered to the prospective teachers.

CHAPTER SIX

THE REFORMATION

Introduction

While the Reformation is usually considered to have been initiated by Martin Luther in 1517, (when he nailed his famous Ninety Five Theses to the door of the Court Church at Wittenberg, Saxony), its religious antecedents extend back several centuries prior to this date. Any questionable doctrine, belief, or proposal for reform was normally and conveniently set aside as "heresy," and punished accordingly. In 1022 Robert II (the Pious) of France decreed that thirteen heretics be burned at the stake, the first such execution to be recorded since the year 385 A.D. In 1184, Pope Lucius III delegated the problem of resolving heretical guilt or innocence to his bishops by instituting the Episcopal Inquisition, while in 1227 Pope Gregory IX appointed a board of Papal Inquisitors in direct response to the Albigensian heresy in South-west France. The heresy was one which related to oriental concepts of mysticism and asceticism, and was distinctly anti-clerical. It flourished during the late twelfth and early thirteenth centuries and was savagely repressed at the instigation of the Papacy. The Dominican Order of Friars (the Black Friars) was founded c. 1215 by St. Dominic (1170-1221) for the specific purpose of counteracting the heresy, and it was this Order which subsequently was designated to administer the operations of the

Inquisition.[1]

The Waldensian heresy of approximately the same period arose out of the teaching and preaching of Peter Waldo of Lyons, France (d. 1217) who had undertaken a pilgrimage to the Holy Land and, upon his return, had exhorted his followers to resort to the fundamental precepts of the early Christian Church, including the renunciation of all property, acceptance of which, by the Papacy, would have signified the complete destruction of its temporal powers. The Waldensians were quickly dispersed from eastern France and northern Italy, but in due course they were to influence small reform groups elsewhere in western and central Europe.

During the period of the Renaissance there had begun a significant decline of clerical influence upon society in western Europe, along with a marked rise in arrogance of secular rulers, who, while deferring to the Papacy in all matters relating to their respective eternal souls, lost no opportunity here on earth to challenge

----

1.   In 1252, Pope Innocent IV authorized the use of torture by inquisitors to obtain evidence. Since a person accused of heresy was immediately assumed to be guilty, and therefore obliged to furnish his own evidence of innocence, recalcitrant heretics under torture were merely privileged to determine the nature of their inevitable execution: those who confessed their guilt might be hanged, those who maintained their innocence would be burned. The Inquisition was most active in Spain during the sixteenth century in the attempt to rid the country of Jews and Moslems. The Spanish Inquisition was not finally abolished until 1834; only eight years earlier, there had occurred at Valencia the last public burning for heresy in Spain of two persons, one a Jew, the other a Quaker.

its temporal powers. Philip IV of France felt
so irritated by the pronunciations of Pope
Boniface VIII (1294-1303), that he procured the
latter's imprisonment (an ordeal from which
Boniface later died), and then so manipulated
Papal elections and affairs that there resulted
the so-called Babylonian Captivity of the Papacy
(1305-77) when the residence of the Pope was transferred from Rome to Avignon in Southern France.
This was succeeded by the Great Schism (1378-
1417) when western Europe suffered the spiritual
ordeal of having to make a decision of obeisance
between a Pope at Avignon and a Pope at Rome.

It was precisely at this period when John
Wyclif (1320-84), a professor of theology at
Oxford, advocated such widespread innovations
in the Church that, had they been accepted, they
would have advanced the Reformation by a century
and a half. He asserted the claim for the supremacy of the State over that of the Papacy, (especially, of the Papacy at Avignon); he placed
emphasis upon the Bible, and not the Church hierarchy, as the ultimate authority in matters per-
taining to moral behavior;[2] and he contended that
the measure most desirable for salvation was the
complete renunciation of all ownership of property by both Church and laity. Unfortunately
for Wyclif there occurred in 1381 in England
the Peasants' Revolt, which so terrified the
landed aristocracy and the growing, prosperous
merchant class of London that they immediately
renounced support for any religious reform which
at all threatened property rights, even if confined to those of the Church. Wyclif was
favored by reason of his political friends, to

----

2. in pursuance of which he provided a trans-
    lation of the New Testament into English in
    1381, while his followers completed an English
    translation of the Old Testament in 1394.

have escaped martyrdom, but a number of his followers, termed the Lollards,[3] were not so fortunate and were either hanged or burned at the stake.

An interesting sequence of events led to the
dissemination of many of Wyclif's proposals for
reform into central Europe, more particularly into
Bohemia. Richard II (1377-99) of England had
married Anne, sister of King Wenceslaus IV of
Bohemia. She and her courtly retainers had become
familiar with Wyclif's views, and the movement for
reform spread to her brother's kingdom, where
political overtones furthered acceptance.[4] In
1391, Bethlehem Chapel had been founded in Prague
as a meeting place for the reformers, and in 1402
John Huss[5] was appointed as its minister. Out-
spoken, eloquent, and viturperative, he was excommunicated in 1409, an event which did little to
silence his denunciations of Church venality, immorality, and simony, particularly when, in 1411,
Pope John XXIII made an offering of indulgences
to finance a Papal crusade against the King of
Naples. In 1414 the Council of Constance met in

----

3. so named because of their alleged habit of
   mumbling (or 'lolling') prayers.

4. The native Czechs had developed resentment
   towards the growing population of Germans who
   had infiltrated into the silver and nickel
   mining areas, where many had become wealthy
   merchants and entrepreneurs. Moreover,
   Wenceslaus had had to overcome considerable
   opposition from prominent German archbishops
   before eventually being elected as Holy Roman
   Emperor.

5. an abbreviation of John of Husinetz, his
   native village.

the attempt to bring to an end the divisions within the Papacy, and Huss was rashly encouraged to appear before it to defend his viewpoints on reform, and to seek acceptance of them. Instead, he was imprisoned, and in 1415, was burned at the stake. This event did not end reform in Bohemia, where for more than half a century the Hussites prevailed. They became subject to more determined persecution towards the end of the fifteenth century, and many of them fled Bohemia into the neighboring German states, including Saxony, where in good time Martin Luther was to be influenced by them.

Reform movements were negligible in Spain where the main resources of the country were mobilized against the Moslem occupants until their final elimination from Granada in 1492. Thereafter, the power of the Inquisition was too ruthlessly applied for any change or modification in Church policy to occur.

Likewise in Italy, reformers had to contend with the Papal army, and their only chance of success lay in the support of rulers eager to embarrass the Pope in furtherance of their own personal territorial ambitions. Arbitrary withdrawal of such support left the reformers entirely at the mercy of the Papacy, which usually ensured that they were quickly silenced. Such was the fate of the Dominican monk, Savonarola, who, indignant at the laxity and immorality of the Church and the citizens of Florence, succeeded (initially, with the aid of Charles VIII of France who had invaded Italy in 1494) in overthrowing the Medici dynasty and in establishing an ascetic theocracy for a period of four years. His fulminations against the Papacy resulted in his excommunication, while his fanatical excesses resulted in the withdrawal of public support and led to his eventual death at the stake (1498).

What emerges from the foregoing brief summary
of religious reform movements in western Europe
up until 1500, is the obvious conclusion that they
were all destined to fail since the political climate was not conducive to independent support and
action by the then prevailing rulers.   Perhaps
France, through the action of Philip IV in initiating the Babylonian Captivity of the Popes at
Avignon in 1305 came closest to establishing
religious autonomy and a separate national church,
but his sons had no male heirs and the abrupt
change of dynasty from the House of Capet to that
of Valois, resulted in the prolonged and disastrous
Hundred Years War (1337-1453) with England.   Not
until 1491 was the territory of France consolidated
into a national state.   A century later it was for
a brief period ruled by a Protestant (Huguenot)
monarch, Henry IV (1589-1610).[6]

Following the Norman Conquest of 1066, the
Kings of England made repeated efforts to weld all
the territory known as the British Isles into one
political unit, but with only limited success.
In 1284, Edward I conquered Wales, but his son
Edward II suffered a disastrous defeat at the
hands of the Scots at the Battle of Bannockburn
(1314), as a result of which, Scotland pursued a
destiny independent of England until 1603 when
the Protestant King James VI of Scotland was recognized also as James I of England and Wales.
Successive revolts in Ireland made that country a
perpetual thorn in the flesh of the English, who

----

6.   In 1593, he converted to Catholicism in order
     to reduce the religious tensions within the
     country, and in 1598 he sponsored the Edict
     of Nantes to protect the liberties of the
     Huguenots.   The Edict was revoked in 1685 by
     Louis XIV.

felt forced to occupy the island lest it become
allied with a continental enemy, (usually France
or Spain). The humiliation of final defeat by
France in the Hundred Years War led to further conflict within England, a civil war known as the
Wars of the Roses (1454-85). It ended with the
victory at the Battle of Bosworth of Henry Tudor,
first of that dynasty, who was crowned Henry VII.
It was he and his son, Henry VIII, who welded the
country into a formidable national state.

In Germany, the destruction of the Hohenstaufen
dynasty by the Papacy in the thirteenth century
also effectively destroyed the Holy Roman Empire
as a political power since thereafter it consisted
merely of a loose confederation of states. In
the fourteenth century, the long papal exile at
Avignon encouraged certain of the rulers of the
more powerful of these states to take precipitate
and unilateral action in furtherance of independence. In 1328 Louis of Bavaria marched to Rome
to have himself crowned Emperor in defiance of
Pope John XXII who had not approved of his election.
Ten years later, in confirmation of this action,
the German Diet announced that the imperial title
was one bestowed by the Imperial Electors alone,
and that, henceforth, papal approval and corona-
tion were not necessary. In 1356 the Emperor
Charles IV proclaimed the Golden Bull, a series
of decrees which gave the Electors considerable
independence of imperial authority, independence
which, during the sixteenth century enabled the
Elector of Saxony to protect Luther, and made
necessary the Treaty of Augsburg of 1555, whereby
the religious persuasion of individual princes
was to be imposed upon their respective citizens,
and was to be mutually recognized and acknowledged
by each of the separate independent states.

The example set by Saxony was followed only
a decade later by Sweden where King Gustavus Vara

openly avowed his support for church reform, while in 1536 King Christian III of Denmark and Norway gave his blessing to the formal establishment of a Lutheran State Church.

In England, Henry VIII (1509-46) was plagued by the problem of ensuring dynastic succession by a male heir. Of six children born to his first wife, Catherine of Aragon, only one, (the future Bloody) Mary, survived.[7] Unsuccessful in his Papal divorce proceedings, he married Anne Boleyn in 1533 and was accordingly excommunicated by Pope Clement VII. Henry responded promptly with the Act of Supremacy (1534) whereby he created a new national Church of England with himself at its head. Despite his dominant political aspirations Henry remained a true Catholic at heart, albeit of English persuasion.[8]

Released from all Papal restraints and prohibitions, Protestants everywhere asserted their freedom to read and interpret the Bible in their own way, with the inevitable consequence of dispute, discord, and dissention, and the proliferation of many varied and different sects. "Heresies" were as characteristic within Protestantism

----

7. At the age of 2, she was betrothed to the 7 month old (future King) Francis I of France. This meant that, with no male heir, the throne of England could automatically pass to the King of France.

8. He had at an earlier date voiced his unswerving support of the (Roman) Catholic faith and in 1521 he had issued his famous Assertion of the Seven Sacraments against Martin Luther for which Pope Leo X had accorded him the title of "Defensor Fidei," (Defender of the Faith), an inscription which still accompanies the representation of British monarchs on all coinage.

as they had been within Catholicism, and, persons
expressing deviant viewpoints were as prone and
subject to persecution, harassment, and hostility
as at any time in history. In England, a bitter
civil war (1642-9) culminated in the decapitation
of Charles I, the reigning monarch of the realm.
Likewise, in the English American Colonies, it
was only the United States Constitution (1789)
which eventually brought peace among the warring
Protestants.

Yet, where the new beliefs had not prevailed
there was even greater turmoil. In France, the
toleration Edict of Nantes (1598) was revoked in
1685, leading to mass expulsion of the Protestant
Huguenots. Germany, still earlier, had been
devastated by the Thirty Years' War (1618-48)
between Catholics and Lutherans, neither of whom
displayed any mercy towards Calvinists and Anabaptists. The Treaty of Westphalia (1648) which
ended the war did establish religious peace in
Germany, and it also brought political freedom to
the Netherlands, where Spanish Catholics and
Dutch Calvinists had been at war for eighty years.

In western Europe religious strife between
Christians virtually ceased after 1700, and the
east-west line of demarcation then established
has remained virtually unchanged. South of this
line lay the Catholic countries of Spain, Portugal, France, Italy, Bavaria, and Austria; north
of it lay the Protestant countries of England,
Wales, Scotland, the Netherlands, Scandinavia,
and Northern Germany. In this northern zone only
Poland and Ireland still remain predominantly
Catholic, and only in Ireland does the religious
bigotry and intolerance characteristic of the
Reformation period continue to prevail.

Education

Outside the predominantly Catholic countries
of Spain, Italy, and France, the immediate impact
of the Reformation upon education in western
Europe was disastrous. While no precise figures
exist, and even most estimates are suspect, it
has been calculated that no less than one-third
of the land (and its resources) in Britain,
Germany, and Scandinavia was owned by the Catholic
Church, and the wealth derived from such ownership
was in part applied to necessary activities at the
place of origin, activities which normally included the maintenance of schools.

What occurred in England was not typical of
Protestant states. Having established the new
national Church of England under the Act of
Supremacy (1534), Henry VIII proceeded upon the
dissolution of the monasteries, and sequestered
all the revenues of the confiscated properties
for his personal expenses and for essential state
business.[9] The result was the widespread closure
of monastic and cathedral schools most of which
were never reopened.[10] In countries where powerful
barons and counts existed, the dispossed ecclesiastical lands were promptly appropriated for the

----

9. The nursery rhyme, "Little Jack Horner" derives its origin from this period. Jack
   Horner was a stewart of Mells Abbey, Somerset,
   and when directed to bring the Abbey property
   deeds and documents to London he withheld
   some for his own advancement; hence the
   "plum" which "he pulled out."

10. The Chantries Act of 1548, transferring en-
    dowments to the monarchy specifically for
    educational purposes was also grossly mis-
    applied and the proceeds were diverted else-
    where.

purpose of extending territorial domains, again
without consideration for the educational services hitherto provided. In England, also, the
doctrine of the ruling aristocracy that education
was merely a personal service to be provided by
an individual family, or, on a voluntary basis,
by some interested charitable organization,
delayed involvement in education by the state
until well into the nineteenth century. Elsewhere in Europe, Lutheranism and Calvinism
advanced radical new viewpoints regarding the
relationship of Church, State, and education.
Martin Luther (1483-1546), like his great contemporary, Erasmus, was a scholar concerned with
church reform, but, unlike Erasmus who pleaded
for caution and a detached, non-violent approach,
Luther was a man of temper and action. He became
an Augustinian monk and a professor of theology
at Wittenberg University. Dismayed at corrupt
practices within the Catholic Church, he earnestly
sought answer in the Scriptures, and he believed
he found it in St. Paul's Epistle to the Romans
(1:17): "The just shall live by faith," and not
by their works. At this very time Pope Leo X[11]
was promoting a sale of indulgences to provide
money to rebuild the Church of St. Peter. As an
outward clash became inevitable, Luther encapsu-
lated his newly-formed principles into 95 Theses
and nailed these to the door of the church at
Wittenberg on October 31, 1517. By 1521, he had
been excommunicated and the Diet of Worms had
declared him a heretic. It was at this juncture
that he became ensured of the protection of

----

11. of whom it has been stated that he might
    have been an excellent Pope had he been
    religious.

96

Frederick the Wise, Elector of Saxony[12] so that
Luther, unlike his predecessors of reform, became
not a martyr but the Father of the Reformation.
Recognizing his privileged status, he gave no
support to the Peasants' Revolt of 1524-5, but
instead advanced the role of the State as the
final authority and arbiter in all temporal as
well as religious affairs. Since Luther had
declared the Bible, and not the Pope, to be the
ultimate authority in spiritual matters, he undertook the translation into German of the New Testament[13] in 1522, while in 1524 he composed his
Letter to the Burgomasters and Councillors of all
towns in German Lands, urging the Establishment
and Maintenance of Christian Schools. It was now
imperative, Luther asserted, that if the individual
Christian, and not the priest or the Pope, was to
be given the opportunity of determining the salvation of his eternal soul, he should likewise be
given full opportunity of being taught to read
the Scriptures, wherein he could instruct himself as to the accredited paths of righteousness.

Luther stressed the role of the family as a
crucial factor in the upbringing of a child, and

----

12. Frederick had earlier appropriated money
    which Pope Alexander VI had requested for
    a crusade against the Turks. Frederick had
    indicated his readiness to release the
    money when the crusade materialized. Since
    it never did, (and the Turks eventually
    were to besiege Vienna in 1529), Frederick
    donated the money to the University of
    Wittenberg.

13. At a later date (1533), he also translated
    the Old Testament as well as Aesop's Fables,
    of whose moral precepts he was fully in favor.

in 1530 he preached his powerful and influential
sermon, <u>On the Duty of Sending Children to School</u>,
wherein he elaborated upon the function of a
formal academic educational institution in sup-
plementing and furthering the moral foundations
firmly provided by a stable home environment. It
was for the State, he alleged, to furnish the
necessary organization, facilities, and supervision of education for all students within the
confines of its territorial boundaries.

Apart from his initial protection by
Frederick of Saxony, Luther was also favored by
the political situation whereby the advance of
the Turks up the Danube Valley made it expedient
for the Catholic Holy Roman Emperor, Charles V,
to seek the cooperation of German Protestants.
In 1529, the Diet of Speyer convened by Charles
formally permitted Lutheran church services in
the Lutheran States of Germany but also demanded
toleration of Catholics within these States; at
the same time it forbade Lutheran church services
in the Catholic States, a provision to which the
Lutherans rigorously "protested," hence the
origin of the term "Protestant."

Luther was privileged not merely by having
a political mentor by way of Frederick of Saxony,
but also by being associated with a fervent intellectual admirer, Philipp Melanchthon (1497-
1560),[14] a very capable educational administrator.
Professor of Greek at Wittenberg University he
published a <u>Discourse on Reforming the Studies</u>
<u>of Youth</u> (1518), and then proceeded upon his
great contribution to Lutheranism: his systematic plans for school organization, which, basically, provided for vernacular schools for all

----

14. He was christened Philipp Schwarzerd, mean-
     ing "Black Earth", which he himself con-
     verted into a Greek translation.

students in their early years, to be followed by
classical secondary schools, as well as for
institutions of higher education. Provision for
supervision by state officials was also included.
Cities and States all over Germany adopted his
suggestions, as also did the countries of Denmark,
Sweden, and Norway.

Melanchthon derived many of his ideas from
Johannes Bugenhagen (1485-1558) also a professor
at Wittenberg, who had advocated German vernacular
schools, Latin schools, as well as public libraries, and from Johann Sturm (1507-1589) of
Strassburg who in 1537 created the prototype of
the German Gymnasium. Sturm's school consisted
of ten grades, within each of which there was
provision for ability grouping. Religious piety
was stressed, along with the formal teaching of
Latin, with emphasis upon grammar and style, but
to the exclusion of the German language. In
1537 Sturm published his Book on the Right Method
of Founding Schools for Literary Education (De
literarum ludis recte aperienidis liber), and he
was to exercise great influence upon subsequent
secondary school developments in Germany.

In comparison with many other of the Protestants of his day Luther was a conservative reformer. Ulrich Zwingli (1484-1531) of Zurich,
for example, modeled his new organization strictly
on the New Testament, embodying his precepts in
a document consisting of Sixty Seven Theses.
While approving of the subordination of Church
to State, he advanced the theory of representative government. In 1523 he wrote The Christian
Education of Boys, the first work on 'Protestant'
education ever to be published. It was written
with the humanist approach, and emphasized, at
secondary level, the teaching of Scripture,
Ancient Languages (Latin, Greek, Hebrew), Mathematics, Science, Music, and Physical Education.

Zwingli was killed in battle in the conflict between the Protestants and Catholics in Switzerland.[15]

Zwingli was unfortunate not to have been
privileged to take full advantage of the unique,
prevailing political circumstances of his day,
whereas his contemporary, John Calvin (1509-1564),
was most certainly able to do so. In 1510 Pope
Julius II, in return for the recruitment of Swiss
mercenaries from Geneva, agreed that the town
council be allowed to supervise all monasteries,
and convents, as well as to regulate public morals.
The city council of Zurich emulated the precedent
created at Geneva, but (temporarily, at least) its
pioneering activities in this direction were
abruptly terminated by the action of neighboring
Catholics, with the fatal consequence referred to
in the foregoing paragraph.

Calvin, born in Picardy in Northern France,
a literary scholar[16] and trained as a lawyer,
apparently experienced a sudden conversion in
1532, following exposure to Protestant propaganda.
Fearing persecution, he went to Basle in Switzerland where in 1536 he published in Latin, The
Principles of Christian Religion (Christianae
religionis institutio), a work which was to dominate the literature of the Reformation. In it he
declared that man was innately evil and corrupt

----

15. Zurich later became a center of the Ana-
    baptists (= to be baptised again, as an adult),
    a very radical group, which in time, was to
    subdivide into the moderate Baptists on the
    one hand, and the more radical sects of the
    Mennonites, Hutterites, and Amish, on the
    other.

16. he published a tract on Seneca's De Clementia.

but that the Lord God had, in his divine mercy
and wisdom, accorded to certain "elected" individuals the power and strength to overcome their
initial, inherited disabilities: hence the doctrine of Predestination. The "elect" were to
demonstrate their privileged position by their
disciplined efficiency, prosperity, and diligence
for the spiritual welfare of the less privileged
majority, in furtherance of which not only was
the (eventual) Puritan Work Ethic[17] to be evolved,
but the reformed Church itself was to regulate
all details relating to faith, ritual, and morals,
while the State was made responsible for enforcing
all the regulations decreed by the ordained ecclestiastical authorities.

In the meantime, Calvin had moved from Basle
to Geneva, but in 1538 he was forced into exile
for three years because of his unorthodox views,
and during that period he taught courses in
religion at Johann Sturm's school in Strassburg,
an experience of immense value since he was here
indoctrinated into matters concerning the relationship between religion and education, as well as
into the principles of efficient organization.

Invited back to Geneva in 1541 he prepared
a set of Ecclesiastical Ordinances which he then
proceeded to implement. In effect, he created an
authoritarian theocracy to be controlled by the
Elect, within which all personal, family, and
public conduct was carefully regulated and supervised. Strict censorship was introduced and since
heresy was declared to be treason, it was punish-
able by death. The tenets of the new faith

----

17. sometimes termed the Divine Right of Capital-
     ists, since Calvin removed the Catholic ban
     on loans, although interest payments were
     not to exceed 5%.

demanded an educated ministry and a literate
laity, so that Calvin instituted an academy of
higher learning and a system of secondary schools
(Schola Privata) and of elementary schools (Schola
Publica). Graduates from the academy spread the
gospel of Calvinism into France (where the
Huguenots were, in time, to establish no fewer
than eight universities and thirty two colleges),
England, Scotland, and Holland, and thence into
the American Colonies. Calvin introduced many of
Sturm's ideas into the Genevan secondary schools,
but substantially reduced the proportion of time
spent in the classical languages in favor of the
vernacular French. The fact that Calvinism declared that all persons were born to sin focused
particular attention to discipline in the elementary schools. Children being considered naturally
prone to evil were subjected to harsh corporal
punishment for violation of school regulations,
and they were constantly directed to apply themselves to school studies.

The most famous and influential of Calvin's
disciples was undoubtedly John Knox (1505-59) of
Scotland. Educated at St. Andrew's University
he entered the priesthood. During the 1520's
Lutheran doctrines had percolated into Scotland,
but its adherents were persecuted and its most
fervent proponent, Patrick Hamilton, was burned
at the stake in 1528. In the course of subsequent decades the principles of Swiss Protestantism, first those of Zwingli, then of Calvin, had
spread into the country, due not least to the
evangelistic enthusiasm of George Wishart,
executed for his conscience in 1546, and it was
his preaching which led to the conversion of
John Knox. Soon after, Scotland was subjected
to an attack by France and Knox was captured,
whereupon he endured nineteen months as a galley
slave. Released in 1549 he then spent a tumul-
tuous decade fleeing from persecution either in

England, Scotland, or France. A man of fanatical personality, immense energy, and vituperative eloquence, he was not easily tolerated, and so had to abide his time in seething frustration until the opportune moment arrived for appropriate action.

This came when the Scottish nobles, irritated by the infiltration of Frenchmen into the court of Mary, Queen of Scots (betrothed to the future Francis II, King of France), assembled in 1557 as the "Lords of the Congregation of Jesus Christ" to sign the first Scottish Covenant whereby they resolved to demand complete liberty of worship and establish reformed churches throughout Scotland. They became even more insistent after the burning in 1558 of Walter Milne, the last known martyrdom of a Scottish Protestant, and they sent word to John Knox that he could be ensured of their protection upon his return from Geneva.

Knox accordingly sailed for Scotland in 1559 taking advantage of the death of the Catholic (Bloody) Mary of England in 1558, who was succeeded by the Protestant Queen Elizabeth. In 1560 the Scottish Reformation Parliament accepted a Confession of Faith written by John Knox which became the official creed of the Presbyterian Church, and,to its great credit, no dissenting religious adherent was ever thereafter martyred in Scotland.

Knox, together with his advisers, now prepared a First Book of Discipline, which included a comprehensive educational program for all classes within the community, the poor as well as the rich, girls as well as boys, and it, as well, made provision for adequate renumeration for teachers. To his intense chagrin, these plans were never implemented during his lifetime,

since too much of the expropriated monies derived from the confiscated monastic lands had
passed into the hands of rapacious landowners.
Nevertheless, Knox's plans for Calvinist education retained for Scotland an element of democracy
which was completely absent from England, but yet
through Puritan influence they were to be conveyed across the Atlantic to a New England.

There emerged in Central Europe yet one other
major educationist of the Reformation period:
John Amos Komensky (1592-1670), universally
better recognized as Comenius, who indirectly
provided a much needed antidote (by way of a more
humane approach) to the harsh rigors of the
Calvinist classroom. Comenius was born at
Nivnitz, Moravia. He attended Heidelberg University, and while in Germany, fell under the
influence of Wolfgang Ratke, a Protestant school
reformer. Comenius himself, a member of the
Moravian Brethren (a sect which had developed
from the teachings of John Huss) became in turn
a teacher, a pastor, and a school superintendent,
but as a result of the Thirty Years War (1618-48)
he and his followers were forced into exile to
Lissa (Lezno) in Poland. It was here that he
embarked upon those educational writings which
were to gain him so much fame during his own
lifetime. In 1632 he completed his Great Didactic
in Czech, (his native language), a work which
remained untranslated into Latin until 1657. In
it, he envisioned a comprehensive school system
designed to accommodate all citizens, and not
merely an intellectual or aristocratic elite.
He proposed four successive periods of schooling
each of six years:

a) The School of the Mother's Knee, from
birth to the age of six years, where, as the
title indicates, the family was to take precedence and function as the formative medium in

in the development of the child. Comenius wrote
The School of Infancy, a book of guidance for
parents, in which he stressed the importance of
family piety, health care, social activities,
and appropriate experiences in sense perception.

b) The Vernacular School, for ages seven
through twelve. Here, children were to be given
instruction in the native tongue, and were expected to spend four hours a day on lessons, two
in the morning (to develop knowledge and understanding in reading, writing, number, history,
geography, and religion) and two in the after-
noon (with attention to activities, such as
crafts and music). Comenius wrote six elementary
school texts, one for each year, and being somewhat obsessed by nature metaphors he entitled
them, in sequence, as follows: The Bed of Violets,
The Bed of Roses, The Garden of Letters, The
Labyrinth of Wisdom, The Spiritual Bed of Balsam,
and The Paradise Park of the Good. In these
books Comenius clearly demonstrated the necessity
for the teacher to recognize the stages of childhood development, and the need to prepare appropriate materials accordingly. He pleaded for
instruction and learning to be made pleasurable
and attractive since, he said, schools have
become

> not as their name previously indicated,
> places of amusement and delight, but
> grinding houses and places of torture
> for youth among certain peoples, espe-
> cially when youth were instructed by
> incompetent men, altogether uninstruc-
> ted in piety and the wisdom of God;
> such who had become imbecile through
> indolence, despicably vile, and af-
> fording the very worst example,
> through calling themselves masters
> and preceptors; for these did not
> imbue youth with faith, piety, and

sound morals, but with superstition,
impiety, and baneful morals, being
ignorant of the genuine method, and
thinking to inculcate everything by
force, they wretchedly tortured the
youth.

c) <u>The Latin School</u>, for ages thirteen
through eighteen. Comenius proposed a veritable
encyclopaedic course of study at secondary level,
to include classical languages (Latin, Greek,
Hebrew) sciences (physics, astronomy), mathematics, ethics, dialectic, music, theology, and
with emphasis upon history (ancient and modern)
as an integrating subject designed to unify and
permeate the entire subject offerings. The
medium of instruction was to be the vernacular
language and not Latin, but recognizing the need
for competency in the latter, Comenius published
his <u>Janua Linguarum Reserata</u> (The Door of Languages Unlocked), probably his most popular work.
Selecting 8,000 of the most common Latin words,
he combined them into 1,000 sentences of increasing syntactical difficulty, which in turn he
grouped into 100 sections, each relating to a
different topic. The book was an immediate success, it was translated into at least a dozen
languages, and made him universally famous.

d) <u>The University</u>, for ages nineteen through
twenty-four. Since Comenius favored higher education for the intellectual elite only, he proposed
that entry be accorded only to those who passed
a rigorous examination at the close of the secondary stage. He recommended that most students
would profit by specialization in studies for
which they had indicated competency and interest,
but that a certain gifted minority should be
encouraged to pursue a broad curriculum so that
they might attain Comenius' great ideal of
Pansophia, i.e. encyclopaedic universal knowledge
and wisdom, although, as he stated:

Do not imagine that we demand an exact
or thorough knowledge of all the arts
and sciences from all men. This would
neither be useful of itself, nor on
account of the shortness of life can
it be attained by anyone. It is the
principles, the causes, and the purposes of all the main facts about
the world that we wish everyone to
learn. For we must do all in our
power to ensure that no man in his
journey through life will ever encounter anything so unknown to him
that he cannot pass a sober judgment
upon it, and turn it to its proper use
without serious error.

A central feature of the Pansophic ideal
was to be a "College of Universal Knowledge,"
wherein scholars of all nations could be free to
assemble to discuss matters and disseminate
materials relating to their humanistic and scientific investigations. Comenius believed that the
universities of his day no longer felt obliged
to adhere to the earlier mediaeval objective of
cosmopolitanism and universalism, partly because
of the rise of nationalism and partly because
acute religious dissent had narrowed the horizon
of scholarship and independent thought.

His idea was taken up by Samuel Hartlib
(1600-1662) a Polish merchant who had settled
in England and was a remarkable, energetic personality. He persuaded Comenius to come to
England and he was instrumental in putting forward a proposal in Parliament in 1641 for a
Pansophic College. Unfortunately, the Civil War
between the Parliamentarians led by Oliver
Cromwell and the Royalist adherents of King
Charles I broke out precisely at this time and
the project was (temporarily) dropped.

Comenius then worked on the production of
textbooks in Sweden for four years, following
which he spent a further four years in Transylvania.
It was here he wrote a tract, On Manners and Laws
of a Well-ordered School in which he recommended
boarding facilities, with adequate classroom and
residential accommodation, as well as the primary
need for the appointment of an efficient headmaster, who could be assured of the cooperation
of supportive parents. More important was
Comenius' school text, the Orbis Sensualium Pictus
(The World in Pictures), considered to be one of
the first illustrated textbooks in education.
Comenius stressed that "words should always be
taught and learned in combination with things."
Wherever possible, nature rambles and field trips
should be systematically organized, but the world
was vast and the obvious alternative was to produce a text wherein 'words' and 'things' were illustrated. As might be expected from Comenius'
educational philosophy, the Orbis was encyclopaedic
in scope, and Latin words and phrases were accompanied by translation into the vernacular (initially, German). Comenius' visual approach did not
end with his textbook, since he also advocated
that classroom walls should be made attractive
with maps, pictures of famous men and great events,
together with "models of all kinds to assist the
memory to retain ideas and facts." Following his
return to Poland, an outbreak of war with Sweden
forced him to flee to Amsterdam where he spent
the remainder of his life.

As mentioned above, Samuel Hartlib, a formidable educational propagandist in England, had
become much attracted with the possibility of
translating many of Comenius' visionary concepts
into practice. Hartlib himself displayed utopian
propensities since in 1641 he published a discourse entitled A Description of the Famous Kingdom of Macaria wherein he described the means

whereby the scientific method could be applied
to all manner of human activities but especially
those related to agriculture, industry, health,
and human welfare. In 1647 he presented to
Parliament a tract, Considerations tending to the
happy accomplishment of England's Reformation in
Church and State, a comprehensive proposal which
included a labor office to propagate and implement work opportunities, an international bureau
to facilitate exchange of educational, intellectual,
and religious ideas, and a patent office to regis-
ter, and widely disseminate knowledge of new
inventions. All these facilities were to be incorporated in a great Office of Address, to be
domiciled in one of the colleges at Oxford. Un-
dismayed by the non-acceptance of his proposals,
Hartlib went on to publish his Essay for Advancement of Husbandry Learning, (1651) which incorporated a project for a College of Agriculture.
Again, nothing of tangible consequence emerged,
yet within a brief interval of time following his
death an institution of considerable significance
in Britain received in 1662 its official charter:
The Royal Society of London for Improving Natural
Knowledge.[18] Known generally as the Royal Society,
it has retained ever since its inception an
honored status as an academy of gifted scientists
and intellectuals.

Hartlib was indefatigable in his efforts to
interest his friends and colleagues in education.
He was instrumental in persuading John Milton to
write a tractate Of Education (1644), in which he

----

18. It is believed that as early as 1645 weekly
    meetings were held in London of "divers
    worthy persons, inquisitive into natural
    philosophy and other parts of human learning,"
    while in 1648 a Philosophical Society had
    been formed at Oxford.

presented a comprehensive course of studies for youth aged 12 through 21, focusing upon Latin as the basic subject throughout. Prior to the age of 16, the ancillary subjects were to include arithmetic, geometry, geography, astronomy, natural philosophy, and agriculture, with due respect to the contribution of ancient classical authors. Other languages including Greek, Hebrew, and French were also to be studied. After the age of 16, a wide variety of practical subjects was to be offered, such as trigonometry, architecture, fortification, engineering, navigation, medicine, and anatomy, together with an extended series of courses on classical literature.

Another of Hartlib's acquaintances was John Dury (1596-1680), who actually spent a few years ministering to the English residents of Hartlib's home town of Elbing in Poland. In 1649 he published The Reformed School wherein he sought to propagate many of the educational principles of Comenius. Dury's ideal was the small community school with boarding facilities and a staffing ratio of no more than one teacher to twelve boys. Piety was to be stressed since Dury considered knowledge, as such, to be "the last and least part of education." Given these conditions, the process of teaching and learning should be happy and animated and should result in a strong motivation to pursue further studies in a Christian spirit. Dury also wrote The Reformed Librarie Keeper, a work which did much to arouse interest in the desirability of creating libraries in schools.

Another teacher, strongly influenced by Comenius was Charles Hoole (1610-67) of Rotherham, who not only published an English version of the Orbis Pictus, but also wrote A New Discovery of the Old Art of Teaching School, wherein he advocated a practical and enjoyable approach to learning.

In 1673 Mrs. Bathsua Makin made a plea, in her _Essay to Revive the Ancient Education of Gentlewomen_, for attention to be given to equal status for girls. Strongly influenced by Comenius[19] she was a pioneer in girls' education.

Earlier reference has been made to the initially grievous consequences of the closure of monastic institutions in England since most of the expropriated funds were allocated for purposes other than education, but, in time, restitution did take place, albeit with due circumspection and with no haste. The two universities of Oxford and Cambridge suffered drastically and it is on record that in 1547 and 1550 Oxford had no graduates at all. Prior to the English Reformation, three colleges had been founded during the sixteenth century at Oxford: Brazenose (1509), Corpus Christi (1516), and Christ Church, founded by Cardinal Wolsey in 1525 and refounded by Henry VIII in 1532. The Tudor monarch also established Trinity College, Cambridge in 1546 and financed professorships there in Greek, Hebrew, divinity, law, and medicine.

By the latter half of the same century, the growing prosperity of the English merchant middleclass was becoming manifest in the marked increase in funds being made available for education from private sources. Not only were three further colleges founded at Oxford (Trinity, 1554; St. John's, 1555; Jesus, 1571), and two at Cambridge (Emmanuel, 1584; Sidney Sussex, 1596), but both universities were assured of a supply of students through a significant increase in the number of Public Schools

----

19. Probably by reason of the correspondence between Comenius and her brother, John Pell, the mathematician. Mrs. Makin was also employed as a tutor to the Stuart Royal Family.

whence they drew their student recruitment.
There were only four such schools in existence
before 1536;[20] between this date and the death of
Elizabeth (1603), no fewer than thirteen additional institutions had been established,[21] while
more than one hundred local secondary (grammar)
schools had also been founded in a well distributed pattern throughout England and Wales. John
Brinsley, (1585-1665) a school-master with over
twenty years experience at Ashby-de-la-Zouche,
published in 1612 his Ludus Literarius (The
Grammar School), a most valuable source book providing a wealth of material relating to classroom
practices of the period. Written in the form of
a dialogue between two teachers, the work pro-
fesses to offer sound advice from the more experienced pedadogue (Philoponus), to his younger
colleague (Spondeus), who is in a mood of growing
depression from his encounters with teaching problems. Large classes provide on-going difficulties,
and Philoponus recommends a monitorial system,
(as did Comenius and other contemporaries). The
problem of Latin versus the vernacular language
as the medium of instruction at secondary level
was still an issue of the day, but the need for
competent English teaching in the elementary
school was strongly stressed by Philoponus who
comments

> it were much to be wished that none
> might be admitted to the Grammar

----

20. These were Winchester (1387), Eton (1440),
     St. Paul's, London (1509), and Manchester
     (1515).

21. Sherborne (1550), Shrewsbury (1551), Christ's
     Hospital (1552), King Edwards' School, Birm-
     ingham (1552), Tonbridge (1553), Repton
     (1557), Westminster (1560), Merchant Taylors,
     London (1561), Bedford (1566), Rugby (1567),
     Harrow (1571), Uppingham (1584), and Stony-
     hurst (1592).

schools until they were able to read
English. Yet, where it cannot be
redressed, it must be borne with wisdom and patience as a heavy burden.
Patience shall make it more light.

In a further work, A Consolation for our
Grammar Schooles (1622), Brinsley wrote at length
upon the imperative requirement for well prepared
instructors for the "laying of a sure foundation
of all good learning in our schooles," and he
strongly advocated the establishment of teacher-
training colleges.

Concern by Catholics at the success of the
Protestant Reformation in Northern Europe led to
the movement known as the Counter Reformation.
The thirteenth century "protest" action of the
Albigensians and Waldensians had already resulted
in the founding of the two great Catholic mendicant orders, those of the Dominicans (the Black
Friars) and Franciscans (the Grey Friars), respectively. Recognizing the power and inter-
relationship of sound belief and knowledge, St.
Dominic adopted the policy of establishing houses
in the great university towns, and within his own
lifetime the Dominicans came to be well-established
at Paris, Bologna, and Oxford. At these and many
other universities, including Salamanca, Padua,
Cologne, and Vienna, the Dominicans became recognized as the great teachers of the age, amongst
whom Thomas Aquinas and Albert the Great took
precedence. Their academic influence had gradually declined over the centuries, but at the
time of the Protestant Reformation, they had been
placed in charge of the Inquisition, albeit now
within the narrower confines of the Catholic
states only.

The Franciscans were also prominent as
university teachers during the earlier centuries

113

of their existence, with Roger Bacon of England
emerging as one of the seminal thinkers of his
age. More so than any other Order, however, the
Franciscans suffered considerable internal discord, and in time came to devote the major part
of their service to the welfare and humanitarian
needs of the less privileged members of society.

At the time of the Protestant Reformation
the Catholic Church was on the defensive but it
was at this critical period in its history that
there emerged what was probably the most formidable single educational institution ever established: The Society of Jesus. Founded by
Ignatius Loyola (1491-1556) in 1534, it received
papal sanction as an Order of the Church in
1540, and by 1542 it had opened its first college
at Coimbra in Portugal, and had spread so rapidly
overseas so that its second college was at Goa,
India, founded by Francis Xavier, also in 1542.
The energy of the Society was phenomenal: by
the year 1600 there were in existence either in
Europe, Asia, or the Americas, almost 250 colleges
or universities. The basic thrust of the Society
lay in the direction of the education of a force-
ful, intellectual elitist and dedicated priesthood whose purpose it would be to lead and direct
rather than merely serve and respond to the con-
ventional, quotidian, and parochial needs of the
normal parishioners of the Church.

Loyola had received training as a soldier
and the Order was organized along military lines.
Its chief officer was the General, who was ac-
countable directly to the Pope. The regions
under his administration were subdivided into
provinces, each presided over by a "provincial."
The first Constitution of the Society drawn up
by Loyola in 1541 was conceived in somewhat
general terms and the colleges tended to develop
their own individual curricula, thus creating
problems of content and teaching methods. The

fourth General, Claudius Aquaviva, decided to resolve the dilemma and appointed a committee of six members from different provinces whose duty it became to formulate a standard academic plan. Published in 1591, it was subjected to experiment and revision for eight years and received its final format in 1599 as the Ratio atque Institutio Studiorum Societatis Jesu.[22]

The colleges were conceived as training institutions for a well-informed, disciplined body of efficient teachers. With Latin as the medium of instruction, the basic curriculum consisted of three parts:

    a) the humanities: Latin and Greek literature and history;
    b) the arts and natural sciences: rhetoric, logic, physics, metaphysics, mathematics;
    c) theology: the acme of the entire course.

The teaching methods were defined in detail and were not to be deviated from. The Ratio Studiorum provided guidance as to which of the works of the classical authors were acceptable for study,[23] the manner in which the text was to be explained, and the procedure to be adopted in discussion. Regular examinations were conducted, and the students were encouraged to compete in disputations and debates and to engage in play production. Discipline was strict but humane. Teachers were expected to be firm, but to achieve loyalty and devotion by the influence of character

----

22. more commonly abbreviated as the Ratio Studiorum (the Plan of Studies). It remained unaltered until 1832.

23. The first Papal Index of prohibited books was issued under Pope Paul IV (1555-9).

and personality and not through punishment.

For over two hundred years the Jesuits provided the most thorough and best organized system
of secondary schools and colleges in the western
Christian world.[24]   The Order was ultimately suppressed by Papal decree in 1773,[25]   not by reason
of failure, but because it had proved itself to
be too successful, and had aroused the jealousy
and envy of temporal monarchs and rulers.

The Jesuits were not without rivals, and two
institutions of note made their appearance in
France during the first half of the seventeenth
century, directly or indirectly as a result of
the inspiration of one of the foremost graduates
of a Jesuit college of his day;   Rene Descartes
(1596-1650).   His scientific mind rebelled
against the rigidity of the Jesuit teaching approach, with its unremitting demands upon the
unquestioning acceptance of narrowly defined concepts and viewpoints.   Instead, he demanded that
students be encouraged to think, reason, and
enter into discussion for the purpose of eluci-
dating facts and truths.   He incorporated his
many proposals and precepts in a tract entitled
A Discourse on the Method of rightly conducting
the Reason and Seeking Truth in the Sciences
(1637).   Equally as important was his insistence
upon writing and communicating in his native
language, French.

The first new institution (in time) was the

----

24.   By 1700, there were in existence over 20
      Jesuit universities and more than 700 colleges.

25.   The decree was rescinded in 1814 by Pope
      Pius VII.   In the intervening period the
      Jesuits set up their headquarters in Russia.

teaching congregation of the <u>Oratory of Jesus</u>,
founded in 1611 by Pierre de Berulle (1575-1629),
along the lines of the Italian Oratory founded
in 1575 by St. Philip Neri (1515-1595). It was
initially designed to offer appropriate instruction for young men desirous of entering the priesthood, but it extended its activities to provide
a comprehensive education for the sons of noble-
men. The Oratorian teachers stressed the importance of competency in reading, writing and
speaking the French language. [26] Latin was duly
introduced as a subject but with emphasis upon
the content of classical literature rather than
upon form and grammar. The curriculum included
mathematics, sciences, geography, and particularly
history, not merely that of the ancients, but
also of mediaeval and contemporary France. The
Cartesian principle of freedom of inquiry in the
search for truth remained a foremost objective
of the Oratorian schools until they were suppressed in 1792 in consequence of the French
Revolution.

The Oratorians displayed remarkable resil-
ience in face of constant attack by the Jesuits
who were firmly of the belief that the open
minded approach led to dissent and heresy, and
would result in still further disruption within
the Catholic church. While the Oratorians survived and even outlived the Jesuits, the second
teaching congregation, the <u>Little Schools of Port
Royal</u>, was less fortunate, but yet came to exert
lasting influence upon education in France. The
congregation took its name from the Cistercian
abbey of Port Royal situated to the southwest of
Paris. In 1635 Jean Duvergier (Saint Cyran) was
appointed as spiritual director. He had studied

----

26. The efforts of the Oratorians in this dir-
     ection were to receive no little impetus
     from the founding of the Academie Française
     in 1629.

at Louvain where he had come under the influence
of Cornelius Jansen (Bishop of Ypres 1636-8), a
theologian who believed in the doctrine of predestination. Like the Calvinists, the Jansenists
stressed the importance of education whereby the
"elected few" might be better equipped to serve
as community leaders. A modest beginning was
made by the opening of a school in 1637,[27] but
the movement suffered a severe setback by the
imprisonment of Saint Cyran for his Jansenist
views and his death in 1643. Undaunted, a group
of his followers, including a gifted teacher and
textbook writer, Claude Lancelot, placed the
school on a firm basis in 1646. Stress was laid
upon the teaching of the French language, and
classical literature was studied with the view
to achieving a better understanding of French
rather than Latin. Class size was limited to
five or six students so that each member could
receive individual attention both as regards his
intellectual capacity as well as his moral and
spiritual development.

The principles and objectives of the Little
Schools were widely publicized through the writings of able proponents, such as Pierre Coustel:
Rules for the Education of Children; Pierre
Nicole: A Treatise on the Education of a Prince;
and Antoine Arnauld: Rules for Humanistic
Studies. Another prominent Jansenist who joined
the Port Royal community was Blaise Pascal (1623-
62) author of the French classic, Pensees sur la
religion, but it was his Provinciales, (Provincial
Letters), a sarcastic indictment of the Jesuits,
which brought about the downfall of the Little
Schools. Incensed by his criticisms the Jesuits

----

27. The term 'Little School' (ecole petite) was
     used to avoid confusion with the Jesuit
     schools and the schools attached to the
     University of Paris.

brought pressure to bear in the French Court, and
all the schools were closed in 1661 by a decree
issued by Louis XIV.

The direct educational impact of the political and religious ferment which accompanied the
Protestant Reformation has been outlined in the
foregoing paragraphs. What is not so evident is
the impact of the slow but certain advance of
scientific discovery during the sixteenth and
seventeenth centuries. This may be attributed to
several factors: in the first place, Protestants
as well as Catholics were more concerned with the
eternal than the temporal world, so that both
religious persuasions tended either to disregard
matters of science or to consider them highly
suspect in fomenting heresy and disbelief in the
accepted interpretations of the Bible.[28] In the
second place, knowledge concerning the various
discoveries was confined to academic circles in
the higher institutions of learning, and even
there "Science" itself was seldom an accredited
discipline except perhaps as "Astrology."[29]

Despite these limitations, even a mere list-
ing of some of the scientific advances of the
period is impressive. Copernicus set the scene
when his work on the heliocentric theory was published in the year of his death (1543). Tycho
Brahe (1546-1601) a Dane, never abandoned his own
belief in the geocentric theory, yet accomplished
a major achievement when, without the benefit of
a telescope, he catalogued the positions of no
----
28. Luther for example, rejected the heliocen-
    tric theory since, in the Bible, Joshua had
    commanded the sun, and not the earth to
    stand still.

29. Astrology was taught as a subject at the
    University of Salamanca until 1770.

fewer than 777 stars. His colleague at Prague
was Johann Kepler (1571-1630)[30] who extended
Brahe's catalogue to more than a thousand stars,
and who formulated planetary laws which substan-
tiated the heliocentric theory, and which were
later to provide the bases for Newton's inquiries
into the nature of gravitation. It was the invention of the telescope by Galileo (1564-1642)
which literally opened up a New World in space
although he placed himself in jeopardy on several
occasions by his statements that the heliocentric
theory was a fact and not a mere hypothesis.
The microscope was also made available (c. 1590)
during this period through the work of Zacharias
Janssen of Middleburg in the Netherlands.

The measurement of heat was made possible
by thermometers devised by both Galileo (1603)
and Sanctorius, (1612) while the measurement of
pressure was simplified by Torricelli's barometer
(1643), and William Gilbert, physician to Queen
Elizabeth initiated the science of electricity
with his work On the Magnet (1600). Vesalius
(1514-64) of Brussels instituted the science of
anatomy with his volume On the Structure of the
Human Body (1543), and by 1628 William Harvey had
made public his research on the nature of the
circulation of blood.

In the field of mathematics, Michael Stifel
in his Arithmetica Integra (1544) introduced
plus and minus signs, and only a decade or so
later, Robert Recorde's Whetstone of Wit (1557)
introduced the "equals" (=) sign. Further significant advances were made by Simon Stevinus
who demonstrated the value of decimals (1585),

----

30. While Kepler was absorbed in his scientific
    studies, his mother underwent imprisonment
    following false accusations of witchcraft.
    She died soon after her release.

and by Napier who devised a system of logarithms
(1614). Later in the seventeenth century
Leibnitz and Newton published their respective
contributions to the development of calculus.
Exploration and colonization had led to new or
improved mathematical instruments such as the sex-
tant and astrolabe, while Mercator's Projection
(1569) enabled map making and surveying to be
placed on a more systematic basis.

The universities in general did little to
promote the new developments, although chairs in
science and mathematics were introduced at Cambridge in 1663. The more progressive intellectuals,
concerned with this apathy, wrote extensively on
the need for new institutions whose objective
would be the study of the new sciences and of new
scientific methods. Reference has already been
made to the Pansophic project of Comenius and to
Hartlib's Office of Address. In 1640, Richelieu
in his Testament Politique formulated plans for
a college intended to specialize in the "mechanical arts", to include physics, geometry, arithmetic, mechanics, trigonometry, optics. astronomy,
geography, mapmaking, and history.[31]

Although not a scientist, Francis Bacon
(1561-1626), (Baron Verulam) Lord Chancellor of
England, was the foremost philosopher of science
of his day. A legal expert, and well educated
in the classics, he had no qualms in publicly
declaring what he considered to be his real
avocation in life:

----

31. These efforts, on either side of the English
    Channel, went not without subsequent reward:
    The Royal Society was founded in 1662, and
    the Academie des Sciences in 1666. In
    Germany, the Berlin Academy was established
    in 1700.

> I found that I was fitted for nothing
> so well as for the study of truth; as
> having a mind nimble and versatile
> enough to catch the resemblances of
> things (which is the chief point) and
> at the same time steady enough to fix
> and distinguish their subtler differ-
> ences; as being gifted by nature with
> desire to seek, patience to doubt,
> fondness to meditate, slowness to
> assert, readiness to consider, care-
> fulness to dispose and set in order;
> as being a man that neither affects
> what is new nor admits what is old,
> and that hates every kind of imposture.
> So I thought my nature had a kind of
> familiarity and relation with Truth.

In 1605 he published The Advancement of
Learning condemning the universities as being
institutions merely for training in the ministerial and legal professions at the expense of
providing basic knowledge and content in the
arts and sciences. He insisted upon freedom of
inquiry since, to him, education existed only so
that "the rightness of the way" could be dis-
cerned. Bacon's greatest contribution was his
Novum Organum (1620): The New (Scientific)
Method, wherein he elaborated upon the necessity
of the inductive or empirical approach by col-
lecting, experimenting, and classifying facts and
data, before drawing conclusions and making gen-
eralizations. Since the purpose of knowledge
was to enable mankind to control nature it was
imperative to determine which cause produced
which effect:

> Man, who is the servant and inter-
> preter of nature, can act and under-
> stand no further than he has observed,
> either in operation or in contempla-
> tion, of the method and order of nature.

In the attempt to understand the world he gave warning against four False Ideas (Idola) which could limit comprehension: Idola Tribus: idols of the tribe (mankind), which presume there is greater order in nature than there actually exists; Idola Specus: Idols of the Cave, which furnish prejudices; Idola Fori: idols of the marketplace, where words and passions limit reason; and Idola Theatri: idols of the playhouse (or pulpit), which lead to the acceptance of mistaken ideas simply because they are uttered by those in authority.

Bacon attempted to compile an encyclopedic summary of all knowledge by way of clarifying and demonstrating his scientific method, and in a later work, The New Atlantis, he sought to describe how science could be harnessed to improve the world. This was one of a number of utopian writings characteristic of the period of the Reformation which was one of sustained political and religious turmoil when idealists yearned for heavens in this world as well as in the next.

In 1516 Sir Thomas More published a work in Latin at Louvain entitled Nusquama (Lat: Nowhere). The first English translation did not appear until 1551, when the name had been euphoniously changed to Utopia (Gk: ou, not; topos, place). More describes a fictitious conversation with a certain Ralph Hythlodaye (Gk: skilled in nonsense) who had supposedly sailed to the New World with Vespucci, and had visited the paradise island of Utopia. There, the natives had established a communal society, (but based on slavery), owning nothing, so that every person had an abundance of everything. A daily routine of six hours work was imposed upon everyone to ensure an adequate contribution towards the overall needs of the citizens. Money was unnecessary, but gold was used to purchase mercenary soldiers

for the defense of the state. Monogamy was practised but divorce by consent was permitted,[32] as
was marriage by priests. Religious toleration
was the rule, except for atheists. A national
system of education had been established, and
provision had been made for election of representatives to the state assembly. The overtones
of Plato's Republic are very evident throughout
the entire work.

Rabelais (1494-1555), in his Thelema, de-
picted an ideal monastery characterized by friendship and devotion to learning. It was a work
derived in part from his personal experiences in
both Franciscan and Dominican institutions (which
he eventually abandoned for his studies in medicine) and in part from his personal observations
of less reputable monastic institutions.

The most tragic of utopian writers of the
Reformation was Tommaso Campanella (1568-1639).
Born and bred in the impoverished region of
Calabria in Southern Italy he became involved in
conspiracies to free the territory from Spain.
Captured and convicted, he spent 26 years of his
life in prison (1599-1626), and it was there that
he wrote Civitas Solis (City of the Sun), completed in 1602, but not published until 1622.
His ideal community was located on a mountain in
Ceylon, and he envisaged a state governed by pure
reason. Slavery was non-existent, and compulsory
work was limited to four hours per day, simply
because of the devoted enthusiasm of the citizens
who had devised a hierarchy of employment-status
whereby the most demeaning drudgery in normal
civilizations received top priority and was considered to be ennobling of character. Provision

----

32. Henry VIII's on-going problem was that his
    first wife, Catherine of Aragon would not
    consent to a divorce, which might otherwise
    have been allowed by the Pope.

was made for communally-held property, for elected government officials, as well as for a unique system of education with all knowledge being posted on the city walls, so that early schooling was considered unnecessary. At a later stage, however, ample provision was made for a most comprehensive and all-inclusive curriculum of studies, within which the humanities, mathematics, the sciences, and practical subjects were given due recognition.

Not long afterwards, in 1619, another Italian author, Johann Valentin Andreae (1586-1654) published his Christianopolis (The Christian City), whose most significant feature was the status accorded to science. Central to his scheme was a college which included laboratories for mathematics, astronomy, natural science, chemical science, pharmaceutical science, as well as demonstration theaters for anatomy and physiology.

It is uncertain whether Francis Bacon was familiar with the foregoing utopian publications, but living within the age of hitherto unprecedented scientific invention and innovation, he was certainly at liberty to indulge in likewise hitherto inconceivable, ideal, scientific commonwealths, without knowledge of, or recourse to contemporary authors. His New Atlantis (1624) was an ideal state situated on an island, and its focal feature was Salomon's House, a veritable labyrinth of scientific research. Since Bacon was of the belief that the whole purpose of science and education was the betterment of human and societal conditions on earth, all manner of experiments were to be conducted and adequately financed along the basic principle that appropriate knowledge derived from research should be applied to enhance the quality of life.[33]

33. In 1626, Bacon himself became a martyr to his belief. While attempting to demonstrate the principle of refrigeration by stuffing a chicken with snow, he caught a chill and died.

In 1656 James Harrington published The
Commonwealth of Oceana, a less romantic and more
politically practicable conception than most of
its thematic precedents, so much so that many
reviewers have regarded it as a more than possible inspiration for the Constitutional Convention of the United States. Harrington maintained
that political authority was based on economic
power, and in this he had ample evidence of the
strength displayed by the powerful merchant middle class in England which had, only a few years
earlier, created an army sufficiently formidable
to overthrow the dominant ruling aristocracy, and
to execute a monarch who had claimed unquestioned
obedience on the grounds of the "divine right of
Kings." Harrington declared that the office of
chief state executive should be one held for a
definite and limited period of time, that his
powers should be defined in a written constitution, that a bicameral legislature would serve
his Commonwealth best, and that all elections
should be conducted by secret ballot. It is of
no little wonder than when the monarch was restored to power in England, Harrison was imprisoned (1661) for his republican views.

With the phenomenal output of sectarian,
propagandist, idealistic, scientific literature
published during the sixteenth and seventeenth
centuries it is very evident that the Reformation
and all its concomitant dimensions might well
have been delayed for one or more centuries had
it not been for one decisive factor: the invention of the printing press. In 1454, Johann
Gutenberg of Mainz produced the oldest extant
printed work, and 46 copies still survive of his
famous Bible [34] published two years later. Within twenty years, presses had been set up in Italy
----
34. It was the Vulgate version, and about 300
     copies were originally printed.

France, Holland, Switzerland, Hungary, Spain,
and England. Since the Protestant Reformers
wished their adherents to read the Bible in the
vernacular, their good intentions would have been
of little avail without the prolific output of
the printing press. Luther's German version
became readily available after 1520, while in
1535-9, Myles Coverdale produced the first
Authorised Version of the Bible in English.[35]
In 1560 the Puritans produced the Geneva Bible,
and in due course, the English Catholics published the Douai Bible (1609).

Copies of original or translated classical
texts facilitated the work of pedagogues all over
western Europe. During the seventeenth century
knowledge of scientific discoveries became widely
disseminated, thus encouraging still further freedom of research and inquiry, which in turn eased
the path of the emancipated intellects of the
eighteenth century period of the Enlightenment.

35. Unauthorised translated versions had been
     produced by John Wyclif (c. 1382) and
     William Tyndale (by 1535).
     The Second Authorised Version was published
     in 1568, and the Third (The King James)
     Version in 1611.

CHAPTER SEVEN

EDUCATION IN THE AMERICAN COLONIES

Introduction

Rivalries between the major political states
in Western Europe were to be expanded on a global
scale during, and subsequent to, the Great Age of
Discovery and Exploration. The latter was initiated by Portugal which,having annexed the African
port of Ceuta in 1415, proceeded on a systematic
basis to dispatch its sailors southwards along the
west African coast, so that Cape Verde was reached
by 1445, the Cape of Good Hope by 1488, and India
itself by 1498. Two years later, Cabral, blown
off course enroute to India, landed in Brazil, and
so within two years, one hitherto insignificant
country had fortuitously linked the continent of
Europe with two New Worlds, one in the East and
one in the West.

Next on the scene was Spain which, following
centuries of a laborious process of political unification, culminating in the capitulation of
Moorish Granada in 1492, sought quickly to place
limits upon the hitherto unrestricted territorial
acquisitions of her neighbor, Portugal, by the
papal bulls of 1493, and the Treaty of Tordesillas
of 1494, which divided the whole unexplored world
between these two countries.

For virtually a whole century the other western states of Europe showed little interest in
political affairs outside their own immediate
boundaries. England commissioned John Cabot, a

Genoese sailor (like Columbus), to explore the possibility of a western route to the East in 1497 and 1498, while France financed another Italian, Verrazano, to do likewise in 1524. A decade later, Jacques Cartier discovered the mouth of the St. Lawrence River. Neither England nor France followed up these discoveries, an indifference in direct contrast to Spain which, by 1535, had explored, conquered, and annexed virtually the whole of the Americas south of (but including) modern Florida and excluding only the east coast of Brazil (formally alloted to Portugal).

But by the end of the sixteenth century, marked changes began to be evident in the political situation in Western Europe. In England and Holland, the fervor of the Protestant Reformation had been accompanied by an eruption of aggressive nationalism, and the defeat of the Spanish Armada in 1588 represents a significant watershed in international affairs. Thereafter, the English and Dutch, confident, arrogant, and assertive, moved into North America, the Caribbean, Africa, India, and the East Indies, everywhere challenging the hegemony of Spain,[1] although in so doing the the two powers themselves became arch-rivals for almost the entire period of the seventeenth century, towards the close of which France replaced Holland as England's major colonial competitor.

On the North American continent, England's first efforts at colonization proved to be a disaster. In 1585 and again in 1587 settlements were established at Roanoke (in North Carolina) under the sponsorship of Sir Walter Raleigh, but

----

1. In 1580, Philip II of Spain annexed Portugal, which until 1640 was virtually defenceless against incursions into her colonial possessions by Holland and England.

no trace of any colonists was found in 1591 when, after a lapse of four years, an attempt was made to re-establish contact. Sixteen years later, a better organized and financed expedition sent out by the London Company brought 105 colonists to a settlement they named Jamestown on May 13, 1607. Under the guidance and leadership of John Smith and John Rolfe, and reinforced by annual immigration, the colony prospered and numbered 2,000 by 1619, a significant date in American history for two reasons: in the first place, the colonists established the House of Burgesses, the first representative assembly in the Americas; secondly, the first negroes imported into the English American colonies were disembarked from a Dutch ship.

One year later, in 1620 a group of 102 Protestant Separatists, the Pilgrims,[2] (whose original destination was Virginia) arrived on the Mayflower in Provincetown Harbor on Cape Cod and settled at Plymouth. Inspired and encouraged by its able leader, William Bradford, the colony overcame its many hardships and was to retain an independent status until almost the end of the seventeenth century.[3]

In 1628, the unsettling political and economic conditions prevailing in England impelled

----

2. They represented a doctrinaire viewpoint which completely rejected the concept of an established state church. In 1608 many Separatists had fled England to Holland, but fearing absorption into the Dutch way of life, they sought refuge in 1620 in the New World.

3. It was eventually merged with Massachusetts Bay Colony in 1691.

the first group of Puritans[4] to leave England to seek a new life in the New World. For the most part they were well-educated, middle-class merchants who emigrated not merely to "New England" but to any congenial environment in the New World[5]. In 1630, a large contingent of 500 Puritans led by John Winthrop arrived with a charter of the new Massachusetts Bay Colony and settled in the area they named Boston. Seeking religious freedom for themselves, they were intolerant of any dissent. In 1636 they banished Roger Williams who migrated to Providence, which in due course (1663) secured a charter from Charles II as the "Rhode Island and Providence Plantations."

Puritans moving southwestwards founded Hartford in 1635-6 and New Haven in 1637; in 1662, these and other settlements obtained a charter which established the colony of Connecticut.

The fourth of the New England colonies was New Hampshire, first settled in 1623, but by 1642 the territory had fallen to the control of the Massachusetts Bay Colony, and it was not until 1679 that it was constituted as a separate colony.

In North America, the term 'Virginia'[6] had

----

4. In origin, the Puritans were those members of the Church of England (the Anglican Church) who simply sought to "purify" that Church from all traces of Catholicism.

5. Between 1620 and 1642, the number of Puritans emigrating to the Americas has been estimated as follows:
    14,000 Massachusetts
     4,000 Other parts of New England
    18,000 West Indies
    18,600 Barbados

6. named in honor of the "Virgin" Queen Elizabeth.

originally been applied by Sir Walter Raleigh to a large undefined territory along the east coast. It was later (1612) more specifically delimited by Captain John Smith as lying between 34° N and 44° N latitudes (i.e. from the northern boundary of North Carolina to Maine). In due course not only were the four New England colonies created out of the territory of "Virginia', but so also were six others to the south. In 1632, Charles I granted a charter to the Catholic George Calvert (first Lord Baltimore) who proceeded to establish a colony named Maryland,[7] as a haven for members of his faith, but with tolerance for other Christian persuasions.

Carolina was settled by Virginians moving downstream along the Appalachian river valleys, though not until c. 1660 was the first permanent English colony established. Soon afterwards (1663), Charles II granted "Carolana" (renamed 'Carolina') to eight favorite members of the English Court, and in 1712 the territory was formally separated into North and South Carolina. Georgia, the last in time of the Thirteen Colonies, was created out of South Carolina and given to James Oglethorpe in 1732,[8] partly to serve as a strategic buffer colony against the Spaniards of Florida and partly to function as a refuge for persecuted Protestant sects in England.

The development of the five English Middle colonies in North America was complicated by the existence of settlements by two other European countries: Holland and Sweden. In 1614, the Dutch constructed Fort Nassau (near Albany) upstream on the Hudson River, while in 1626 Peter

----

7. in honor of Henrietta Maria, the Spanish wife of Charles II.

8. the first settlement was at Savannah in 1733.

Minuit made his famous purchase of Manhattan Island for $24, where New Amsterdam was founded as the capital of the colony of New Netherland (administered by the Dutch West India Company).

In 1638, the Swedes established Fort Christina (present-day Wilmington) on the lower Delaware River, where the Dutch also settled, a situation which gradually led to mutual antagonism, and to the eventual elimination of Swedish colonial aspirations by the Dutch in 1655. The latter, in turn, were eliminated by the English in 1664, not only from the region of the Delaware but also from New Netherland and New Amsterdam. The territory was renamed New York, in honor of its new proprietor, James, Duke of York, (brother of Charles II) to whom was also bestowed the area now known as New Jersey.[9]

Thus by 1664 the English were in sole control of the entire seaboard of eastern North America from (modern) Maine[10] to the southern Carolinas. The hinterlands remained unoccupied. After the Restoration of Charles II in 1660, repressive legislation by the Anglican Parliament imposed severe restrictions upon all dissenters, and it was at this time that William Penn conceived the idea of creating a colonial refuge for Quakers, but not until 1682 did he succeed in his project. Penn drafted a Frame of Government for the new colony of Pennsylvania, which included provision for freedom of worship and democratic representation.
----

9.   Until 1738 the Governor of New York was also governor of New Jersey.

10. Maine was part of Massachusetts territory until 1820 when, under the Missouri Compromise, it was admitted into the Union as a 'free' state to balance the admission of Missouri as a 'slave' state.

The religious tolerance which prevailed in Pennsylvania attracted thousands of colonists from western and central Europe, but even so, certain groups of settlers finding Quaker rule distasteful moved into the "Three Lower Counties" of Pennsylvania and were granted quasi-autonomy in 1702, although the governor of Pennsylvania remained the chief executive until 1776, (following which date Delaware fought in the Revolutionary War as a separate state).

The outstanding feature of the English American colonies was the remarkable degree of freedom and independence accorded them by the Mother country, in contrast to the highly centralized control over their overseas settlements exercised by France and Spain. Huguenots, for example, were expressly forbidden from emigrating to French Canada, while for most of the colonial period the entire territory of Spanish America was administered from Spain as two viceroyalties [11] (New Spain and Peru, respectively), rigidly controlled by the Council of the Indies. The Spanish colonists were given no opportunity to develop any form of representative government, and it has remained the tragedy of the entire continent of Latin America that, despite the independence achieved by the new states of the continent created during the first decades of the nineteenth century, the lack of tradition and practice in democratic methods has resulted, for two centuries, in a seemingly interminable sequence of military and autocratic regimes.

----

11. A third, New Granada, was carved out of New Spain in 1739, and a fourth, La Plata, was separated from Peru in 1776.

Education

Among the more remarkable facts of colonial settlement in the Americas was the early recognition by both Spanish and English of a need to establish institutions of higher learning. All such institutions were sponsored with the sole objective of training priests and preachers, whose function it was to administer to the spiritual needs of colonists: Catholic priests served Catholic communities; Protestant ministers responded to the tenets of the respective divisive sects characteristic of the new persuasion.

In Latin America, even after four hundred years of debate there remains uncertainty as to which institution may legitimately consider itself to be the 'first' university. The claim is advanced by a) Santo Domingo in the Dominican Republic, (which cites a papal bull of 1538 according university rank to a Dominican school in the city); b) the University of San Marcos, Lima, Peru, founded in 1551 on the basis of a grant from Charles V, but which did not open until 1572; and c) the Royal and Pontifical University at Mexico City, also founded in 1551 and the first to offer courses (1553).

No fewer than twenty-five colleges and universities were established either by the Spanish Crown or by the Church and the religious orders during the colonial period for the exclusive education of the ruling class and with the Castilian dialect as the universal language. Instruction was, for the most part, in the hands of the priests and clergy, and many of the charters were modeled after that of Salamanca in Spain (founded in 1243) which gave the university considerable independence, at least in theory and on paper, from political interference.

135

While the dominant objective of the universities remained that of the training of priests,
the curriculum, consisting basically of theology
and canon law, was gradually expanded in the major
institutions to include medical studies,[12] Indian
languages, astronomy, and mathematics.[13]

The most productive educational agencies in
Spanish America were the Franciscan, Dominican,
and Jesuit Orders. The Franciscans were active
in Mexico where they received substantial support
from Viceroy Antonio de Mendoza. They were, initially, strong proponents of the establishment of
schools for the native Indians in the belief that
they could then be more easily assimilated into
Spanish culture. The first recorded school for
Indians was opened in 1523 by Pedro de Gante who
administered there for forty years and taught the
natives the arts and crafts of church decoration.
The conversion and education of Indians received
substantial impetus after 1531, in which year a
native Indian, Juan Diego, was said to have
thrice encountered at Guadaloupe an apparition of
the Virgin Mary in the guise of an Indian maiden.
She directed him to have a shrine built in her
honor, and as proof of her appearance, her image
became imprinted on a blanket.[14] Impressed by the

----

12.   In 1768 an independent School of Medicine was
      established at Mexico City.

13.   A distinguished intellectual and professor of
      mathematics, Carlos de Siguenza y Gongora,
      who taught at Mexico City University during
      the latter years of the seventeenth century,
      was greatly respected in Europe for his
      scholarship.

14.   The blanket still hangs over the high altar of
      the Shrine at Guadaloupe, near Mexico City.

miracle, the Franciscan Juan de Zumarraga,[15] first Bishop of Mexico, a compassionate and sincere friend of the Indians, accelerated the movement to establish churches and schools for them. The neighboring Bishop of Michoacan, Vasco de Quiroga, was also active on behalf of Indian culture, and, influenced by Sir Thomas More's Utopia, he set up communal villages for their benefit.

By 1600, however, the initial enthusiasm for providing education for the Indians had waned appreciably,[16] although craft teaching continued, as evidenced by the products of their work in the more than 10,000 churches of Mexico founded during the colonial period. The task of conversion of the Indians to the Catholic faith was continued uninterruptedly by all the religious orders, who unstintingly dedicated themselves to the spiritual welfare of their parishioners, and who devotedly and laboriously studied the native languages and resolved them into print, thereby making available Scripture translations in the vernacular.

In Latin America, as in Catholic Europe, by far the most vigorous and enterprising teaching order was that of the Jesuits, and again, in America as in Europe, they focused upon elitist education at secondary and higher levels for the exclusive purpose of training competent Catholic

---

15. It was Bishop Zumarraga who introduced into Mexico in 1537 the first printing press in the New World.

16. This was, at least in part, due to the opposition of the Dominicans who were apprehensive of what they considered to be the corrupting influences of schooling. The Dominicans were the foremost agents of the Inquisition, introduced into Mexico in 1571.

priests and administrators. The fact that more
than double the number of colleges and universities
were founded in colonial Latin America as compared
with colonial Anglo-America, may most certainly be
attributed to the resolute and uncompromising
efforts of the Jesuit Order in that direction.

The Society of Jesus had been accorded papal
sanction as an Order of the Church in 1540, and
its enterprise is evident in that within one
decade of that date the Order had extended its
mission activities westwards into Latin America
and eastwards as far as Japan. In the Americas,
apart from their widespread religious and educational operations, the Jesuits displayed genuine
and obstinate concern for the physical and economic well being of the natives. Their best-
known Indian missions were established in the La
Plata basin[17] where they successfully organized
the indigenes into substantial communal settlements, (in some instances comprising more than
100,000 natives), intended to be economically
self-supporting by the cultivation of cotton,
tobacco, sugar, yerba mate and the production of
animal hides, with the profits of any export sales
being applied towards the enhancement of the
native welfare and culture. The Jesuits demanded
discipline and a working contribution from their
employees, but in turn they provided, with altruistic humanity, technical skills for improving
agricultural output as well as for cooperative
marketing. Their efficiency in these operations
aroused the envy and wrath of the Spanish and
Brazilian planters and landowners, but not until
after two centuries of highly successful projects
were they finally elimated in Latin America as
well as in Europe when, under the papal edict of
----

17. Territorially covering the modern political
     units of Paraguay, Uruguay, Northern Argentina
     and Southern Brazil.

1773, the Order was dissolved.[18]

In the Anglo-North American colonies a very
distinctive educational pattern emerged within the
first half century of successful settlement. The
earliest immigrants were Anglicans who settled in
Virginia, but their major objective lay in personal
financial advancement rather than in the establishment of a new faith in a New World. Moreover,
since the Church of England, described as being
the least Bible-centered of all the Protestant
sects, had little interest in mass literacy, education was not considered a subject requiring any
particular attention or promotion. It is on record
that a few schools were established,[19] but these
earliest efforts were apparently obliterated by
the Indian massacres of 1622. The Anglican Church
regarded education as a matter of private concern,
with each family accepting responsibility for the
appropriate instruction of its members. Private
tutors were favored by the wealthy landowners
whose sons and heirs were then sent to one or
----

18. Their mission work in Northern Mexico and
    California (under Eusebio Kino and Juan Maria
    Salvatierra) was inherited by the Franciscans
    led by Junipero Serra and it was the latter
    who was largely responsible for the founding
    between 1769 and 1823 of the famous mission
    chain in California extending from San Diego
    to San Francisco.

19. The Virginia Company had made money available
    for schools in 1618 and there was even a pro-
    posal to fund an Indian College at Henrico.

other of the colleges of Oxford and Cambridge.[20]
The cause of education in Virginia was appreciably
retarded by the negative attitudes adopted by many
of its prominent citizens, notably Sir William
Berkeley (1606-77), governor of the colony for
over thirty years, who declared:

> I thank God there are no free schools
> nor printing, and I hope we shall not
> have them these hundred years, for
> learning has brought disobedience and
> heresy and sects into the world and
> printing has divulged them and libels
> against the best government. God keep
> us from both.

The colonists were nevertheless sufficiently
concerned about one particular dimension of education, that of apprenticeship, to enact laws[21]
emulating those passed in England during the reign
of Elizabeth: the Statute of Artificers of 1562,
and the Poor Law of 1601, both of which were designed to prevent indolence and idleness on the
part of the poor, as well as (in Virginia) the
native Indians and slaves. By the provision of
training facilities for trades and crafts not only
was an adequate labor force guaranteed, but the
burden to the community for welfare service was

----

20. The only college in the South during the colon-
    ial period was that of William and Mary,
    founded in 1693 at Williamsburg as the result
    of the energetic initiative of the Anglican
    James Blair, who functioned as its president
    from 1693 to 1743. The "college" began as a
    grammar school and graduated its first student
    in 1700.

21. A Virginia law of 1642 required guardians and
    master craftsmen to provide adequate training
    for apprentices.

substantially reduced.

Where and when they existed, elementary schools
in the South were charitable institutions. The
most prominent agency in their establishment was
the Society for the Propagation of the Gospel in
Foreign Parts of the Anglican Church, founded in
1701 with its headquarters in England where funds
were raised and then made available to the colonies.
Responsibility for the licensing of teachers (mainly clerics) was delegated to the Bishop of London,
since no American Anglican Bishop was ever appointed. The Society remained in being until the
close of the colonial era, and while a few secondary schools were opened,[22] it directed its energies mainly towards the creation and maintenance
of elementary schools.[23] The unfortunate consequence was that, in the South, schools became
associated with the stigma of charity and were
therefore, wherever possible, to be avoided by
respectable members of the community, who other-
wise appear to have lacked a sense of public
responsibility and obligation towards education.

The situation in Virginia was exacerbated by
the 1714 Schism Act which required that all school
teachers be members of the Anglican Church. Dissenters within the colony could not be expected
to support any legislation promoting education,
while in reprisal the Church itself placed every
obstacle in the way of dissenters wishing to open
schools of their own. It was not until after
1730 when thousands of Scots-Irish immigrants

----

22.   one of the earliest was a Latin grammar school
      at Charleston, 1712.

23.   While the South was the region within which
      the Society was most active, it extended its
      operations north through Pennsylvania and
      New York into New England.

(mainly Presbyterians) settled in Virginia and other Southern states that the influence of the Church of England was finally broken.

In Georgia, the Moravian Brethren were among the first to establish schools for both whites and Indians, and they made every effort to implement the educational precepts of Comenius[24] (the foremost member of their faith). But the colony of Georgia had been founded and chartered (1732) for the specific purpose of providing a bulwark against the northern encroachment of Spaniards from Florida, and the pacifist sentiments of the Moravians led to antagonism between them and the English settlers, in consequence of which the Moravians decided to depart to Pennsylvania, where in 1741 they settled in Bethlehem. It was here that they set up Nazareth Hall Academy, the first exclusive school for girls in the English colonies.[25]

Governor Oglethorpe of Georgia invited John and Charles Wesley to the colony in 1733, but it was the enthusiastic and evangelistic Methodist preacher, George Whitefield, who was most active, and it was he who was mainly responsible for the establishment of the Bethesda Orphan House in 1739, where instruction was offered in reading and writing, together with training in weaving, tailoring and carpentry, (along the lines of August Francke's school in Halle, Germany. In 1764,

----

24. It is believed that, in 1636, Comenius may have been offered the position as President of Harvard College, but that he did not accept.

25. The oldest girls' school in the (present) territorial United States was the New Orleans Ursuline Convent School of 1727. Ursuline nuns had first arrived in Louisiana from France in 1724.

Whitefield attempted to convert the school into a "seminary" of literature and academic learning but it did not prosper.

In the American colonies north of Virginia a much more positive philosophy existed with respect to community responsibilities for the schooling of the younger generation. Even though many of the early efforts fell far short of expectations, the early settlers, albeit limited and confined by the circumscribed horizons of their religious faith, set the foundations for much of the present-day North American school system.

The Puritans arrived in 1628 under the aegis of the Massachusetts Bay Company which, in the same year agreed to furnish "salary, grounds, and diet" to three ministers who promised

> to do their true endeavors in their places in the ministry as well as in catechizing, as also in teaching, or causing to be taught, the Company's servants and their children.

in 1631, the colonists passed a law which made membership in the (Congregational) church and ownership of property the two conditions of voting. In the same year the General Court (the legislative body) passed censure upon the citizens of Salem for employing a certain Mr. Williams to "the office of teacher," since he had voiced his opinion that magistrates should not be permitted to impose fines upon persons not attending church services.

The Puritans had emigrated from England for the purpose of enjoying freedom of worship according to the principles of the Calvinist faith put into operation by John Calvin at Geneva, where he had set up a theocratic state. The Massachusetts Bay Bible Commonwealth had no intention of

143

advocating religious liberty for other faiths
for, to quote the Reverend Nathaniel Ward:

> God had sifted a nation that he might
> send choice grain into the wilderness...
> I dare take me to proclaim that all
> Familists, Antinomians, Anabaptists,
> and other Enthusiasts shall have free
> liberty to keep away from us and such
> as will come to be gone as fast as
> they can, the sooner the better. He
> that is willing to tolerate any re-
> ligion either doubts of his own, or
> is not sincere in it. Experience will
> teach churches and Christians that it
> is far better to live in a state united
> whereof some part is corrupt, than in
> a state whereof some part is incorrupt
> and all the rest divided.

In 1635, the Puritans founded the Boston
Latin Grammar School, financed out of the public
treasury, hence its claim as the first public
school in the Anglo-American colonies. It was
modeled upon the "Free Grammar School" of Boston,
England, (with which the Reverend John Cotton had
been associated since 1613) whose statutes had
required regular attendance at church, school
prayers, study of the Bible along with the Collo-
quies of Corderius, a text by Maturinus Corderius,
the schoolmaster who had taught John Calvin. Similar grammar schools were soon to be established
by the Puritans at Charlestown and Ipswich (1636),
Salem (1637), Dorchester and Newbury, (1639).

Since, to the Puritans, the Calvinist doctrine
of "justification by faith," implied that all persons be literate in the Scriptures,[26] action was
_____
26. The Puritans were advocates of a State church,
    but to be governed by the Congregations (and
    not by bishops) i.e., by the "priesthood of
    all believers."

taken by the General Court in 1641 instructing
the Church Elders to formulate a suitable cate-
chism for young people. In 1642 all heads of families and master tradesmen were required to give
instruction to their children or apprentices "in
the grounds and principles of religion" once a
week, in the content of the "capital laws" of the
Colony, and in the basic rudiments of reading the
English language. The Act of 1642 did not establish schools nor did it specify the need for
teachers. It proved unsatisfactory, even though
it was supposedly supervised by duly appointed
"selectmen" in each community. Hence, to remedy
the exposed deficiencies, the General Court passed
in 1647 the "Old Deluder Satan" Act, so-called
from the Preamble which read:

> It being one chief project of the old
> deluder, Satan, to keep men from knowl-
> edge of the Scriptures, as in former
> times by keeping them in an unknown
> tongue, so in these latter times by
> persuading from the use of tongues,
> that so at least the true sense and
> meaning of the original might be
> clouded by false glosses of saint-
> seeming deceivers, that learning may
> not be buried in the grave of our
> fathers in the church and commonwealth
> .....it is therefore ordered, that
> every township in this jurisdiction,
> after the Lord hath increased them to
> the number of fifty householders, shall
> then forthwith appoint one within their
> town to teach all such children as shall
> resort to him to write and read, whose
> wages shall be paid by the parents or
> masters of such children, or by the
> inhabitants in general...It is further
> ordered, that where any town shall in-
> crease to the number of one hundred
> families or householders, they shall

set up a grammar school, the master
thereof being able to instruct youth,
so far as they be fitted, for the university.

Initially, a fine of Five Pounds was imposed
upon each community for non-compliance with the
Act. In order to provide for public school support, a tax on property was legislated at Dedham
in 1648, this being the first known instance of
such a tax in the American Colonies. By the time
of the American Revolution, the property tax had
become virtually the universally accepted financial source for the establishment and maintenance
of elementary schools.

The Act of 1647 specified no provision for
teacher-training, and made only the vaguest
reference to teacher qualifications.[27] A substantial number of the immigrant Puritans were persons
of intellect, many with degrees from Cambridge
University, England, where Emmanuel College had
emerged as a vigorous Puritan institution. They
were fully cognizant of the need to ensure a well-
educated ministry and competent leadership of the
theocratic state which they had founded, objectives
summarized in the following paragraph:

> After God had carried us safe to New
> England and we had builded our houses,
> provided necessaries for our liveli-
> hood, reared convenient places for God's
> worship and settled the civil govern-
> ment; one of the next things we longed
> for and looked after, was to advance
> learning and perpetuate it to posterity,
> dreading to leave an illiterate ministry

----

27. except that teachers were expected to be persons "of discreet conversation and well
versed in tongues."

to the churches, when our present
ministers shall lie in the dust.[28]

In 1636, the General Court of the colony
voted Four Hundred Pounds towards "a schoole or
colledge," which in 1637 was ordered to be at
"Newetowne" (renamed Cambridge one year later).
In 1638 John Harvard, a graduate of Emmanual College, Cambridge, and a puritan minister, bequeathed
260 books and Seven Hundred and Eighty Pounds (a
sum equivalent to half his estate) to the new
college which thereupon was named in his honor.[29]
Its first president and only teacher was Henry

----

28. quoted from New England's First Fruits, and
    inscribed on the gates of Harvard University.

29. Dissension within the Massachusetts Bay Colony
    led to the migration of groups of conservative
    Calvinists to Connecticut. In 1701 the Gen-
    eral court of the latter colony granted them
    a charter for the founding of a college,
    which, for the first sixteen years of its
    existence, endured a peripatetic career with
    no permanent housing. In 1717, a large gift
    of books made a building necessary, and this
    was erected at New Haven. At the same time a
    valuable cargo of products from India was do-
    nated by Elihu Yale (a native of Boston and a
    former governor of Madras, India), and this
    led the trustees to bestow his name upon the
    college on the occasion of the first commence-
    ment held in the new building in 1718.

    The third Calvinist college in the Ameri-
    can colonies was Dartmouth, New Hampshire,
    chartered in 1769.

    The fourth of the colonial colleges of
    the New England region was Brown College,
    Rhode Island, of Baptist foundation, chartered
    in 1764.

Dunster, and the curriculum consisted of Bible
studies and the Bible languages (Latin, Greek, and
Hebrew), together with logic, ethics, philosophy,
astronomy, and geometry. The annual college enrollment throughout the seventeenth century probably
averaged no more than 20 students, but it was from
this corpus (as well as from the supply of new,
educated immigrants), that teachers became available: ministerial students taught in schools
thereby receiving a meager but still desirable pit-
tance which could contribute towards college
tuition and maintenance expenses; qualified and
ordained ministers themselves frequently functioned
in the dual role as church pastors and grammar
school teachers.

Not all qualified teachers were ministers:
by far the best known of colonial school teachers
was Ezekiel Cheever, who having attended St. Paul's
School, London, came to America at an early age,
and thereafter taught for no less than seventy
years in schools at New Haven, Ipswich, Charlestown, and Boston. He died in 1708 at the age of
94, and was eulogized in a poem by his former
student, Cotton Mather, as well as, over a century
later, by Nathaniel Hawthorne in "The Whole History
of Grandfather's Chair" (1841).[30]

In New England elementary school teachers
were expected to undertake a variety of extra-
curricular activities including acting as court
messengers, leading the Sunday choir, ringing the
bell for public worship, conducting certain church
services, and even digging the graves. In the
words of Meriwether:[31]

----

30. Two other colonial teachers of note were Elijah
     Coolett of Cambridge, Massachusetts, and
     Francis Pastorius, who taught at the William
     Penn (Charter) School, in Pennsylvania.

31. Colyer Meriwether: Our Colonial Curriculum,
     1607-1776 (1907) p. 16.

Is it to be wondered at that the calling
was loathed, and that tramps and ped-
dlers, the very driftwood of society,
men of broken futures, discharged soldiers, often presided in the school
house? But some rugged souls went
through the mills and survived as men.

a major problem confronting education in the
American colonies was that of the supply of books.
In the first instance, many were imported from
England, including Lily's Latin Grammar (made compulsory in English schools by Henry VIII in 1540),
the Grammatica Anglicana, (the first English Grammar, written in Latin, 1594), and A Perfect Survey
of the English Tongue (1624) by John Hewes.[32]
The first printing press in the colonies was that
established by the Reverend Jose Glover in Cambridge, Massachusetts in 1638. One year later,
the Cambridge Press was instituted, and in 1640
there appeared The Whole Booke of the Psalmes,
with an introduction by Richard Mather, (progen-
itor of the famous family of American men of
letters).[33]
----

32.   The first English Grammar written by a native
       American was that of Hugh Jones, professor of
       Mathematics at the College of William and
       Mary, and published in England, 1724. The
       first English Grammar to be printed in America
       was that of Samuel Johnson, President of King's
       College (N.Y.), 1765.

33.   Two other books which appear to have been in
       circulation by 1660 were: a) A New Discovery
       of the Old Art of Teaching School by Charles
       Hoole, and b) The English Schoolmaster by
       Edmund Coote, who informed his reader on the
       title page that he "needeth to buy no other
       (book) to make him fit from his Letters to the
       (Latin) Grammar School."

In elementary schools the horn book was in universal use. This was simply a wooden pad upon which was tacked a sheet of paper covered with a layer of transparent horn. Upon the paper itself there were usually written the numerals, the alphabet, the Lord's Prayer, and a few religious precepts. When available, catechisms were circulated, taught, and memorized, the most famous being John Cotton's Spiritual Milk for American Babes Drawn out of the Breasts of Both Testaments for Their Souls Nourishment.

In the 1690's there appeared the New England Primer which "taught millions to read and not one to sin." It consisted of no more than eighty pages and included an illustrated rhymed alphabet beginning with:

> In Adam's fall
> we sinned all

and ending with:

> Zaccheus he
> Did climb a tree
> His Lord to see

It was a book of gloom and despondency, designed to remind students of the dire peril of wandering from the true (Calvinist) faith, as well as of the omnipresence of death and the possibility of eternal torment.[34]

----

34. as illustrated by the following verse:

> I in the burying place may see
> Graves shorter there than I
> From Death's arrest no age is free
> Young children too may die.
> My God, may such an awful
> Awakening be to me!
> O! That by early grace I might
> For death prepared by.

The colonial Dutch settlement of New Netherland, with its capital at New Amsterdam, was under
the control of the Dutch West India Company. The
settlers were Calvinists and were therefore just
as zealous in religion and education as were
their colleagues in the faith in New England.
Their educational theories were based on the Canons
of the Synod of Dort (1618), part of which read:

> Schools in which the young shall be
> properly instructed in the principles
> of Christian doctrine shall be insti-
> tuted not only in cities, but also in
> towns and country places where hereto-
> fore none have existed. The Christian
> magistrates shall be requested that
> well qualified persons may be employed
> and enabled to devote themselves to
> the service; and especially that the
> children of the poor may be gratuitously
> instructed, and not be excluded from the
> benefit of schools.

Even though the colony was transferred to the
English Crown in 1664, Dutch schools, traditions,
and the language long persisted in the region,
and in 1766 the Dutch Reformed Church founded
Queen's College (New Jersey), which later became
Rutgers University.[35]

In the Middle American colonies the Quakers
were the most active group in education. George
Fox, founder of the Society of Friends, believed
that schools should be open to all classes and
races, and he placed emphasis upon moral and

----

35. King's College, New York, chartered in 1754
     was founded by Anglicans. Its name was
     changed in 1784 to Columbia College, and in
     1896 to Columbia University.

151

religious instruction. He objected to the classical curriculum of the Latin grammar school because of its inadequacy in the preparation of a Christian minister, and he was a firm advocate of some form of practical and apprenticeship training.[36] William Penn had the foregoing observations in mind when he exhorted his fellow believers to be liberal in the matter of school provision:

> Spare no cost, for by such parsimony
> all is lost that is saved, but let it
> be useful knowledge such as is consis-
> tent with truth and godliness, not
> cherishing a vain conversation or idle
> mind; but ingenuity mixed with industry
> is good for the body and the mind too.
> I recommend the useful parts of mathe-
> matics, as building houses, or ships,
> measuring, surveying, dialing, naviga-
> tion; but agriculture, especially, is
> my eye. Let my children be husbandmen
> and housewives; it is industrious,
> healthy, honest, and of good example.

Penn's Frame of Government for Pennsylvania, passed by the first colonial legislature in 1682, had provision for a system of public schools, but it was not implemented. Private elementary schools under Quaker jurisdiction were widespread. At secondary level, the William Penn Charter School, a free school, was founded in 1700, and while it offered classical studies the curriculum was in time extended to include some of the practical subjects recommended by Penn. It remains noteworthy that of all the major religious groups in colonial America the Quakers were alone in not

----

36. Fox himself published a school Primer in 1659, and his Instructions for Right Spelling and Plain Directions for Reading and Writing True English appeared in 1702.

establishing an institution of higher learning.

Following a visit by Penn to Germany, a heavy immigration of Lutherans to Pennsylvania occurred. They were firm advocates of Christian principles in education, but, finding difficulty in the matter of teacher competency they appealed for assistance to their brethren in Germany, in consequence of which Heinrich Muhlenberg was sent to Pennsylvania in 1741. He founded a college to train ministers and drew up a code of conduct and behavior for school teachers.

A large influx of Scotch-Irish Presbyterians also arrived in Pennsylvania, where they put into practice Christian education precepts formulated by their founder, John Knox, in his Book of Discipline. Stressing the need for an educated ministry a "Log College" was opened by William Tennant at Neshaming in 1726, and while, in reality, it was no more than a Latin Grammar School, it became the model for the more ambitious training institute for Presbyterian ministers and teachers founded in 1746 and named the College of New Jersey. Initially opened at Elizabeth, Maryland, it was transferred to Newark and finally to Princeton, where in 1756 its first permanent building, Nassau Hall (the largest educational building in the colonies) was opened.[37]

Despite the obvious concern for education expressed by some of the colonists of the early seventeenth century, it was becoming evident that the initial enthusiasm had waned perceptibly by the beginning of the eighteenth century. In the domain of elementary education, many communities

----

37. The institution retained the name of the College of New Jersey until 1896 when it became designated as Princeton University.

in New England preferred to pay the fines imposed rather than accept the burden of establishing and maintaining schools, even when those fines themselves were increased from five to twenty pounds in 1701, and to thirty pounds in 1718.

At the other end of the spectrum, only three small colleges, those of Harvard, William and Mary, and Yale, respectively, had been founded in over one hundred years of settlement, and the primary function of all three remained that of the training of ministers. The colleges recruited their students from the Latin grammar schools which functioned purely as preparatory institutions whose curricula were limited to reflect and serve the needs of the colleges. Hence, considerable dissatisfaction came to be expressed with respect to the nature and content of the education provided by the Latin grammar schools. The colonial population had expanded from possibly 50,000 in 1650 to approximately 250,000 by 1700, and by the time of the Revolution this had increased to 2,500,000.[38] Already, by 1700, a marked westward movement of settlement had occurred which had appreciably loosened church-colony ties.[39] Significant changes were also occurring in the character of the economy, which had become enriched through extensive trade and commerce. The larger colonial cities, exclusively sea-ports, were engaged in profitable product exchange not only with England, but also with the West Indies, Africa, and, not least, among them-

----

38.   The first census of the United States in 1790 recorded a total population of 3,929,214.

39.   permitting the development of small independent school districts, each with its autonomous school board, setting a precedent which became a tradition in the school system of the United States.

selves, by reason of the climate contrasts between Massachusetts in the north and the
Carolinas in the south, making possible a great
variety and diversity of products.

Consequently, two new major dimensions of
education emerged: on the one hand, the delimita-
tion and demarcation of new settlements demanded
competency in the practical subjects of arithmetic,
surveying, and draughtsmanship; on the other hand,
overseas commercial exchanges required not only
proficient ship navigators, but also accurate
bookkeepers and accountants, along with persons
with at least some minimal qualifications in
French and Spanish.

Obviously, the Latin Grammar School was in
no way equipped and adapted to cope with the
rapidly changing economic circumstances of the
age. Hence, there arose an alternate and resili-
ent system of schooling which did apply itself
with remarkable flexibility to the demands of a
new economy: this was the private school or
academy. It was a concept which originated in
England subsequent to the Restoration of Charles
II in 1660, when many restrictions were placed
upon those persons non-conforming to, or dissenting
from the religious doctrines and practices of the
Church of England. Preachers and teachers set up
private schools wherein they felt free not only
to propagate their own beliefs (albeit still
under penalty) but also to introduce a greater
variety of the more "modern" and/or practical subjects referred to in the foregoing paragraph.

The new movement spread only slowly in the
American colonies but when academies did appear
they had none of the religious motivation of their
English counterparts: instead, they were established to provide a viable alternative to the
Latin Grammar School where the curriculum was
circumscribed by college entrance enquirements.

155

It was not until the mid-eighteenth century that an organized effort was made to provide the new academy with a systematic design and structure. This was Benjamin Franklin's pamphlet of 1749 entitled <u>Proposals Relating to the Education of Youth in Pennsylvania</u>,[40] in which he propounded a very comprehensive curriculum, whose main feature lay in the emphatic affirmation of the importance of English as opposed to the Classical Languages. Stress was laid upon reading, writing, composition, and speech, while in the study of History, Franklin pleaded that more attention be given to the arts, trade, commerce, moral development and religion, as opposed to the endless study of chronological events, particularly wars. His roster of practical subjects included geometry, astronomy, navigation and surveying; arithmetic and bookkeeping; natural science, agriculture and gardening; painting, carpentry, and printing; and physical education.

Franklin succeeded in gaining considerable support for his proposals except that his sponsors insisted that a Latin school be incorporated into the new institution, and to his great and lasting disappointment, when the Academy was opened in 1751, the teacher of classics was appointed principal of the entire institution, and his salary was double that of the teacher of English.[41]

----

40. In it, Franklin made no reference to the Dissenting Academies in England, and he was probably unaware of the first German Realschule (providing vocational and modern studies) founded in Berlin by Julius Hecker in 1747.

41. The first teacher of English was David James Dove, a most competent instructor who, however, left within three years.

Thus Franklin's Academy fell far short of its founder's expectations. When the College of Philadelphia was chartered in 1755,[42] the Academy became little more than a Latin preparatory school, and the English department was relegated to the status of an elementary school.

Yet, Franklin's inspirational ideas were not entirely lost. Other academies were founded,[43] which although basically oriented towards college preparation, maintained a broader curriculum of modern and practical studies for students less capable of profiting from the academic disciplines.

---

42. It became the University of Pennsylvania in 1791.

43. The more famous of the earliest Academies were: Dummer's Academy, opened 1763, a graduate of which was Samuel Phillips (senator and governor-general of Massachusetts) who in 1778 sponsored Phillips Andover Academy. Samuel's uncle, John Phillips, endowed another Academy at Exeter (Phillips Exeter), opened in 1783.

CHAPTER EIGHT

THE ENLIGHTENMENT

Introduction

In terms of its direct political origins, the eighteenth century Period of Enlightenment (The Age of Reason) emanated from the defeat of the Spanish Armada by the English in 1588. Thereafter, released from the threat of invasion and conquest by Spain, the northwestern states of Europe became embroiled in rival, aggressive, overseas expansion, spearheaded by the creation in England and Holland of the formidable, commercial, monopolistic enterprises, chartered as the English and Dutch East and West India Companies, respectively. The French were less active until the reign of Louis XIV. The overall consequence of these activities was the rapid growth of a prosperous middle class whose wealth excited the cupidity of the ruling monarchs.

In England, Charles I rashly brandished the banner of the Divine Right of Kings, and ignored all the evidences of the rising hostility and angry resentment of his subjects against arbitrary taxation. The result was civil war and his execution (in 1649). These events were followed by the repressive Puritan dictatorship of Oliver Cromwell, which was, however, of brief duration, and was terminated by the restoration of the monarchy (under Charles II) in 1660.

It was now the turn of members of the Established Church of England to be repressive, and they embarked upon a systematic program of persecution directed against all religious dissenters, many of whom sought refuge in the American colonies. In 1685, James II, an avowed Catholic, succeeded to the throne, and he proved to be as insensitive as his father, Charles I, to the changing political climate in England, but fleeing to timely exile, he succeeded in avoiding a similar fate.

It was at this juncture that Parliament, wearied by over half a century of internal crises and conflicts arising out of the capricious actions of the English kings decided to enact two historic documents.[1] First was the Bill of Rights of 1688 which established a constitutional monarchy under parliamentary supervision, and the second was the Toleration Act of 1689 which permitted freedom of worship for all Christians, other than Catholics and Unitarians.[2]

It was in vindication of the Bill of Rights that John Locke propounded (in the second of his two Treatises on Government, 1690) his famed Social Contract theory, wherein he proclaimed the "natural right" of subjects to rebel against lawless and oppressive rulers. It was this theory which to their great advantage was endorsed by the proponents of American Independence in 1776, of the French Revolution in 1789, and of the several freedom movements which emerged in Latin

----

1. The Habeas Corpus Act of 1679 had already effectively limited the power of the ruler and his ministers to imprison without trial.

2. All persons not conforming to the tenets of the Church of England were still banned from attending the universities of Oxford and Cambridge and were ineligible to stand for Parliament.

America during the early decades of the nineteenth century.[3]

In contrast to England, France made no progress during either the seventeenth or the eighteenth century towards the goal of political democracy. The Estates-General, initially emerging during the thirteenth century as a political institution representative of the Catholic Church, the nobility, and the townsmen, had not met since 1614, and was not again called into session until 1789 (by Louis XVI). This belated act, in place of generating reform, directly precipitated the Revolution, and with it the abrupt termination of the monarchy.

The immediate ancestors of Louis XVI were the long-reigned autocrats, Louis XIV (1643-1715) and Louis XV (1715-74) respectively, neither of whom was prepared in any way to surrender one iota of political power to any of the Estates within their realm.[4] At the same time, they did little to advance the cause of absolute monarchy particularly during the eighteenth century, when their successive military adventures in the War of the

----

3. The development of representative government was yet further advanced (albeit by accident) by the accession of the Hanoverian, George I, in 1715. Since he knew little or no English, parliamentary affairs fell under the control of his ministers, and it was during the long party "reign" of Robert Walpole that the (unofficial) title of Prime Minister was evolved.

4. It was Louis XIV, who in 1685, in an effort to enforce political unity, revoked the Edict of Nantes (1598) which had guaranteed religious freedom to Huguenots.

Spanish Succession (1701-13), the War of the
Austrian Succession (1740-48) and the Seven Years
War (1756-63), not only reduced the country to
the verge of bankruptcy but also resulted in the
loss of its colonial possessions in Canada and
India.

Yet what remains remarkable is the fact that
despite the uncongenial political atmosphere,
French culture attained an unsurpassed zenith during the period under review. The seventeenth
century had already produced a galaxy of poetic
and dramatic writers including La Fontaine,
Corneille, Racine, and Moliere. Now, the Age of
Reason was to produce a galaxy of writers of equal
brilliance, but whose attention was directed (with
due and necessary caution, to avoid incurring the
wrath of the Establishment) to the theme of
social criticism. Already, the scientific intellectual giants of the seventeenth century from
Galileo to Newton had conclusively demonstrated
the existence of "natural laws" governing the
movement of planetary bodies within the universe,
so that for the first time in history its mechan-
istic principles had been made comprehensible to
mankind. It was inevitable that speculation then
became focused upon the possible existence of
identical natural laws governing the activities
of people in this world, laws which, if discovered
and applied, could lead to utopian Heavens on
Earth.

In the domain of politics, the outstanding
writer of the age was Montesquieu (1689-1755)
who, in his L'Esprit des Lois (1748), made an
exhaustive survey of the influences, both benign
and pernicious, of such factors as climate,
physiology, economics, governmental structures,
and religion upon society. It was in this work
that he advanced his famed proposal for the
separation of the legislative, executive, and

judicial powers of government, together with provision for a system of checks and balances.

All governments of the period exercised close,
rigid control and supervision over the commercial
enterprises of their respective countries, to the
intense irritation and frustration of all merchants
and tradespeople. Both Francois Quesnay (1694-
1774) of France, and Adam Smith (1723-90) of
England prescribed reforms in the domain of economics and both were to publish works of immense
import. It was Quesnay[5] who initially propounded
the doctrine of "Laissez-faire," the free-market
economy, and it was Adam Smith who became its
classic advocate in his scholarly Inquiry Into the
Nature and Causes of the Wealth of Nations (1776).

The most penetrating critical analysis of
the social system was the monumental Encyclopedia,
a compendium of knowledge which ran to more than
twenty volumes under the direction of Denis
Diderot (1713-68). Even though the work was carefully edited, many of the contributors, including
Voltaire and Rousseau, as well as Diderot himself,
suffered imprisonment at some time or other for
their sarcastic commentaries upon, or "treasonable"
allegations against, the political and religious
hierarchy which governed France. With so little
response by the latter to the cumulative surge of
denunciation, disparagement, and invective throughout the entire period of the eighteenth century,
it is of little wonder that it was doomed to

----

5. In 1768 Pierre-Samuel du Pont, a devotee of
   Quesnay, wrote a book entitled Physiocratie
   (=Government according to natural laws);
   henceforth, the term "physiocrats" was applied
   to persons who upheld Quesnay's economic doctrines. Du Pont emigrated to the U.S.A. in
   1813 to found the famous dynasty associated
   with the chemical industry.

disappear in the eruptive convulsion of the
Revolution.

Of major interest remains the fact that the
pursuit of and quest for a new 'natural order' of
society not only in France but in all the major
states of Western Europe as well as in colonial
America, was accompanied by thoughtful investigation into the manner in which the younger generation should best be educated to play a constructive
role in an ever-changing society. The format and
content of this investigation will be discussed
in the succeeding section.

Education

A major outcome of the Reformation was not
simply the emergence of a Protestant Movement,
but rather the proliferation of a host of diver-
gent sects within the Movement itself. The fact
that the Bible, and no longer the Pope, became
the ultimate authority as the basis of doctrinal
beliefs and actions permitted all manner of interpretation of the Holy Script, and was accompanied
by arrogance and intolerance of one sect towards
another.

In England, the Reformation had resulted in
the creation of a 'national' Church, but many of
the rites and rituals of the Catholic faith had
been retained, leading to the development of a
divisive group seeking to "purify" the Church of
what it considered to be the unnecessary and irrelevant trappings of a dangerous foreign power.
Some of these "Puritans", finding their efforts
to no avail, emigrated to the American Colonies,
but the majority remained in England and Wales to
engage in a Civil War, which, while in the first
instance they won, eventually they were to lose,
since with the restoration of King Charles II in
1660, the Old Regime of the Established Church
set about a vigorous program of persecution of all
those dissenting from the now time-honored ritual
practices of the Church of England. By this date
the dissenting sects had expanded to include the
Anabaptists, the Quakers, and Presbyterians[6] who

----

6. The Anabaptists (ana= Greek, again) believed
   in adult baptism, basing their beliefs upon
   the baptism of Jesus Christ by John the Baptist.
   The Quakers who "trembled at the word of God"
   were initially led by George Fox (1624-91) who
   founded the Society of Friends. The Presbyterians (Greek, presbuteros = elder) recognized only the authority of members of their
   Church, and, for the most part, were adherents of the theological principles of John
   Calvin.

were extremely active in disseminating the tenets of their faith. Hence, the Parliamentary proponents of the Established Church enacted a series of laws specifically designed to curb the disquieting missionary activities of the dissenters.

In 1662 the Act of Uniformity made mandatory the provision that all preachers and teachers subscribe to an oath of loyalty to the King, and, further, that they declare full acceptance of the Book of Common Prayer of the Anglican Church.

In 1665, the "Five Mile Act" (as part of the repressive "Clarendon Code") forbade all dissenting ministers to reside within five miles of any town, or to teach in any public or private school therein.[7]

The Dissenters responded in energetic fashion and proceeded to establish a new educational institution, the Academy. In essence, this was a secondary grammar school designed in the first place to offer appropriate courses in religious studies and the classics for those young students proposing eventually to become ministers of the gospel. At the same time, it offered a broad curriculum of studies, not only so that its future ministers should be well educated, but that students preparing to enter into one or other of the alternative acceptable professions should be adequately prepared to function within the ever-evolving

----

7. To his credit, Charles II, the "Merry Monarch", made every effort to alleviate the harsh consequences of these enactments. In 1672, for example, he decreed that 1200 Quakers be released from prison, and, typical of his tolerance, was his oft-time quoted statement: "Presbyterianism is no religion for a gentleman, and Anglicanism is no religion for a Christian." Charles II was received into the Catholic Church upon his deathbed.

political and economic climate of the period.
Included in the Academy curriculum was provision
for classical and modern languages; for ancient
and contemporary history, and for science, mathematics, astronomy, navigation, surveying, and
bookkeeping.

The Academy proved to be a successful institution despite the many handicaps initially imposed upon it, and, following the Act of Toleration of 1689 when it emerged as a legitimate
educational institution, it proceeded to prosper,
(in the absence of any alternative schooling
other than that of the independent "Public Schools")
throughout the entire eighteenth and nineteenth
centuries until, in 1902, the (Balfour) Education
Act set up in England a state system of public
secondary schools.

John Locke (1632-1704) was a product of the
aristocratic schooling of his day. His father, a
lawyer, had served in Cromwell's Parliamentary
("Roundhead") Army, and had sent his son to Westminster School, which he (John) had hated and
wrote:

> I am sure he who is able to be at the
> charge of a tutor at home may there
> give his son a more genteel carriage,
> more manly thoughts, and a sense of
> what is worthy and becoming, with a
> greater proficiency in learning into
> the bargain, and ripen him sooner into
> a man, than any school can do.

Locke went on to Oxford where eventually he
taught Greek and Rhetoric, but then went on to
study medicine. He performed a successful operation upon Lord Ashley (later, the first Lord
Shaftesbury) who, in gratitude became his patron,

and employed Locke as tutor to his son.[8] Ashley
was much involved in political intrigue and was
forced into exile, accompanied by Locke, who was
compromised by his intimate association with the
family. Locke spent six years in Holland (1683-
89) where he wrote two famous essays: the first,
An Essay Concerning the Human Understanding (later
published in 1690) was the text wherein he propounded his theory of the Mind as a passive,
receptive "tabula rasa" (blank slate) upon which
is imprinted all new impressions and experiences,
with the implication that the teacher-tutor has
the responsibility of imparting most of the appropriate knowledge to be conveyed during the formative period of childhood and adolescence.

In a subsequent study entitled Some Thoughts
Concerning Education (published in 1693) Locke
outlined the criteria upon which an adequate curriculum should be based. Of primary importance
was the Roman precept, "Mens sana in corpore sano,"
(A healthy mind in a healthy body). In this,
Locke not only drew upon his classical and medical
background of knowledge but he was acutely conscious of the devastating consequences of the Great
Plague of 1665 in England, and of the need to develop a sound physique to counteract (if possible)
the ravages of such a scourge.[9]

----

8. At a later date, Locke, assisted Shaftesbury,
   one of the chief proprietors of Carolina, to
   draft a constitution for the State.

9. The normal infant mortality rate of the sixteenth and seventeenth centuries was prodigious. Queen Anne of England gave birth to no
   fewer than 15 children all of whom she survived since all died before the age of 21.
   It was this tragedy which ended the Stuart
   dynasty in England and initiated that of the
   German Hanoverians.

Locke's remedies were austere: he prescribed
a "hardening" process, recommending light clothes
in winter, hard beds for sleeping, and even leaky
shoes for wet weather. All these precepts were
to be appropriately modified in the event of any
obvious real danger to health, since Locke was only
too acutely aware of the hardships imposed upon
himself during his own school days. He was by no
means the only person in England concerned with
school child abuse at this period. In 1669 a
"Children's Petition" had been presented to
Parliament,

> as a modest remonstrance of that in-
> tolerable grievance our youth lie
> under in the accustomed severities
> of the school discipline of this
> nation.

The Petition fell on deaf ears so that thirty
years later (1698) a further appeal sought legislative action

> to remedy the foul abuse of children
> at schools, especially in the great
> schools of this nation.

Locke recognized that some degree of discipline was fully appropriate in the upbringing
of the child:

> If ... a strict hand be kept over
> Children from the beginning, they
> will in that Age be tractable and
> quietly submit to it as never having
> known any other.

Parents, when concerned with child discipline, should themselves be models of behavior for
their children. They should exercise their
authority in an unmistakably firm yet friendly
manner. They should censor their offspring in
private, but be careful to praise them in public,

so as not to impair the development of worthy self-esteem.

With regard to schooling, whether public or private, Locke was concerned that due recognition be given to the principle that the basic objective of education should be the development of <u>character</u>:

> Of good breeding, knowledge of the world, virtue, industry, and a love of reputation, he (the student) cannot have too much; and if he have these, he will not long want what he needs or desires of the other.

He identified four major attributes: those of Virtue, Wisdom, Breeding, and Learning, respectively:

> <u>Virtue</u> he defined as "the true notion of God..from whom we receive all our good."

> <u>Wisdom</u> is "the product of a good temper, application of mind and experience together" (therefore unattainable at school level so that it became all the more imperative that children be exposed to the Great Thoughts of the past).

> <u>Breeding</u> implied the development of "a disposition of the mind not to offend others" as well as a means of expressing disagreement without giving unnecessary offense.

> <u>Learning</u> to Locke, was "the least part of education":

> When I consider what ado is made
> about a little Latin and Greek,
> how many years are spent on it,
> and what a noise and business
> it makes to no purpose, I can
> hardly forbear thinking that
> the parents of children still
> live in fear of the school-
> master's rod which they look on
> as the only instrument of
> education.

Locke next examined the several subjects of
the school curriculum. First, he favored adequate
instruction in the vernacular langage. He saw no
reason why learning should not be a pleasant experience with ample opportunity for appropriate
play activities especially when a foreign language
(albeit classical or modern) be taught. He strongly advocated that foreign language teaching be
introduced in a flexible manner by conversation
rather than by a rigid set of grammatical rules,
destined at the outset to destroy all manner of
interest and curiosity in the new subject.

Locke believed that a modern language such as
French, (appropriately accompanied by studies of
the country and the culture of the people of
France) should precede that of the study of Latin
and Greek, and also that classical studies, whatever their nature, should place emphasis upon
their timeless contribution to philosophy and culture rather than upon the boring analytical grammatical study of Latin and Greek. He suggested
that the time saved in not learning Latin or
Greek be better expended in learning something
of the new sciences of the seventeenth century.

He strongly advocated the teaching of mathematics as a discipline well structured to promote
the development and enhancement of reasoning
power through "observing the connection of ideas

and following them in train." He expressed doubts
about the value of Reading if it led only to shal-
low judgment and over-dependence upon the statements and conclusions drawn by other persons. He
favored the combination of a wide reading program
with relevant field experiences:

> since some men scarcely allow them-
> selves time to eat and sleep, but
> read and read and read on, yet make
> no great advances in their intel-
> lectual faculties.

He strongly deplored the current practice of
his day of mandatory verse writing in the classical languages, a practice from which he had no
doubt suffered during his own school days:

> If any student have a poetic vein, it
> is to me the strangest thing in the
> world that the father should desire
> or suffer it to be cherished or im-
> proved. If he proves a successful
> rhymer, and once gets the reputation
> of a wit, I desire it may be con-
> sidered what company and places he
> is like to spend his time in, nay,
> and estate too; for it is very seldom
> seen, that anyone discovers mines of
> gold or silver in Parnassus.

Concerned mainly with the education of "gen-
tlemen,"[10]Locke gave full approval for such

----

10. Locke did write an essay on Working Schools,
    to be set up for children (of working parents)
    from the age of 3 years onwards so that their
    parents could feel free to seek employment.
    The children were to be taught morality and
    appropriate crafts to earn their keep, and
    their basic diet was to consist of bread and
    soup (warmed in winter). They were to be
    suitably apprenticed as soon as possible.

activities as dancing, riding, fencing, music (for
relaxation, rather than for acquiring skill) and
craftwork (for enjoyable leisure time). He also
recommended travel promoted as a two-part program:
the student was likely to derive great benefit
from his journeys abroad first between the ages
of 7 and 16, if accompanied by a tutor, and later,
after the age of 21, if he travelled alone.
Between the ages of 16 and 21 Locke claimed that
all travel experience was wasted since the student
was innately prone to recall and emulate "the
worst and vainest practices."

    In contrast to England, where, with the few
exceptions of Church of England "charity schools,"
education was regarded as the responsibility of
the individual family, the Scottish Presbyterian
Church, responding to the precepts of Calvin, had
set up elementary schools in every parish (maintained by the Kirk) and Burg schools in every
town (maintained by the municipal authorities).
In the American Colonies this same system had
been promoted by the Massachusetts Legislature
in its famed 1647 'Deluder Satan' Act, but in
practice, this initial enthusiasm for education
had tended to lapse. This was certainly not the
case in Scotland where promising students were in
every way encouraged and assisted to advance
their studies at one or other of the four established universities: St. Andrews (1411), Glasgow
(1453), Aberdeen (1494), and Edinburgh (1582).
David Hume (1711-76), the renowned Scottish philosopher of the Enlightenment, was a product of
this invigorating, aggressive, and well-established
school system.

    During the period of the Enlightenment France
produced two outstanding educators, one a practitioner, the other a theorist. The practitioner

172

was Jean Baptiste de La Salle (1651-1719) who,
in 1684, founded the Order of the Brothers of the
Christian Schools (The Christian Brothers) at
Rheims. Its members were laymen, not priests, and
they took a vow of obedience for one year only, a
vow renewable annually. La Salle focused upon
elementary education for the poor, and, in his
schools only the vernacular was used. Recognizing
the need for trained teachers he established one
of the earliest training colleges (seminaries) in
France. He was an indefatigable organizer, and
when King James II of England fled to France in
1688, La Salle was requested to establish a school
for the children of the monarch's large retinue
of fellow-exiles, which he did, and successfully.
He is further credited with founding a reformatory
boarding school at St. Yon, Normandy, for young
delinquents, for whom he devised a practical curriculum of craft training to enable the offenders
to better rehabilitate themselves as useful citizens.

Since the Christian Brothers eliminated or at
lease de-emphasized the teaching of Latin, but at
the same time depended on charity, they received
little support from wealthy patrons anxious for
their offspring to enter the established professions for which a knowledge of Latin was de rigeur.
Hence, the Order made only laborious progress during the eighteenth century, although at the time of
La Salle's death, schools had been founded in at
least 22 towns in France and in Rome. In 1725
Pope Benedict promoted the Order to the status of
a papal institute.[11]

----

11. At the time of the French Revolution it still
    had less than a thousand teachers and only
    36,000 students. Yet the Order has flourished
    and today represents the largest single
    teacher Order in the world (with 17,000 teach-
    ers) and it retains much of the dynamic inspir-
    ational qualities and organizational capacities
    bequeathed to it by its founder.

By far the most prestigious educational institution in France during the eighteenth century was that of the Society of Jesus. Despite the ferocious and incessant attacks upon the order by the French philosophers and Encyclopedists, it continued to prosper, and its demise in France in 1762 was far more a consequence of Church and State politics than it was of opposition by the proponents of Reason. The latter were, indeed, even more incensed that, after 1762, control of education passed not to the State, as a secular institution, but to the other religious Orders in France, namely the Christian Brothers and the Oratorians.[12]

The inexorable advance of scientific ideas had slowly begun to erode much of the prestige of a Church which blatantly ignored proven factual evidence and instead maintained many beliefs based upon legend, myth, and superstition. As mentioned earlier, scholars in England had, under the patronage of Charles II established the prestigious body of scientists, the Royal Society, in 1662. Elsewhere in Europe identical societies known as Academies were in quick succession founded in Berlin (1701), Uppsala (1710), St. Petersburg (1724), and Stockholm (1741), with no fewer than fourteen Academies being established in France alone during the eighteenth century. It was the Academy at Dijon which in 1749 offered a prize for an essay on the topic of whether the revival of the sciences and arts had led to the corruption or to the purification of morals. Announcement

---

12. In 1763, Louis Rene de La Chalotais, a vigorous opponent of the Jesuits, had published his Essai d'education nationale, pleading for a more patriotic-type education as opposed to that of Catholic Orders owing allegiance to a foreign power (the Papacy).

of this competition appeared in the Mercure de France which Rousseau happened to be reading on the way to visit Denis Diderot imprisoned at Vincennes. Initially prepared to write in positive support of the contribution of the arts and sciences, he was apparently persuaded by Diderot to adopt a negative stance, and was duly awarded the first prize of the Academy, an event which brought him immediate and national fame.

Jean Jacques Rousseau (1712-78) was born in Geneva and was left motherless soon after his birth. He suffered acutely from ill health throughout his life, a condition which led him to write in his Confessions (1778): "The saddest event in my life was my birth." He fathered five children all of whom he placed in foster homes so that he experienced nothing of the joys and tribulations of personally rearing his own sons and daughters. Yet it was Rousseau who emerged as the great educational theorist of the period of the Enlightenment, and who was to exert an astonishing influence upon education well into the twentieth century.

The Enlightenment was the period of Reason, which, however, Rousseau rejected in place of Naturalism and Romance. He advanced the thesis that mankind had once existed in a state of bliss and in harmony with the environment: the age of the "noble savage." But the acquisition of property had produced inequality, so that the institution of government had been created in order to ensure protection of these 'unequal rights.'13 It was therefore in the best interests of mankind to seek a return to Nature and it was in furtherance of this plea that Rousseau wrote his famed work, Emile (1762), whose opening sentence reads:

----
13. Hence the statement in the Social Contract (1762): "Man is born free and everywhere he is in chains."

175

> Everything is good as it leaves the
> hands of the Creator: everything
> degenerates in the hands of man.

Rousseau had already published The New Heloise
(1761) wherein he had stated:

> Nature wants children to be children
> before they are men....Childhood has
> ways of seeing, thinking and feeling
> peculiar to itself; nothing can be
> more foolish than to substitute our
> ways for them.

The New Heloise was a romantic novel written
in the form of letters. Its heroine was Julie
who lived in a menage·a·trois. She bore three
children, and presumably Emile was conceived as
an appropriate sequel wherein Rousseau expanded
upon his views on the ideal education for Julie's
children.

Emile was to be reared in isolation from all
companions except for a tutor:

> The first education should be purely
> negative. It consists by no means of
> teaching virtue or truth, but in secur-
> ing the heart from vice and the intel-
> lect from error....May I set forth at
> this point the most important and the
> most useful rule in all education?
> It is not to save time but to waste
> it....The mind should remain inactive
> till it has all its faculties.

Rousseau had earlier[14] condemned the educa-

----

14. in his Discourse on the Origin and Foundation
    of Inequality Among Men, the essay which he
    had submitted to the Dijon Academy competition
    of 1753, but for which he had received no
    award.

176

tional system of his day:

> Even from our infancy an absurd
> system of education serves to adorn
> our wit and corrupt our judgment.
> We see on every side, huge insti-
> tutions where our youth are educated
> at great expense and instructed in
> everything but their duty. Your
> children will be ignorant of their
> own language, when they can talk
> others which are not spoken any-
> where.

In contrast, Emile was for the first twelve
years of his life to enjoy freedom to follow his
own inclinations within a prepared environment
without any formal instruction in reading,[15]
writing, or number. He was permitted to listen
to music and to draw so as to develop an apprecia-
tion of aesthetic and creative expression.

At the age of 12, a new and more formal
phase of instruction was scheduled. Emile's first
book was to be Robinson Crusoe, since it provided
a practical model of initiative, resourcefulness,
and independence. The boy's natural curiosity
was to be aroused by exposure to scientific won-
ders in astronomy, physics, and geography, and
Rousseau was emphatic concerning the method of
teaching:

> Put the problems before him and let him
> solve them himself. Let him know noth-
> ing because you have told him, but
> because he has learnt it for himself.
> Let him not be taught science, let him
> discover it.

----

15. To Rousseau "The child who reads does not
    think, he does nothing but read, he gets no
    instruction; he learns words."

The study of history through the reading of biographies was recommended, and Emile was to learn a craft, preferably carpentry, since it combined utility with "elegance and taste." Rousseau approved of sex guidance for the adolescent boy but heartily rejected any religious instruction:

> My readers, I foresee will be surprised to see me take my pupil through the whole of the early years without mention of religion. At fifteen he was not aware that he had a soul, and perhaps at eighteen it is not yet time for him to learn. For if he learns sooner than is necessary he runs the risk of never knowing. No doubt there is not a moment to be lost if we must deserve eternal salvation, but if the repetition of certain words suffices to obtain it, I do not see why we should not people heaven with starlings and magpies as well as children.

These and similar passages brought down upon Rousseau the certain wrath and anger of the Church which immediately had the entire book proscribed and forced its author into exile to escape prosecution.

In later adolescence (15 to 18 years), Emile was to enter fully into adult society with whose complexities he was now expected to cope by reason of his matured personality. A little later he would be ready to meet and associate with a girl companion, Sophie, whom he would eventually marry, (following two years of enforced separation to test their mutual love).

In contrast to his radical ideas concerning the education of Emile, Rousseau was unrepentantly conservative in his remarks (in The New Heloise)

upon the education of girls.[16] He fully accepted
the contemporary viewpoint of the status of women,
which he summarized as follows:

> The more womanly a woman is, the better.
> Whenever she exercises her own proper
> powers she gains by it. When she tries
> to usurp ours she becomes our inferior.
> Believe me, wise mother, it is a mis-
> take to bring up your daughter to be
> like a good man. Make her a good woman,
> and you can be sure that she will be
> worth more for herself and for us.

What Rousseau achieved in Emile was to provide
a very well written and readable education tract
encompassing the entire period of infancy, childhood, and youth. He formulated what is now termed
a child-centered curriculum, which permitted the
individual full freedom of expression (within a
controlled environment)[17] and of benefitting

----

16. An earlier French writer, Francois Fenelon
    (1651-1715), later Archbishop of Cambrai, ex-
    pressed far more progressive ideas than did
    Rousseau on the education of women. In 1687
    he published a treatise On the Education of
    Girls, in which he advocated the training of
    women teachers, as well as of future mothers.
    The latter, he claimed, should receive adequate
    instruction not merely in home living but also
    in the competent management of family estates.

17. Rousseau was by no means alone in stressing
    the influence of environment in the upbringing
    of children. His contemporary, Claude Adrien
    Helvetius (1715-71) in a posthumous work en-
    titled On Man, His Intellectual Faculties, and
    his Education, completely discounted the in-
    fluence of heredity, declaring that by dis-
    covery of the "natural laws" of education,
    Society could be completely transformed.

either positively or negatively from his uninhibited actions (except where they involved physical
harm and danger). The teacher's function was to
provide for a wealth of educational experiences,
but then to withdraw so as to permit the boy to
engage in happy discovery. Rousseau insisted
that the primary purpose of all education was the
development of a sound, well-balanced character
capable of exercising mature judgment upon entering adult life. While he accepted the fact that
the capacity to reason was important, Rousseau
declared that the objective of emotional stability
demanded priority, and it was in the expression
and promotion of this belief that Rousseau parted
company with many of his former colleagues of the
Age of Reason.

At the time of the English Civil War a much
more prolonged, bitter, and economically disastrous civil war, The Thirty Years War (1618-48),
had raged in Germany between Catholics and Protestants. It so exhausted both sides that tacit
agreement was finally concluded regarding religious
toleration. A further significant outcome was a
reform movement within the Lutheran Church known
as Pietism. Founded by Jacob Spener (1635-1705),
it sought freedom from rigid doctrinal precepts
and, instead, emphasized personal devotion, spiritual priesthood, and emotional warmth. A scholar
of note, Spener became the principal founder of
the University of Halle (1694) where the medium of
instruction was German, not Latin, and where he
was eventually joined by August Hermann Francke
(1663-1727).[18] Both were uncompromising in their
criticism of the school instruction of their day.
They complained that little attention was being

----

18. who had been expelled from the University of
    Leipzig because of Pietist views.

given to moral education via Scripture study, and
that too much time was being expended upon formal,
boring exercises in Latin syntax and grammar with
scant reference to the value content of significant
passages for translation. Francke, like his contemporary, La Salle of France, was an organizer of
incomparable energy and unremitting enthusiasm.
The list of his impressive accomplishments includes
the founding of an elementary school for poor children, an elementary school for middle-class children, orpnanages for boys and girls, a Pedagogium
for children of the nobility, a teacher-training
seminary, the Canstein Bible Institute (for the
publishing of religious texts and tracts), and
perhaps of greatest historical significance, the
first German "gymnasium" (secondary academic school)
which gave prominence not only to the classics but
also to the German language, science, and vocational subjects.

Francke was fortunate to attract the patronage of Frederick William I of Prussia, a progres-
sively-minded ruler who decreed (1713-17), that
all parents were to send their children to school,
(wherever such facilities were available),[19] and
that the local community was to be responsible for
the payment of fees of poor children. A further
decree (1737) provided state aid for the building
of schools and for the payment of teacher salaries.

Among Francke's students at Halle was Johann
Julius Hecker (1707-68), who, encouraged by
Frederick II (the Great) of Prussia, (who was even
more interested in education than his father), in
1747 set up the first German Realschule,[20] a

----

19. Several hundred schools had been established
    in Prussia, along the lines of Francke's model
    institutions in Halle.

20. Its complete title was the "Economic-Mathemati-
    cal Realschule."

secondary school for non-academic students. Its
main purpose was to provide a school:

> for those young people who are not
> destined for study but who are still
> found fitted to wield the pen, in
> business, management of estates, fine
> arts, mathematics, etc. These we will
> strive to strengthen in their natural
> capacities and to give the first essen-
> tial introduction to their preparation.

It was Frederick the Great who gave Hecker
the task of formulating the famous School Code of
1763 which laid the basis of a national system of
elementary education in Prussia. The Code established standards of competency in literacy, number,
and religion, through state examinations prepared
and directed by the clergy. Detailed provisions
set out curricula, teacher-qualifications and textbooks, while inspectors were to be appointed to
ensure the overall efficiency of the school system[21]

In 1787 a state system of education was instituted in Prussia by the creation of the Oberschul-
kollegium (Higher School Board) with full authority
over all school education, and this Board in 1788
initiated the Abiturientenprufung, (the school-
leaving examination), competency in which guaranteed entry to the universities. Consequently, in
Prussia control of education passed out almost
entirely from the Church to the State, and teachers
became officials appointed by representatives of
the State.

While it was the Pietists who exercised most
influence upon Prussian education throughout the
eighteenth century, the precepts of Rousseau

----

21. In 1765 a similar School Code was instituted
     for Silesia, (which Frederick the Great had
     forcibly acquired from Austria).

became widely read and disseminated in the German States during the later decades of the same century. Among the prominent educators profoundly impressed by _Emile_ was Johann Bernhard Basedow (1724-90), as eccentric a genius as Rousseau himself, on the one hand demonstrating an immense talent for devising and organizing educational institutions which incorporated progressive concepts at least a century ahead of their time, and on the other, pathetically incompetent to establish warm personal relationships with colleagues inspired by his ideas.

Born in Hamburg, Basedow ran away from home after an unhappy childhood, and developed unorthodox habits which led him to abandon the opportunity of pursuing studies at the University of Leipzig. He eventually became a teacher in both Danish and German schools, and these experiences led him into writing two influential tracts: the _Methodenbuch_ ("A Book of Methods for Fathers and Mothers of Families and for Nations," 1770), and a four-volume _Elementarwerke_ ("The Elementary"). Among the many ideas which Basedow outlined in these texts were provision for:

a) the physical wellbeing of students by way of games, exercise, and ample opportunity for outdoor activities and instruction, which in turn should afford language experiences to be incorporated into the normal schoolday curriculum;

b) moral and religious development, by affording students facilities to form social groups wherein they could discuss their problems with a competent advisor;

c) the teaching of foreign and classical languages, first by conversation and then by reading;

d) practical instruction directed towards

skill competency which would enable students to earn a living.

Basedow, even before the publication of his writings, had, in 1768, issued his <u>Appeal to the Friends of Mankind and to Men of Power Concerning Schools and Studies and Their Influence on Public Welfare</u> with great success, since contributions were received "from the Emperor Joseph II, from Catherine the Great of Russia, from Christian VII of Denmark, from the Grand Prince Paul, and other celebrities, the total sum received being over 2,000 pounds.." With these contributions and with the aid of Prince Leopold of Anhalt-Dessau, Basedow set up his Philanthropinum, where "for the first and probably for the last time, a school was started in which use and wont were entirely set aside, everything done on 'improved principles.'" Yet, two years later, there were only 13 students at the school, (including two of Basedow's own children). Basedow himself was soon forced to leave because of incompatibility with his teacher-colleagues. The school finally closed in 1793, yet Kant in his treatise, <u>On Pedadogy</u>, wrote:

> it was the only School in which teachers had liberty to work according to their own methods and schemes, and where they were in free communication both among themselves and with all learned men throughout Germany.

Until the eighteenth century education in Russia had remained unchanged for centuries, and had been virtually confined to activities within the Orthodox monasteries, a situation characteristic of Western Europe a thousand years earlier. But a new era had opened with the accession of the Romanov dynasty in 1613. There followed

almost a century of wars against Poland and
Sweden culminating in Peter the Great's defeat of
the latter, leading to the permanent acquisition
of Russian territory fronting the Baltic Sea.   In
1703 the city of St. Petersburg was founded, and
Peter, immediately recognizing the now imperative
need for naval power, himself set out to acquire
the necessary technical skills in the shipyards
of Holland and England.   Impressed by achievements
in Western Europe,[22] he established upon his return,
a School of Mathematics and Navigation (1701), an
Engineering and Artillery School (1712), a Naval
Academy (1715), and an Academy of Sciences (1725).
Most of the instructors at these institutions were
foreign experts (usually German or English) commissioned by Peter.   During the reign of Elizabeth
I (1741-62) still further progress was made by the
founding of the University of Moscow (1755), an
institution of advanced learning sponsored by the
poet-scientist Michael Lomonosov, who had studied
in Germany.

Elizabeth was succeeded by Catherine II, the
Great (1762-96), a Prussian princess[23] who became
the first Russian ruler able to read and write.
Catherine was a person of considerable talent who
corresponded regularly with the French Encyclopedists.   In response to her request, Denis
Diderot in 1770 drew up a Plan d'une Université
pour La Russe, but it was not implemented, neither
was her decree of 1775 which attempted to establish schools in every large village and township

----

22.   Tradition has it that in his youth he was
      tutored by a Scotsman named Menzies.

23.   She had married the future Peter III, an im-
      becile, who died under mysterious circum-
      stances within a year of his accession (1762).

in Russia. Nevertheless, Catherine persisted in her efforts and in 1786 a <u>Statute of Public Schools</u> was put into effect. The program was placed under the direction of Jankovitch de Mirievo, (an Austrian subject of Croatian descent), who had been strongly impressed by educational reform in Prussia.

When the Society of Jesus was proscribed in Western Europe, Catherine siezed the opportunity to advance the cause of education in Russia by inviting the Jesuits to settle and teach in her country, and many did so. She was also interested in education for girls as well as for boys and in 1764 she sponsored the Smolny Institute at St. Petersburg, the first secondary school for girls in Europe to be established and maintained by the State.[24]

Catherine displayed all the virtues of a liberated monarch of the Enlightenment for the greater part of her reign, but the excesses of the French Revolution brought about a marked reaction to popular education, which, in Russia, was to endure into the twentieth century.

----

24. For the first twenty years of its existence, the medium of instruction was French.

CHAPTER NINE

EDUCATION IN THE NINETEENTH CENTURY

Introduction

The nineteenth century was a period of industrialization which resulted in marked global
political, economic, and social changes. The
Industrial Revolution had begun during the late
eighteenth century in England, where ample resources of coal and iron ore had combined, in
opportune and propitious manner, with a unique
surge of human inventiveness. The results were
first made apparent in the cotton industry, and
the factory system there developed made necessary
a concentration of workers. As the process
spread, it brought about an accelerated rise of
urban settlements, which in turn created overall
problems relating to the welfare of communities
in the mass. Since the monotonously repetitive
operations of the typical factory required little
skill, recourse was made to child and female
labor which was readily available at cheap rates,
a practice which quickly produced widespread
abuse.

The very variety of problems precipitated a
plethora of solutions: politically, they ranged
from the mandates imposed by dominantly autocratic
regimes through the whole gamut of liberal, radical,

scientific and utopian socialist proposals, and even beyond into Marxist-communist and anarchist tenets. In terms of economics, early nineteenth century laissez-faire principles emerged during the later decades of the century as Social Darwinism which, in its most simplistic format equated ends with means to such degree that, to its proponents, acceptance into Heaven was within the grasp of any prosperous mortal being on Earth, irrespective of the manner whereby his wealth had been procured; alternatively, poverty was declared simply as the outcome of sin.

A very different approach was propounded by the host of humanitarian and philanthropic movements which proliferated during the same century, and which sought to alleviate the grosser inequities of industrialism, especially such as were related to slavery, serfdom, imprisonment, intemperance, and child and female employment. Their persuasive tactics happily tended to coincide with the aspirations and ambitions of the commercial middle classes which sought to gain improved economic and social status through representative assemblies. The subsequent extension of the suffrage led inevitably to progressive legislation in all the forementioned areas of concern, albeit not without resistance, friction, and trauma.

Of particular interest in education is that while all the major countries were subject to identical problems, their individual responses showed remarkable variation in terms of concrete proposals, goals, and achievements, a situation which reflected current national political, economic, and social tradition, philosophy, and structure.

In the United States, education received no mention in the Constitution, so that it fell within the purview of the residual powers of the individual states, and there it has remained for two centuries. Yet, there slowly emerged over the entire country the democratic concept of "education for all" irrespective of class, creed, or color.

In England, the tenets of the Established Church hierarchy long rejected parliamentary interference in what it considered to be the prerogative of the individual family to make decisions regarding the education of its members. Voluntary efforts were given indirect or direct financial support, and it was not until it had become patently obvious that their valiant contributions were pathetically inadequate that formal legislation was enacted in support of elementary education in 1870, and secondary education in 1902.

France, subjected to the convulsions of the French Revolution and Napoleonic Imperialism, devised a highly centralized educational administrative system providing for the evolution of an elite bureaucratic and military class through selective processes at the post-elementary and post-secondary stages of the school structure.

Germany (like Italy), a mere "geographic expression" until 1870, became dominated by Prussia whose powerful and aggressive eighteenth century sovereigns had already determined the course and direction of the ship of state. Consequently, the efforts and energies of the country's administrators came to be expended almost exclusively in the direction of territorial unification, a process culminating in such intense nationalism as to upset the political equilibrium of Central Europe for a period approaching two centuries. The educational systems evolved in both Germany and France bore many resemblances, since both emerged from the military dictates of autocratic rulers, but that of Germany was more comprehensive by reason of the attention devoted to industrial development and training.

The great colonizing powers of Western Europe spread their respective cultures overseas; but much of the educational work accomplished may be attributed not to the action of governments but rather to the devoted voluntary efforts of religious bodies, whose energies however, were greatly circumscribed by limited financial resources. Moreover, the continent of Africa was considered primarily as a vast source of tropical products, as also was the Indian sub-continent. In Latin America, political revolution had created independent nation-states ruled for the most part by creole minorities with little regard for the remainder of the population. Consequently, in all these regions, the nineteenth century tended to be a period of stagnation, or of extremely limited progress.

It is therefore of interest to make reference to two non-European states where sophisticated indigenous cultures had emerged, and which, when confronted by western culture, exhibited contrasting reactions. In China, where the Confucian ethic had prevailed for almost two millenia there was considerable resistance to any change resulting from foreign incursions. Japan, which also possessed a stable society, reacted to contact with the West in a vastly different manner, and readily adopted both American and European techniques and methods to such a degree that the country developed not only as the foremost technological nation in Asia, but also as one of the major industrial states in the world.

A more detailed study of nineteenth century educational developments in the United States, England, France, Germany, China, and Japan now follows.

THE UNITED STATES

For almost the first forty years or so of the
existence of the new nation-state, there was comparatively little change in education. The
Constitution of 1789 had made no direct reference
to education, so that action with respect to the
provision of schools fell entirely within the jurisdiction of the individual states. Even before final
independence had been assured under the Treaty of
Paris (1783), each of the thirteen colonies had
moved to set up a state government with a state constitution clearly affirming the principles upon
which the new democratic society in America was to
be based. Several of these early constitutions
recognized the duty of the state to promote instructional facilities for its young people. In 1776
the state constitution of Pennsylvania included
provision for a school or schools to be

> established in every county by the
> legislature for the convenient instruc-
> tion of youth, with such salaries to
> masters, paid by the public, as may
> enable them to instruct the youth at
> low prices, and all useful learning
> shall be duly encouraged and promoted
> in one or more universities.[1]

Similar provisions were incorporated into the constitutions of North Carolina (1776), Vermont, and
Georgia (1777), although little of practical import resulted. Perhaps, and as might be antici-
pated in terms of historical perspective, the best
expressed single statement relating to the incum-
bent duty of the state to discharge its obligations

----

1. Stuart G. Noble, <u>A History of American Educa-
tion</u> (p. 117).

with respect to education was that written by John
Adams in the Massachusetts Constitution of 1780:

> Wisdom and Knowledge, as well as virtue
> diffused generally among the body of the
> people, being necessary for the preser-
> vation of their rights and liberties,
> and as these depend on spreading the
> opportunities and advantages of educa-
> tion in the various parts of the country,
> and among the different orders of the
> people, it shall be the duty of the
> legislatures and magistrates, in all
> future periods of the Commonwealth, to
> cherish the interests of literature
> and the sciences, and all seminaries
> of them....[2]

Those lands ceded to the new United States in
1783 and which were not part of the original
Thirteen Colonies were initially designated as territories. An ordinance of 1785 provided for the
survey of the Northwest Territory and made provision for the sixteenth section of every township
to be reserved for the support of education. The
Ordinance of 1787 which set up governmental procedures of the Territory also made the statement
that "Religion, morality, and knowledge being
necessary to good government and the happiness of
mankind, schools and the means of education shall
be forever encouraged." In this way it was hoped
that the westward moving settlers could maintain
and propagate the cultural standards with which
they had been familiar in the East.

Earlier reference has been made to the interest
in education displayed by several of the Founding
Fathers notably Franklin and Jefferson. Washington
in a message to Congress (1790) favored the estab-

----

2. Noble. op. cit. p. 117.

lishment of a national university, and he declared
that:

> Knowledge is in every country the
> surest basis of public happiness.
> In one, in which the measures of
> government receive their impres-
> sion so immediately from the sense
> of the community, as in ours, it
> is proportionably essential. To
> the security of a free constitution
> it contributes in various ways; by
> convincing those who are intrusted
> with the public administration that
> every valuable end of government
> is best answered by the enlightened
> confidence of the people, and by
> teaching the people themselves to
> know and to value their own rights.[3]

It is apparently on record that he made a be-
quest valued at 25,000 dollars towards the funding
of a national university (to be located within the
present limits of Washington, D.C.) but it is not
known what became of this money.[4]

The idea of a National University was widely
discussed in the early decades of the new Republic
but it never came to pass. Instead there emerged
what President Ezra Stiles of Yale termed a
"college enthusiasm":

> ....seventeen colleges were
> founded before the end of the
> century, and twelve more by
> 1820....... by 1860, 182 of

----

3. Jared Sparks: The Life and Writings of George
    Washington (Vol. II, p. 9).

4. Noble: op. cit. p. 119.

the country's "permanent" colleges had been established.
Nine out of every ten had some connection with a religious
society.[5]

The University of Georgia was the first state university to be chartered (1785), but the University of North Carolina was the first to be opened (1795).

In New York, an attempt was made to create a comprehensive State system of education along the lines of Condorcet's "University" in France, when in 1784 and 1787 the legislature founded the University of New York under a Board of Regents, to be responsible not only for Columbia College but also for associated academies to whom financial aid was made available.[6] Again, as in France, the State concerned itself only to a minimal degree with elementary education.[7]

In New Hampshire, an effort was made to establish a State university system which would have incorporated Dartmouth College, thereby annulling its charter (first granted in 1769). The college board resisted, and the legal issue was ultimately decided in 1819 by the Supreme Court, whose

----

5. H.G. Good: A History of Education p. 95.

6. These measures led to the incorporation of no fewer than 315 academics between 1787 and 1853 (Kandel: History of Secondary Education p. 403).

7. The administration of elementary education was delegated in 1812 to the Superintendent of Common Schools, an office which represented the first instance of the establishment in the U.S. of a State Schools Superintendent. The office was later abolished in 1821.

decision (written by Chief Justice John Marshall)
affirmed the status of a college charter as a contract which thereby was unilaterally inviolable.

Projects for a national university did not
mature, neither did pleas for a national system
of education. In 1795 the American Philosophical
Society of Philadelphia had offered a prize for

> the best system of liberal education
> and literary instruction, adapted to
> the genius of the Government of the
> United States; comprehending also a
> plan for instituting and conducting
> public schools in this country on
> principles of the most extensive
> utility.

The first prize was awarded to Samuel Knox
for his Plan for a System of National Education
Adapted to the Genius of the Government of the
United States (1797). The second prize was
awarded to Samuel H. Smith for his Remarks on Education (1798). Both proposals were strongly in
favor of a public-supported, non-denominational
school which was to offer a broad curriculum of
studies relevant to the needs of college-bound
and terminal students alike: the Academy, and not
the Latin Grammar School, was to serve as model.[8]
In many respects, these were tributes which, while
he did not live to hear them, would have done much
to relieve Benjamin Franklin of the profound despondency into which he had lapsed by reason of

----

8. An earlier proponent of the comprehensive-
    style curriculum had been Benjamin Rush in his
    Thoughts Upon the Mode of Education Proper in a
    Republic (1786), on the grounds that a school
    should make available to the student everything
    "that is necessary to qualify him in public
    usefulness and private happiness."

the disappointments suffered at the presumed failure of his efforts in Philadelphia. It was indeed
the Academy which was to satisfy the aspirations of
the new nation and not until after the Civil War
was its hegemony every challenged. Like the Latin
Grammar School, (with its more limited curriculum
offerings), the Academy was a fee-paying institution: strong tradition emanating from England
that the education of children was essentially a
private matter subject to decision by the individual family had resulted in firm opposition to the
concept of public-supported schools at any level.
Even in the Puritan communities of New England,
which were presumed to have completely rejected
the foregoing tradition, the Law of 1647 and
similar enactments were being observed more in the
breach than in the observance, so that during the
eighteenth century by far the most effective elementary education in the American Colonies was
being provided by the Society for the Propagation
of the Gospel despite the stigma of charity attached to its funding of (more or less) free
schools. The Society had ceased its activities
after independence in 1783, resulting in the closure of hundreds of schools. Under the circumstances, it was not surprising that the monitorial
system which appeared to be flourishing in England
was seriously advocated as a viable solution.
The first such school was opened in 1806 in New
York with 500 children in one room and 150 in
another.[9] Joseph Lancaster[10] himself came to the
United States in 1818 to promote his system which
was calculated to educate the children of poor in
the three R's as efficiently and as cheaply as
possible.

But voluntary efforts were progressively

----

9. Good. op. cit. p. 137

10. Vide infra p. 210

doomed to fail. Charity alone could not cope with
the country's rapidly growing and changing society.
At the time of its first census in 1790, the United
States had a population of approximately 4 million;
by 1830 it had increased to 13 million and by 1860
it was no less than 30 million. Already by the
1820's concern was being openly expressed by progressive and far-seeing statesmen for the need of
initiating drastic measures to ensure adequate
instruction for the neglected youth of the new
nation. In Massachusetts, James G.Carter (1795-
1845) was the State legislator mainly responsible
for the Massachusetts School Law of 1827 which
attempted to set up a state-wide system of "common"
schools, but since the law had not provided for any
body of supervision it was not until the establishment of the Massachusetts State Board of Education
(1837) that its provisions could in any way be
implemented. Carter's efforts in both directions
were vigorously supported by his legislative colleague, Horace Mann (1796-1859), himself a professional lawyer and president of the State Senate,
who in 1837 resigned to take up the position of
Secretary of the newly constituted Board of Education. He served in this capacity for twelve years
in each of which he published an annual report
which became a model document for the dissemination of educational facts and viewpoints. The
best known is the Seventh Annual Report, which he
wrote following a visit to Prussia in 1843. While
he was not in favor of the rigid, centralized
political and educational administration of that
state, he voiced his approval of its well organized
elementary, secondary, and teacher-training
systems, and of the ample financial support available to the schools. Mann was instrumental in the
founding (between 1839-40) of three of the first
normal (teacher-training) schools [11] in the
----
11. Samuel Hall is credited with having, in 1823,
    established the first teacher-training school
    in the United States at Concord, Vermont.

United States, being fully convinced that any advance in education was predicated upon the supply of well-trained teachers. Mann was an indefatigable propagandist of the need to establish an effective system of education. During his term of office he edited the Massachusetts Common School Journal, which so widely propagated his views throughout the United States that by the outbreak of the Civil War, every state had legislated for the establishment of a state school system.

The state of Connecticut had its able counterpart in Henry Barnard (1811-1900). Again a lawyer by profession and a member of the Connecticut legislature, he labored to establish a board of "Commissioners of Common Schools" (1838) of which he was its Secretary until the board was dissolved only four years later. He moved to Rhode Island where for four years (1845-49) he functioned as the first Commissioner for the State public schools, following which he returned to Connecticut, (which by this time had recognized its sins) to function (1849-59) as its "Superintendent of Common Schools." Both Connecticut and Rhode Island were immediate beneficiaries of Barnard's educational genius,[12] while the remainder of the United States was to profit immeasurably from his written contributions to the American Journal of Education for which he served as editor from 1855 to 1870.

In the domain of elementary education further progress may be attributed to the efforts of, at least, three other noteworthy pedagogues:
      a) John Philbrick, who in 1847 built

----

12. Barnard was subsequently to serve as Chancellor of the University of Wisconsin, (1859-60) President of St. John's College, Annapolis, Maryland, (1866-67), and first U.S. Commissioner of Education, (1867-70).

at Quincy, Massachusetts,
the first school with separate rooms for each class.

b) <u>Edward A. Sheldon</u>, public
schools superintendent at
Oswego, N.Y., who, having
visited Pestalozzian schools
in Europe, returned to propagate the "object lesson"
(realia) approach with which
he had been impressed. In
1861 he established a normal
school at Oswego specifically
for this purpose, whose graduates were instrumental in disseminating the practical
concepts of the new instructional techniques throughout
many of the states.

c) <u>Francis Wayland Parker</u>, again
of Quincy, Massachusetts, who,
much impressed by Sheldon's
ideas, developed them yet fur-
thur. To quote Good:

> At Quincy there was an effort
> to combine subjects. Every
> lesson was to be made a les-
> son in the language arts of
> speech and writing. The spel-
> ling book was wholly discarded
> and spelling was taught in
> writing and reading. Parker
> favored the use of many read-
> ing books in each grade, not
> just one. Every language
> lesson could also be the begin-
> ning of science instruction.
> Lessons on color involved form.
> Number work could use both form

and color. All lessons
were to teach good manners
and morals. History and
Geography were to be com-
bined quite after the manner of Herbart, and Parker
in some passages seems to
hold that history is determined by geography.[13]

Another movement of considerable significance
in American education was initiated by Mrs. Carl
Schurz,[14] who, in 1855, established the first
kindergarten in the United States in Watertown,
Wisconsin. Before emigrating from Germany she had
become acquainted with the work of Friedrich
Froebel, and in her new school she introduced the
child-centered activities with which he was associated. The language of instruction at the Watertown school was German, and it was left to Elizabeth
Peabody, (who had also visited kindergarten schools
in Prussia), to set up at Boston in 1860 the first
English-speaking kindergarten in the United States.
In 1873 William Torrey Harris, superintendent of
schools in St. Louis, Missouri, first set up the
kindergarten as an integral part of the public
school system.

At the time of the Civil War, all the states
of the Union had accepted the legal responsibility
for the development of a public school system. They
had, moreover, in practice, accepted legal responsibility for the funding of 'common' schools, although
except in the northeast, there existed considerable
opposition to the concept of extending the rubric

----

13. Good.op. cit. p. 220-1

14. Wife of Carl Schurz, Secretary of State under
     President Hayes.

of "common school" to include education beyond
elementary level. Only in the more progressive
states and larger cities did secondary (high)
schools receive public funding.

The public high school itself had its genesis
in the opening of the Boston English Classical
School for boys in 1821[15] (followed in 1826 by the
Boston Female High School which closed its doors
two years later). The school, in fact, offered no
classical studies and its avowed purpose was the
provision of an appropriate curriculum for "the
many children of the poor and unfortunate classes
of the community." Students desirous of admission
were required to sit an entrance examination at the
age of twelve, and the successful candidates were
thereafter expected to attend school for three years
to receive instruction in a variety of course-
offerings, to include, in the First Year: reading,
composition, critical analysis, arithmetic, geography, and declamation; in the Second Year: algebra,
geometry, trigonometry, surveying, navigation, and
history; and in the Third Year, natural, moral and
political philosophy.[16] By 1840, it is estimated
that there were twenty-six similar high schools in
Massachusetts.[17]

Progress elsewhere was slow and even though
"the statement of Dr. William T. Harris that there
were only 40 high schools (in the U.S.) in 1860 has
little basis in fact, except that the high school
was not yet fully defined,"[18] it remains a fact that

----

15. In 1824, the name was changed to the "English
     High School;" in 1832, it was changed back to
     the "English Classical School;" and in 1833,
     it finally reverted to the "English High
     School."

16. Kandel. op. cit. p. 428

17. Kandel. op. cit. p. 432

18. Kandel. op. cit. p. 448

as an institution at that date it could hardly be considered comparable in status and prestige to that of the Academy, which, in 1855, numbered 6,185 schools with an enrollment of 263,096 students.[19]

Not until after 1874 did the situation begin to change. In that year the Supreme Court of Michigan ruled (in its momentous Kalamazoo decision) that a tax levied by city authorities for the purpose of maintaining a public high school was legal.[20] Thereafter, other states followed suit so that by 1890 the number of public high schools in the U.S. had risen to 2,526 (with 202,063 students) while the number of Academies had fallen to 1,632 (with 94,391 students.[21]

Several other significant measures affecting education were enacted during the last decades of the nineteenth century. In 1862 the U.S. Government passed the Morrill Act,[22] whereby each state was granted 30,000 acres of public land for each of its senators and representatives. Income from the sale of this land was to be applied towards the founding and maintenance of one or more colleges

----

19.   Gutek. op. cit. p. 366

20.   The suit brought forward by citizens in Kalamazoo was actually one opposed to the use of tax revenues for the teaching of foreign languages which were normally considered to be outside the purview of elementary school instruction.

21.   Gutek. op. cit. p. 366. It is to be noted that the average number of students in each category of high school was below 100, and that approximately one-half of the public high schools were one-teacher institutions.

22.   Named after Justin B. Morrill, Congressman from Vermont.

whose primary purpose was to teach "such branches of learning as are related to agriculture and the mechanical arts....without excluding other scientific and classical studies, and including military tactics."[23]   The second Morrill Act of 1890 made possible the allocation of Federal money to the land-grant colleges, (many of which were later to develop as State universities).

In 1776 there were in existence only ten colleges within the territorial confines of the Thirteen Colonies. The great westward flow of population which had accompanied independence had led to a marked rise in the number of colleges, particularly in the Mid West, where a society, less conservative than that in the East, had fostered a more liberal outlook. Oberlin College, Ohio founded in 1833, was not only the first coeducational college in the United States, but it was also the first to admit negroes. At the same time, there arose a demand in the East and South for higher education for both women and negroes, equivalent to that of the prestigious and old-established exclusively male colleges. Mount Holyoke Seminary (1837) was the first of the female institutions, followed by Elmira (1855), Vassar (1865), Wellesley (1870), Smith (1875), and Bryn Mawr (1880). "Coordinate" women's colleges attached to existing male institutions founded during this period included Barnard College (1889) with Columbia, and Radcliffe College (1893) with Harvard.

The earliest of the exclusively black colleges were Fisk (1866), Hampton (1868), and Tuskegee (1881). Under the provisions of the second Morrill Act of 1890, no fewer than 17 Southern States established land grant colleges for black students.[24]

----

23.   The Iowa State Legislature (in September 1862) was the first to take advantage of the financial provisions of the Act.

24.   Gutek. op. cit. p. 375

During the middle and late nineteenth century, American scholars had increasingly fallen under the influence of German universities where, beginning with establishment of the University of Berlin in 1808, research was recognized as the major and primary activity, so that advanced graduate work was accorded a full, legitimate, and financial status. Of the many advocates of identical programs in the United States, two were outstanding: Charles W. Eliot, for forty years (1869-1909) President of Harvard, and Daniel Coit Gilman, first President (1876-1901) of Johns Hopkins University. Other institutions soon followed suit so that by 1900, no fewer than fourteen had satisfied the exacting qualifications set up for membership in the Association of American Universities established in that year.

During this same period, colleges and universities alike had good reason to feel concerned with the problem of undergraduate admission standards. A vast public school system was in the process of development,[25] courses were proliferating, and "college entrance requirements alone saved the high schools from anarchy and chaos, insofar as they offered recognizable standards of attainment."[26] Moreover, the fact that the new school system provided for as many terminal, as it did college-bound, students extended the controversy into the

----

25. By 1900, there were 6,005 public high schools with an enrollment of 519,251 students (216, 207 boys, 303,044 girls), together with 1978 private secondary schools with 110,797 students (55,734 boys, 55,063 girls). Kandel. op. cit. p. 482

26. Kandel. op. cit. p. 461

domain as to what was the appropriate high school curriculum for either or both.

In 1871 the University of Michigan originated the concept of accreditation by inviting high schools of the state to have their programs evaluated by university faculty. Approval by the latter would permit qualified students of a participating institution to be admitted to the University without further examination. In due course, regional accreditation associations were organized, and this movement was paralleled by attention focused upon the problem of the diversity of college entrance requirements. Again, regional bodies came into being in the effort to provide standardization, the first being the New England Association of Colleges and Preparatory Schools (1885). Eventually, an independent College Entrance Examination Board came into existence and held its first examination in 1901.

One of the country's most influential organizations, the National Education Association, was formed in 1870.[27] Among the more immediate of its tasks was the problem of determining the appropriate course offerings at high school level. In 1892 the Association appointed its now-famed Committee of Ten on Secondary School Studies, with President Charles W. Eliot of Harvard as chairman. The Committee identified 9 subject areas,[28] each

----

27. It developed out of the National Teachers' Association founded at Philadelphia in 1857.

28. These were:
    1. Latin;
    2. Greek;
    3. English;
    4. Modern Languages;
    5. Mathematics;
    6. Physics, Chemistry, Astronomy
    7. Natural History (Botany, Zoology, Physiology);
    8. History, Civil Government, Political Economy;
    9. Geography (Physical Geography, Geology, Meteorology).

of which was assigned to a separate "conference" of ten members, who were expected to respond to a variety of questions, including specific content material, sequence, and time allocation, (both weekly and annual). Reporting in 1893, the Committee issued the following statement clarifying the definitive role of the public high school:

> The secondary schools of the United States, taken as a whole, do not exist for the purpose of preparing boys and girls for colleges. Only an insignificant percentage of the graduates of these schools go to colleges or scientific schools.

Yet the Committee Report placed emphasis upon college preparatory subjects[29] and it elaborated upon four model programs (each of four years) which were offered to high schools as a basis for a structured curriculum. These four programs were, respectively: 1) Classical; 2) Latin-scientific; 3) Modern Languages; and 4) English. Selection between one or other of the four programs was permitted, and the Report further propounded the new and significant principle that all subjects taught for an equal length of time were to be regarded as being equal in value.

The Report made a strong recommendation for the introduction of a number of subjects at a stage earlier than high school, and so gave sustenance and support to an already existing movement which sought to reduce the elementary school years from eight to six, along with a commensurate increase at secondary school level from four to six.

By the close of the nineteenth century, which had seen an increase in population from 5 to 75

----

29. It made no reference either to art, music, physical education, or vocational training.

millions, distinctive patterns were emerging in
the varied domains of educational administration,
school structure, and curriculum at all levels
from kindergarten through graduate studies, so that
the nation was reasonably well equipped in terms
of its pedagogic enterprise to engage upon the
challenges of the twentieth century.

ENGLAND AND WALES

In England, the tradition of non-government interference in education persisted into the latter decades of the nineteenth century: not until 1870 was the first Elementary Education Act passed by Parliament, while measures relating to the establishment of a public (state) secondary school system were not put into operation until 1902.[1]

During the eighteenth century, the most active agencies in the domain of elementary education had been the charitable organizations related to the Church of England and its reform offshoot, the Methodist Church. The former had, in 1698, established the Society for Promoting Christian Knowledge, (S.P.C.K.), which by about 1750 had succeeded in opening almost 2,000 schools for approximately 30,000 students but, thereafter, interest in education for the poor waned considerably, and a progressive decline in numbers set in for the rest of the century.

The Methodist Church was, in terms of education, most active in Wales where, in 1737, the Reverend Griffith Jones of Llanddowror initiated a remarkable system of "Circulating Schools," founded to provide poor persons of all ages with adequate tuition for reading the Bible in Welsh. He outlined the method of organization in his book, Welsh Piety (1743): trained instructors remained from three to six months in responsive communities where classes were held by day or evening, particularly in winter months when farming activities were at a minimum. Jones died in 1761, but his work was continued by

----

1. It had been preceded by the Intermediate (Secondary) Education Act of 1889, which related to Wales only.

his patroness, Madame Bevan, such that, at the time of her death in 1777, the number of Circulating Schools in Wales was 6,465 with 314,051 scholars.[2]   Mismanagement of her estate after her death led to the rapid demise of the Circulating Schools, although,as a by-product,a vigorous Sunday School movement was established in Wales in 1785 by the Reverend Thomas Charles of Bala, and in England in 1780 by Robert Raikes of Gloucester, influential editor of the Gloucester Journal, who, in 1785, sponsored the undenominational "Society for the Establishment and Support of Sunday Schools through the Kingdom of Great Britain." So success -ful was this movement that, by 1787, approximately 250,000 children were in attendance.[3]

The Methodist revival movements of the eighteenth century resulted in an appreciable rise in the social consciousness and sense of responsibility among concerned people towards the lower classes. The excesses of the French Revolution also had their impact, such that the opening decade of the nineteenth century witnessed marked (albeit still limited) advances in the area of elementary education.

In 1797, Dr. Andrew Bell (1753-1832), a clergyman of the Church of England who had worked in India, published an account of an emergency experiment (due to staffing problems) which he had conducted as Headmaster of the Male Orphan Asylum at Madras. The school situation had required him to improvise by selecting the more advanced senior boys and subjecting them to an intensive short period of instruction, following which, they,themselves,became

----

2. C. Birchenough. History of Elementary Education in England and Wales (London: University Tutorial Press, 1914). p. 19.

3. Birchenough. op. cit. p. 19.

instructors of lower grade students. In this way,
it was claimed that one teacher responsible for a
hundred students, could, by training ten boys,
each placed in charge of nine others, easily supervise the work of the entire school at the lowest
possible expense. His seminal concepts fell on
fertile ground: in the first instance, the Church
of England, with its educational traditions rooted
in the charitable Society for Promoting Christian
Knowledge, eagerly accepted the new approach so
that in 1811, "The National Society for Promoting
the Education of the Poor in the Principles of the
Established Church Throughout England and Wales"
was founded, with the Archbishop of Canterbury as
President.

Joseph Lancaster, (1776-1838) a Quaker schoolteacher in London, impressed by Bell's account, set
up his own experimental school involving a thousand
students, which he described in his Improvements
in Education (1803).[4] This resulted in the forma-
tion of the Royal Lancasterian Association, with
James Mill as one of the chartered committee members. Unfortunately, Lancaster proved himself to
be an incapable administrator and in 1814 the
Association was reorganized as the British and
Foreign School Society. From the outset, the Lancasterian Schools excluded all denominational
religious teaching (unlike the schools established
by Bell), and the Borough Road (London) School was
established as an experimental model school for

----

4.   The published reports of Bell and Lancaster
     prompted Samuel Whitbread to introduce his
     Parochial Schools Bill in Parliament in 1807,
     which provided for two years free schooling for
     poor children between seven and fourteen years.
     The Bill passed the House of Commons but was
     rejected by the House of Lords.

the training of teachers.[5]

Contemporaneous with the foregoing innovations were the educational experiments of Robert Owen (1771-1858), a Welsh cotton mill manager, in New Lanark, Scotland. He was a firm believer in the beneficial influence of a well regulated environment. As he wrote in his book, A New View of Society (1813):

> Children are, without exception, passive and wonderfully contrived compounds, which by an accurate previous and subsequent attention, founded on a correct knowledge of the subject, may be formed collectively to have any human character ..... They partake of that plastic quality which by perserverance under judicious management may be ultimately moulded into the very image of rational wishes and desires......Any general character, from the best to the worst, from the most ignorant to the most enlightened, may be given to any community, even to the world at large, by the application of proper means; which means are to a great extent at the command and under the control of those who have influence in the affairs of men.

Owen, a philanthropic idealist, had been appalled by the inhumane conditions which the new factory system accompanying industrialization was

----

5. Both the Bell and Lancasterian systems, (the 'National' and 'British' Schools, respectively) were, in due course, labeled monitorial schools.

imposing upon young children. At his own establishment he set up a pioneer infants' school which,
in time, became renowned throughout Europe. The
school provided opportunity for children to indulge in play and games, to enjoy listening to
stories, to be taught the rudiments of reading,
writing and number, and to have their imagination
stimulated by vivid description of peoples far removed both in space and time. Through Owen's
influence, the Infant School Society was founded in
1824, and it was in this year that he came to the
United States to found a utopian community at New
Harmony, Indiana. Despite the fact that the ven-
ture lasted less than two years, Owen initiated
here the first kindergarten, the first trade school,
and the first community-supported public school in
the United States.

The first instance of State involvement in
education in the nineteenth century was the Health
and Morals of Apprentices Act of 1802: working
hours were limited to 12 per day, and provision was
made for instruction in the three R's. For all
practical purposes the educational clause was a
dead-letter, not merely by reason of indifference
on the part of employers, but also because of the
impossible demand made upon young persons to
attend school after long hours at work.

In 1807, Samuel Whitbread introduced his Bill
into Parliament providing for a nation-wide system
of schools funded from local taxes. The Bill was
accepted by the House of Commons, but was rejected
by the House of Lords.[6]

----

6. This was among the first of many progressive
    social and political reforms of the nineteenth
    century proposed by the Lower House of Parlia-
    ment but rejected by the (non-elected) conser-
    vative and privilege-protecting Upper House.

In 1832, the first Reform Act was passed.
This made provision for wider popular representation of the middle classes in Parliament, and its
effect was quickly seen one year later when the
newly constituted House of Commons voted the sum
of 20,000 pounds "for the purposes of education."
The money was to be administered and spent (on a
matching basis) by the two major voluntary education societies, (the National and British Societies,
respectively) on the construction of school houses.
The grant was renewed annually and promoted considerable activity on the part of the educational agencies
concerned.

In 1839, a Special Committee of the Privy
Council was constituted "for the consideration of
all matters affecting the education of the people,"
with the specific function of determining "in what
matter the grants of money made from time to time"
by Parliament should be distributed. A sum of
10,000 pounds was initially allocated to establish
a State Normal College for teacher-training, but
such strong opposition was raised to this proposal
that it was abandoned in favor of donating the
money to the voluntary societies for the same purpose. The Societies responded quickly, and in 1841
the National Society founded St. Mark's Training
College (Chelsea, London), and a year later the
British Society had appreciably extended its
teacher-training facilities at Borough Road. A
further important development was the appointment
of two inspectors to supervise the fund expenditures,
a move which initiated the influential H.M. Inspec-
torate of Great Britain. Within the next decade,
a pupil-teacher system was initiated, with Queen's
Scholarships to Normal Schools being made available
for the most promising applicants.

State grants for education having increased
substantially after 1833, a Department of Education
was created in 1856 to supervise the spending of
funds, while in 1858 a Royal Commission, chaired by

the Duke of Newcastle, was appointed "to inquire into the present state of popular education in England, and to consider and report what measures, if any, are required for the extension of sound and cheap elementary instruction to all classes of the people." Reporting three years later, the Commission commented adversely upon "the state of popular education," a situation which led to the government's Revised Code of 1861 which introduced a scheme for "Payment by Results," concerning which, Robert Lowe (Vice-President of the Department of Education) made the oft-quoted statement that "if the new system will not be cheap it will be efficient, and if it will not be efficient it will be cheap." A grant of twelve shillings was to be made for each child in school, of which four shillings were reserved in payment for regular attendance; the remaining sum of eight shillings was payable only upon the recommendation of an Inspector of Schools, responsible for conducting an annual examination in reading, writing, and arithmetic, (each of these three subjects being accorded one-third of the sum of eight shillings). As might be expected, appreciable savings in government expenditure upon education resulted.

Nevertheless, the Newcastle Commission Report had clearly demonstrated the inability of the voluntary societies to cope effectively with the education needs of the country. The Reform Act of 1867 extended the franchise to the urban working classes, a measure which led Robert Lowe to state: "We must educate our masters." The Liberal Party Government of the day responded to the situation by the compromise incorporated into the first Education Act of Parliament: the Elementary Education Act of 1870. The prevailing voluntary system was preserved intact, but where deficiencies occurred, non-denominational School Boards were to be appointed with power to build and maintain schools by levying local rates.

Relatively rapid progress was made from this
date onwards. In 1876 and again in 1880 provisions
were enacted concerning compulsory attendance.[7]
The Elementary Education Act of 1891 made education
free or inexpensive for most students, while Payment by Results disappeared in 1897.

The Local Government Act of 1888 completely
reorganized the internal administrative system of
England and Wales, and led to the comprehensive
Education Act of 1902 which made the new County
and County Borough Councils responsible for both
elementary and secondary schools within their
boundaries. The School Boards vanished, and the
nonconformists were, for the most part, content to
permit the "British Schools" to dissolve into the
State system. This was not true of the Established
Church nor of the Catholic Church, and again a compromise ensued whereby State and local financial
aid was made available to their respective school
agencies.

Concern displayed by the State in England and
Wales in secondary education during the nineteenth
century was even more casual and arbitrary than
that relating to elementary education, as described
in the foregoing section. In 1800, a variety of
endowed, fee-paying secondary (grammar) schools were
in existence. For the most part they were schools
with a predominantly classical language curriculum,
whose scholars were expected to proceed to one or
other of the two universities of Oxford and Cambridge, whence students graduated mainly in

----

7. for all children under 10 years by 1880, 11
   years by 1893, and even 14 years by 1900, (although partial exemption by-laws were permiss-
   ible).

theology and law. Standards had long been set by the great "Public Schools" of which there were seven:

Winchester, founded in 1382 by a bishop, William of Wykeham, who, having already sponsored New College, Oxford, providing for 70 scholars in theology and law, but being dismayed with their ignorance of Latin, decided to establish a preparatory school with a classical curriculum.

Eton, opened in 1442, was established by King Henry VI, and ever since that date, had been closely associated with King's College. Cambridge, founded by the same monarch.

Westminster, one of twelve grammar schools endowed by Henry VIII, suffered a temporary demise during the reign of the Catholic Queen Mary, but maintained continuity following re-endowment by Queen Elizabeth in 1660.

The four other schools, Harrow, Rugby, Charterhouse and Shrewsbury,8 were founded by less prominent individuals but were all modeled upon Winchester: initially they were boarding establishments, where poor but academically well-qualified students from all parts of England could receive a free education— it was in this sense that they functioned under the rubric of "public schools." A few sons of the nobility had always been accepted but in time they came to outnumber

----

8. Shrewsbury was unique in that it was a municipal undertaking although chartered and endowed by Edward VI (c. 1552).

the "poor scholars," and the schools
attained the status of private and
privileged fee-paying institutions,
but so well-endowed that they could
always be independent of State aid
and control.[9]

At all times, while classical learning was
emphasized to promote mental discipline, the Public
Schools paid most attention to character and moral
education, implicit in the school motto of Winchester,
"Manners Maketh Man." Formal religious services
were regularly conducted in the impressive chapel
at each school, and strict discipline was enforced
through corporal punishment. Physical exercise
through compulsory games was a daily routine with
the intent of the development of a team spirit
(esprit de corps) as well as of individual self-
control.[10]

Many smaller day, as well as boarding, "public
schools" sprang up all over the country, and, after
the Restoration of 1660, they were accompanied by
the Dissenting (Nonconformist) Academies which
tended to offer a much wider curriculum, including
modern languages, mathematics, science, and practical subjects.

During the eighteenth and the earlier decades
of the nineteenth century the Public Schools generally fell into disrepute. Being well-endowed, they

----

9. Two other schools, St. Paul's and Merchant
    Taylors, respectively, partook of the same
    characteristics as the other seven, except that
    they were day, and not boarding, schools.

10. Hence the remark attributed to the Duke of Wel-
    lington that "the Battle of Waterloo was won
    on the playing fields of Eton."

could afford to remain independent of external pressure, especially that exerted by the growing prosperous middle class which emerged with the Industrial Revolution. The "nouveaux riches" were well able to afford the fees charged by the Public Schools, but in time they became disillusioned with the narrow academic curriculum, which, in fairness, was often difficult to change because of the binding clauses of the original endowments.

Reform came from three directions. First and foremost was the personal influence of a remarkable series of headmasters, among whom Thomas Arnold took precedence. Appointed to Rugby School in 1828 he transformed its ebbing fortunes and made it the pioneer establishment for a new era in the history of the Public Schools. A powerful and authoritarian personality, he combined stress upon discipline, duty, and loyalty with humanitarianism and compassion, and many of his students became influential headmasters and teachers, thus spreading the new gospel throughout the system.

In the second place, a new middle class institution funded by joint-stock companies, was created along the lines of the Public Schools, but with more liberal statutes reflected in their broader curricula. Termed "Proprietary Schools," they originated with Cheltenham (1841) and Marlborough (1843) Colleges, and within twenty years at least a score of similar well-established schools had been founded.

A third significant agent in reform was the State itself which set up a sequence of Royal Commissions. The first, in 1849, under Lord Chichester reported upon "the evils and abuses" of the innumerable charitable endowments, and led, in 1853, to the Charitable Trusts Act. The second, in 1861, under Lord Clarendon, investigated conditions in the nine famous Public Schools, and was followed by the Public Schools Act (1868) designed to free the institutions from their original, specified restrictions and to set up new governing bodies. The third, the Endowed Schools Commission of 1864, chaired by Lord Taunton, inquired into the nature of the education provided by all remaining endowed schools[11] in the country. The Commission, reporting in 1868, was obviously influenced by the conclusions of Matthew Arnold (son of Thomas Arnold of Rugby, and an Inspector of Schools) who had been authorized abroad to study secondary school systems in France, Prussia, Switzerland, and Italy. Greatly impressed by what he had observed, he exhorted the Commission to "Organize your secondary and your superior instruction." Its members responded by advocating more positive action by the State, and they recommended the appointment of a central administrative authority for secondary education. While the government ignored this latter recommendation in the Endowed Schools Act of 1869, it did accept the Commission's interpretation that secondary education implied the provision of facilities for girls as well as boys, so that after 1870 a new era began in girls' education in England and Wales by the allocation of endowments for the establishment of High Schools for girls.

Outside the endowed school system, the status of secondary education was very confused and complicated. A Department of Practical Art had been created in 1852, and, following the great interest aroused in scientific and technical developments by the Great Exhibition held in London in 1851, the Department was reconstituted (as a matter of administrative convenience) as the Department of Science and Art, and soon afterwards was incorporated as a branch of the new Education Department in 1856. Grants were made available to teachers and students on the basis of examinations.

----

11. They numbered 782.

The Elementary Education Act of 1870, together with subsequent legislation, had not only led to the opening of many new schools, but also to the development of "higher grades" presumed to offer instruction beyond the elementary stage to students eager for more advanced education, although there persisted great uncertainty as to the nature of the courses to be offered. At the same time, mounting demands for guidance in the technical field led to the appointment of a Royal Commission on Technical Instruction (1881-84). The significance of the Commission's Report (1884) lay in the statement that "the best preparation for technical study is a good modern secondary school,"12 which, the Commissioners alleged, was an institution much neglected in England as compared with industrial countries of Western Europe.

Ten years later, yet a further Royal Commission13 was appointed

> to consider what are the best methods of establishing a well-organized system of secondary education in England, taking into account existing deficiencies, and having regard to such local sources of revenue from endowments or otherwise as are available or may be made available for this purpose and to make recommendations accordingly.

The first outcome of the Commission's Report (1895) was the establishment, in 1899, of one central Education Authority for England and Wales, the

----

12. The Spens Report (on Secondary Education) p. 52, (London H.M. Stationery Office 1938).

13. The Royal Commission on Secondary Education (1894-95) with Lord Boyce as Chairman.

Board of Education. The second outcome was the
(Balfour) Education Act of 1902, which finally provided a coherent State System for the administration
of secondary schools throughout England and Wales.[14]

It is not without interest to note that action
undertaken to develop a comprehensive system of
secondary education was in the nature of a series
of fill-gap measures between developments at the
elementary stage on the one hand, and at the university level on the other.

In 1800, there were only two universities,
those of Oxford and Cambridge, respectively, in the
whole of England and Wales, a situation which had
remained unchanged since before 1200 A.D. After
the Reformation all non-communicants of the Church
of England were excluded from graduation, and not
until the nineteenth century did the nonconformists
gain sufficient confidence and power to proceed with
the establishment of a secular institution: University College, London (1827).[15] The Established
Church reacted quickly, and founded King's College,
London (1828). Both sides reached a compromise so
that in 1836 the federal University of London was
chartered, and it initially consisted of the two
named colleges.

----

14. The Act empowered the counties and county bor-
    oughs (established in 1888) to provide, main-
    tain, and administer all state-aided secondary
    education institutions. It followed the prece-
    dent initiated in the Welsh Intermediate Act
    of 1889, when identical provisions had been
    stipulated and successfully put into operation.

15. which Thomas Arnold, ever a fervent Churchman
    labeled, "that godless institution in Gower
    Street," since it excluded theology as a dis-
    cipline.

In 1850, two Royal Commissions were appointed, to enquire into the state, studies, and revenues of Oxford and Cambridge, respectively. Both Commissions reported in 1852 and recommended reforms in finance and administration, and the removal of oaths and declarations for all degrees, reforms which were (with modification) made operative by the Oxford (1854), and Cambridge (1856) Acts.[16] Both universities expanded their curricula after mid-century to include honors schools in science, law, history, as well as modern and Asiatic languages. Women came to be admitted by the founding of Girton College, Cambridge in 1872, and Newnham Hall, Oxford, in 1875.

Elsewhere in England, the University of Durham was chartered in 1832, Victoria University (consisting of colleges at Manchester, Liverpool and Leeds) in 1880, and Birmingham University in 1900.[17]

The four mediaeval universities of Scotland remained adequate for the country during the entire nineteenth century, except for internal reforms, and for the foundation of a University College at Dundee in 1881 (to be associated with the University of St. Andrews).

In Ireland, Trinity College, Dublin, received nominal university status[18] from Queen Elizabeth in 1591. It was of Protestant foundation, closely

----

16.   The University Tests Act (1871) finally abolished all oaths and affirmations at both universities, except for Divinity.

17.   In Wales, the University Colleges of Aberystwyth (1872), Cardiff (1883), and Bangor (1884) were, in 1893, incorporated as the University of Wales.

18.   As the University of Dublin.

associated with Cambridge. In 1845, university colleges were established in Belfast, Cork, and Galway, and these were federated as Queen's University (1850). Religious problems remained until the 1870's when the University was renamed the Royal University of Ireland empowered to grant degrees without disability to Catholics and Protestants alike.

FRANCE

Even before the French Revolution, significant changes had become manifest in French education. The abrupt expulsion of the Jesuit Order had created a chaotic lacuna in the domain of secondary education which was only partially compensated for by the accelerated activities of the Oratorians, but the latter did provide a school curriculum of more liberal dimension than that offered by the Jesuits, with more attention being directed towards science, mathematics, modern history, and to the French language (as opposed to Latin).

Despite the prevailing, oppressive, political climate, the French "philosophes" of the Age of Enlightenment had focused upon an immediate and convenient target for their abrasive diatribes, a target which met with the approval of the French monarchy, namely the Catholic Church. The Protestant countries of north-western Europe had long swept aside all Papal restrictions, and the rulers of the Catholic states, visibly motivated by an intense nationalistic outlook now sought like means for political self assertion. Hence the surprising freedom of thought and expression accorded to the "philosophes" insofar as they focused upon the Catholic Church, and not the (French) state, as the butt of their animosities.

Prior to the Revolution, educational reform had been confined to mere discussion of proposals of which there was no dearth. Rousseau's Emile (1762) had paved the way for the more concrete and practical suggestions expounded by, among others, Claude-Adrien Helvetius, Denis Diderot, Etienne Bonnot de Condillac, and Louis-Rene de la Chatolais, who, in an Essay on National Education (1763), probably most ably summarized the contemporary viewpoint of the period:

I do not presume to exclude eccles-
iastics....but I protest against
the exclusion of laymen. I dare
claim for the nation an education
which depends only on the State,
because it belongs essentially to
the State; because every State has
an inalienable and indefensible
right to instruct its members; because, finally, the children of the
State.[1]

With respect to developments in higher education, France had been remarkably well served by no
fewer than 21 universities (as compared with only
two in England and Wales), together with at least
50 technical or practical institutions relating to
such diverse professions as the military arts,
mining, engineering, hydrography, obstetrics,
veterinary science, music, and art.[2]

In July 1789, the Third Estate (consisting of
merchants and peasants) had proclaimed itself as
the National Assembly of France, and on the 14th
day of the same month, the Bastille was stormed.
In quick succession the Assembly reduced the status
of the Catholic clergy to that of state civil servants, and completely reorganized the former
historic provinces of France into 83 administrative
departments. A series of educational plans was
formulated, all of which, to a greater or lesser
degree tended to reflect many of the principles
already advanced by the "philosophes."

----

1. Birchenough; History of Elementary Education,
    p. 20

2. Among the more prestigious institutions were
    the School of Bridges (1775) and the School of
    Mines (1778).

In 1791, Talleyrand (1754-1838)[3] drew up an educational proposal comprised of three parts:
1) free, universal elementary schools;
2) secondary schools for advanced students;
3) institutions of higher learning, one of which to be located in each Department.

No action was taken to implement either the foregoing proposal, or the more comprehensive plan advanced by Condorcet (1743-94). The latter was a gifted mathematician and scientist and a member of the Committee of Public Instruction of the Legislative Assembly to which, in 1792, he submitted his Report on Public Instruction. Condorcet recognized four levels of schooling:
1) free, compulsory, elementary education for students aged 6 - 10;
2) opportunity for post-elementary education either for the gifted, at secondary schools, or for the less advanced, at post-primary schools (for 2 or 3 years). (At both primary and secondary schools, scientific studies were to be given priority over classical languages and literature;
3) scientific Institutes, providing instruction in agriculture and mechanics, were to be established, with one in each Department;
4) higher academic learning was to be pursued at 9 "Lycees," located regionally over the country.

Supervision was placed under the aegis of a

----

3. a former bishop, and a paragon of the art of political survival, serving in turn the monarchist regime of Louis XVI, the governments of the Revolution, and the Restored Monarchy of Louis XVIII.

National Society of Arts and Sciences, composed mainly of scholars, who would be expected to inject acumen and expertise into the entire school system.[4]

In 1795, the National Convention took more direct action.[5] It decreed that free primary schools be established in each commune, and that secondary "central" schools be located on the basis of one in each Department, with five in Paris. Advanced technical schools were to replace all other forms of higher education. By far the most successful practical outcome of the decree was that relating to the "central" schools, (avidly patronized by the French middle class), which survived until the next phase of educational reorganization, that undertaken by Napoleon, who,siezing power by a coup d'etat in 1799, was designated first consul for life in 1802. Seemingly obsessed by an urge to make France the dominant military power in the world, Napoleon set out to create a comprehensive machine which would provide him with, on the one hand, an eminently efficient officer corps to command his armies, and, on the other hand, an effective bureaucracy to administer the projected world-wide empire.

Astute and diplomatic in his imperialistic designs, Napoleon in 1801 negotiated a Concordat

----

4. Condorcet fell foul of the Jacobins, by whom he was placed in prison where he died in 1794.

5. It had already provided financial aid to the Museum of Natural History (1793), established a School of Public Works (1794), created a National Institute of 100 resident scholars (1795), and had set up the Louvre Museum for the purpose of housing the Royal collections of art.

with Pope Pius VII, which, inter alia,[6] permitted
instruction at elementary school level to revert
to the control of the Catholic Brothers of the
Christian Schools. Having established this working compromise, Napoleon next proceeded to organize a national, centralized, and secular structure
of schools and institutions of secondary and higher
education categories. Under the Law of 1802, the
"central schools" of 1795 were replaced by two
major types of secondary schools:

    a) the Lycee, typically a state boarding
       school, which charged fees, but was
       otherwise entirely supported by the
       government. Its six-year curriculum
       placed emphasis upon high academic
       achievement in mathematics, science,
       the classics, and philosophy, (the
       latter to replace all religious teach-
       ing). Thirty lycees were initially
       created. Students wore uniforms and
       underwent military training by regular
       army officers.

    b) The College, a less prestigious institu-
       tion funded, not by the state, but by
       local civic initiative. The curriculum
       content was virtually identical with
       that of the lycee, but with lower achieve-
       ment student expectations.

    Since no State board existed to supervise
the new school structure it was necessary to create
one. A decree of 1808 brought into being the
Imperial University [7] (the University of France),

----

6. Under the terms of the Concordat, the Catholic
   religion was recognized as the "religion of
   the great majority of French citizens" but not
   as the religion of the State.

7. The term "University" as here employed was an
   administrative, and not an academic, concept.

as a central administrative body responsible for the entire supervision of education within the country. The Imperial University functioned as a national office of education under the control of a Grand Master[8] appointed by the Emperor.[9] France was subdivided into 17 subdivisions, termed Academies, each of which was headed by a Rector (supported by an administrative and inspectoral staff), who was to be responsible for the entire educational activities, ranging from elementary through university level, within his specified territorial jurisdiction.

In 1789 there already existed in France 21 universities (all under Church authority) most of which exhibited evident signs of marked deterioration in academic standards. Napoleon himself had little interest in advanced learning, but was determined to destroy all ecclesiastical vestiges of control. For that reason, he undertook a complete reorganization of the universities, and resolved them into the degree-granting faculty bodies of the arts, sciences, law, medicine, and theology, respectively, whose only common denominator, thenceforth, was the Rector of the Academy.[10]

In furtherance of his objective of achieving

----

8. The title was changed in 1824 to that of Minister of Ecclesiastical Affairs and Public Instruction, and again in 1840 to that of Minister of Public Instruction.

9. Napoleon self-crowned himself as Emperor in 1804.

10. Not until late in the nineteenth century and early in the twentieth century did the concept of the "University," as an all-inclusive, academic institution, reappear in France.

French military hegemony in Europe, Napoleon
lavished funds upon the professional schools, in
particular the Grande Ecole Polytechnique and the
Grande Ecole Militaire, which furnished his armies
with engineers and officers. Recognizing that his
new schools could not possibly function adequately
without well-trained teachers, he created, in 1810,
the Ecole Normale Superieure in Paris, a two-year
teacher-training institution of high academic
standards for prospective instructors in the
lycees and colleges.

     The nationalistic and conservative character
of Napoleon's educational reforms strongly favored
their retention by the Bourbon Restoration monarchy
which replaced the Empire in 1814. Additional
schools were opened and they followed the pattern
decreed by Napoleon. The July Revolution of 1830
put an end to the arbitrary and reactionary rule
of Charles X, and initiated the more liberal
regime of Louis Philippe. The change was reflected
in the Loi Guizot of 1833 which required each commune to establish a (secular) primary school,
supported by parental fees, but with provision for
state aid where necessary. Private (religious)
schools were permitted, but teachers therein were
to be certified by the local mayor as well as by
the ecclesiastical authorities. The Law thus provided a framework for a State primary school system.
Responding to the needs of the day, the Law also
established higher primary courses of two to three
years duration, to include basic training in preparation for vocational work in industry, agriculture, or commerce. But, among the most important provisions of the Law was the requirement that
each of the 83 Departments in France set up a
Normal College for the training of teachers. This
represented an educational landmark providing a
pioneer model which came to be widely imitated in
the Western World.

     The year 1848 was one of Revolutions in Europe.
In France it led to the abdication of Louis

Philippe[11] along with a series of revolts whose
suppression was followed by a strong conservative
reaction, reflected in the Loi Falloux of 1850.
This Law was specifically designed to restore the
power of the Catholic hierarchy in France. Convinced that radical revolutions were supported,
if not inspired, by elementary (rather than secondary) school teachers, the Law granted to each
Department the power to close its Normal School
for teacher training. It recognized the right of
the clergy not only to inspect primary schools but
also to validate the teaching certificates of all
teachers in those schools. It conferred upon
each commune the right to establish private
(religious) schools wherein women in the religious
orders were permitted to teach without qualification other than their oaths of obedience.[12]

Still further political turmoil followed the
defeat of France by Germany in 1870, and the abdication of Napoleon III led to the creation of the
Third Republic. Once again, anti-clerical forces
assumed power, and in the field of education, the
outstanding personality was Jules Ferry (1832-93).
As Minister of Public Instruction he sponsored and
implemented a new era in French education through
a series of laws enacted during the decade of the
1880's: in 1881 all tuition fees were abolished
in state primary schools; in 1882 compulsory attendance was required of all students aged 6 to 13
years; in 1886, the Ministry assumed control for

----

11. His abdication led to the Second Republic
    which collapsed when Louis Napoleon seized
    power (1851) and assumed the title of Emperor
    as Napoleon III (1852).

12. In consequence, there were by 1880 five times
    as many private schools as in 1850.

the entire state school system with regard to curricula, examinations, teacher certification, appointments, and salaries.13 No longer were any members of the religious teaching orders permitted to serve in state schools, and all religious instruction in these schools was forbidden.

The State offensive against sectarian (i.e. Catholic) education climaxed in the early years of the twentieth century. Since the legal status of religious orders in France had not been adequately defined under the terms of Napoleon's Concordat of 1801, and since many of the subsequent laws and decrees, whether liberal or illiberal, had been ambivalent and very loosely interpreted, a great deal of confusion regarding the status of non-public school education persisted throughout the entire period of the nineteenth century. A crisis arose following the National Election of 1902 when the radical Prime Minister, Emile Combes, forcibly sponsored the Law of 1904 which prohibited all members of religious orders from teaching in France. At least 20,000 primary and secondary Catholic schools were closed as an immediate result of this Law.14

First concerns over the predominantly classical curriculum of the Napoleonic lycée were voiced

----

13.   In 1828 a post-graduate competitive examination (the Agrégation) had been instituted in 4 subjects: letters, grammar, philosophy, and science. The number of subjects has since been amplified but the principle of teacher appointment on the basis of a national competitive examination remains unaltered.

14.   The number of religious order teachers in France was reduced from c. 1.5 million in 1902 to c. 60,000 in 1910.

towards the mid-nineteenth century, since there appeared to be no provision at secondary level for able students in the domain of science and technology. The first attempt to remedy the situation came in a statute of 1847 which advocated the establishment of a Special Course of three years (L' Enseignment Special)[15] in secondary schools to follow the regular three years course of literacy studies. However, the entire concept was aborted by the events of the 1848 Year of Revolutions. A compromise was put into effect in 1852 when, following upon a common course of three years, students were offered the choice of pursuing either a literacy course (leading to the baccalaureates-lettres) or a scientific course (leading to the baccalaureates-sciences).[16] This system was not considered satisfactory and was suppressed in 1863. An effort to revise the Enseignment Special by Victor Duruy in 1865 faltered by reason of lack of support by parents who considered it to be inferior because Latin, the prestige subject, was not offered.

Repercussions arising out of the defeat of France by Germany in 1870, facilitated the modernization of the secondary school curriculum with the amount of time devoted to classical studies being reduced in favor of the sciences and modern languages. In 1880, Jules Ferry instituted a major reform, whereby the curriculum was restructured to provide for two cycles, each of three years, to be capped by a final year of specialization in philosophy.

----

15. The Special Course comprised a basic core of Latin, Modern Language(s) and Science, together with mechanics, accounting, commercial law, agriculture, and technical drawing.

16. All students continued their studies of Latin, French, modern languages, history, and geography.

The three-year Enseignment Special of Duruy
which, for over fifteen years, had survived as a
vague penumbra bordering upon the more dominant
classical-science secondary curriculum was extended
by Ferry in 1881 to 5 years, (culminating in a bac-
calaureat of Special Instruction), while in 1886,
one further year of study was added. In 1891, the
term Enseightment Special was abolished in favor of
that of Enseignment Moderne.

The basic questions in French education remained unanswered: on the one hand, the classicists
deplored the continued erosion of Latin and Greek
as basic subjects in the secondary curriculum, claim-
ing that French culture and societal values were
inherently enshrined in these disciplines; on the
other hand, the modernists were vehement in their
protests that the schools were not equipping the
younger generation with the scientific and technological background necessary to ensure that France
assume its status as a modern industrial power.

The mounting criticisms of secondary education
led, in 1898, to the appointment of a Parliamentary
Commission on Education, (presided over by
Alexander Ribot), whose recommendations led to the
reforms of 1902, wherein:
   a) a parallel system of <u>classical</u> and <u>modern</u>
      courses leading to a <u>single baccalaureat</u>
      was to be instituted;
   b) the seven year course was divided into
      three parts:
         i) a 4 year cycle,[17] complete in
            itself and leading to a <u>Certificat
            D' Etudes Secondaires</u>;

----

17. providing for a Latin and non-Latin tracking
     system.

ii) followed by a four-track[18] 2 year
cycle leading to the <u>Baccalaureat</u>
(<u>First Part</u>);

iii) with one final year of specialization,
either in philosophy or mathematics,
leading to the <u>Baccalaureat</u> (<u>Second
Part</u>).

The reform represented an important victory
for the proponents of modern studies (especially
the sciences and foreign languages) which were now
accorded parity of status with the classics as
regards university entrance requirements. Further
reform was to await the onset of World War One.

----

18. with alternatives in   a) Latin and Greek
                          b) Latin and Modern
                             Languages
                          c) Latin and Science
                          d) Science and Modern
                             Languages

GERMANY

Not until 1870 was there in Central Europe a country legitimately designated as "Germany," or, more specifically "The German Empire," the brainchild of Otto von Bismarck, who, following his appointment as Chancellor of Prussia in 1862, contrived, with Machiavellian zeal, to prosecute wars in rapid succession against Denmark (1864), Austria (1866), and France (1870) respectively, so as to achieve his ultimate objective: the unification of the German States under the aegis of Prussia.

Prior to 1870, the territorial area of Germany was comprised of several hundred quasi-autonomous provinces, states, and cities, and, ironically, it was Napoleon who, obsessed by his ambition to dominate Europe under the French flag, became responsible for initiating the concluding stages of German unification. Germany west of the River Elbe had been an integral part of Charlemagne's Empire. Several centuries later, the Teutonic Knights in the Crusades of the North had extended the German dominions eastward into the territories of the Slavs, and it was here, as an aggressively military province, that the state of Prussia emerged, a state which in due course came to dominate the German-speaking peoples of Central Europe. During the eighteenth century, three resolute rulers of Prussia, Frederick William I (1713-40), Frederick II, the Great (1740-86), and Frederick William II (1786-97), respectively, not only measurably advanced the political status of the country but also, recognizing the role of education as a formidable agency in the manipulation of a society, gave strong support to the development of a structured school system.

In consequence, while the defeat of Prussia by Napoleon at the battle of Jena (1806) was a humiliating and traumatic experience for the country, the

event resulted in an immediate counteraction of such
intensity in the cultural domain that it proved to
be the catalyst whereby political consolidation was
achieved within little more than half a century
after Jena. The very title of Johann Gottlieb
Fichte's famous Addresses to the German Nation
(1807-8) was demonstratably indicative of the new
mood, and Fichte himself was appointed as the first
Director of the newly founded University of Berlin
(1809), now considered to be the prototype of the
modern university by reason of its emphasis upon
graduate research and upon state recognition of the
independence and freedom of the university faculty
from political control and interference.

In 1808, a Bureau of Education was created within the Ministry of the Interior, with Wilhelm von
Humboldt[1] (1763-1835) as its head. Von Humboldt
was a liberal-minded scholar who, while being a
fervent admirer of the classics, recognized the
changing character of society and the consequent
need to update the curriculum so as to incorporate
studies relating to science and proficiency in
modern languages. His suggestions developed into
the Allgemeine Bildung, a comprehensive curriculum
for the academic secondary school, the Gymnasium.
Von Humboldt further recognized the fundamental precept that a good system of education was predicated
upon an adequate supply of competent teachers so
that he introduced, in 1810, the Examen Pro Facultate
Docendi, a teacher certificate examination which,
henceforward, placed German secondary teachers on
a pedestal as a qualified, professional body with
nation-wide established qualifications.

The termination of the Napoleonic Wars in 1815

----

1. He is not to be confused with his equally emin-
    ent brother, Alexander von Humboldt, the explorer
    and naturalist of South America.

resulted in conservative reaction to reform all over Europe. In Prussia the Bureau of Education (created in 1808) was, in 1817, absorbed into a new Ministry of Religion, Education, and Public Health, which delegated the clergy with more responsibility for the supervision of education. Testimonial confirmation of satisfactory moral character was required of all prospective teaching candidates, while practising teachers, themselves, were expected to demand from their students unquestioning obedience to lawful institutions.

In 1834, success in the Abiturienten Examen[2] was recognized as sole criterion for admission into the universities (whose individual entrance examinations were thereby abolished). This provision substantially enhanced the status of both the Gymnasium and its teachers.

In the field of primary education, by far the most influential educators were Johann Heinrich Pestalozzi (1746-1827), a German-speaking Swiss citizen, and Friedrich Froebel (1782-1852).

Pestalozzi, born in Zurich, was a Protestant of Italian origin, who, in his formative years, had been greatly influenced by his reading of Rousseau's Emile. As a college student he had become politically involved in a patriotic Helvetic Society dedicated to the improvement of Swiss government and education. He was intensely sympathetic to the depraved conditions of the Swiss peasantry, and, uncertain as to a career, he eventually married and settled in 1769 on a farm at Neuhof. Here, he involved himself in an altruistic effort to provide

----

2. It was part written and part oral, provisions which remain characteristic of German school and university examinations.

a good home for at least 20 orphan or poor children, kept employed with farming in the summer, and craft weaving in the winter. Short of funds by 1776 he published in that year, An Appeal to the Friends and Benefactors of Humanity, in which he described his work. His appeal elicitated more money and Pestalozzi expanded his activities by accepting more children. He was, however, a poor business manager and the entire experiment collapsed by 1779, a tragedy which left him in a depressed mood for almost twenty years. Yet, in 1781, Pestalozzi wrote Leonard and Gertrude, a work which brought him fame, together with some means of financial support. Written in the format of a novel, (within which Pestalozzi took the opportunity of disseminating his pragmatic approach to education), it portrayed life in the fictional village of Bonnal where Hummel, an unscrupulous bailiff, was exploiting poor, honest peasants. He was eventually thwarted by the efforts of the local schoolteacher, Leonard, with the cooperation of the village pastor and the benevolent lord of the manor. But it is Leonard's wife, Gertrude, who emerges as the real heroine of the book, since it is she, the ideal peasant house-wife and mother who rears and educates her seven children according to Pestalozzian principles, among which domestic love, emotional stability and progressive training in sensory education take precedence. While approving of much of Rousseau's Emile, Pestalozzi rejected the concept of unlimited freedom, and held the view that, while "Liberty is a good thing, obedience is equally so." He laid stress upon the principle that the process of learning always demanded considerable effort on the part of the child, but it was the function of the teacher to provide a congenial environment for, and a warm human relationship with, the child so as to ease the path of knowledge.

In 1782, Pestalozzi published Christopher and

<u>Elizabeth</u>[3] in dialogue format which apparently had
no appeal. His three subsequent, sequel volumes to
<u>Leonard and Gertrude</u> (1783-7) likewise failed.

A new era of practical endeavor opened for
Pestalozzi in 1799, when, following the Napoleonic
invasion of Switzerland and sacking of the town of
Stanz by the French army, hundreds of children were
left destitute. The Swiss (Helvetian) authorities
were sufficiently concerned to establish an orphanage, and presented Pestalozzi with the challenge
of setting up appropriate facilities. He was quick
to respond and soon put into operation an institution
providing a home of love and security for eighty
children. However, within five months, the French
returned and commandeered the orphanage buildings
as a military hospital. Yet, brief as it was,
Pestalozzi gained great experience from the experiment. Later he was to write:

> I believe that the first development of thought
> in the child is very much disturbed by a wordy
> system of teaching, which is not adapted
> either to his faculties or the circumstances
> of his life. According to my experience, suc-
> cess depends upon whether what is taught to
> children commends itself to them as true
> through being closely connected with their
> own personal observation and experience.

And again:

> I always made the children learn perfectly
> even the least important things, and I
> never allowed them to lose ground; a word
> once learnt, for instance, was never to
> be forgotten, and a letter once well written
> never to be written badly again. I was very

----

3. With the subtitle, <u>My Second Book for the
    People</u>.

patient with all who were weak or slow, but very severe with those who did anything less well than they had done it before.

To which he added:

The pedagogical principle which says that we must win the hearts and minds of our children by words alone without having recourse to corporal punishment, is certainly good, and applicable under favourable conditions and circumstances; but with children of such widely different ages as mine, children for the most part beggars, and all full of deeply rooted faults, a certain amount of corporal punishment was inevitable, especially as I was anxious to arrive surely, speedily, and by the simplest means, at gaining an influence over them all, for the sake for putting them all in the right road.

In 1801 a further opportunity to apply his theoretical concepts in practice came when Pestalozzi was placed in charge of a school at Burgdorf, which developed into a teacher-training institute. A devoted faculty[4] made the school and institute a great success, but the project was forced to close within four years because of the withdrawal of government financial aid. In terms of writing output it proved to be a most prolific period, since within this brief span of time, Pestalozzi published, How Gertrude teaches her

----

4. It included Joseph Neef and Hermann Krusi. Neef and Krusi's son, Hermann Krusi, Jr., emigrated to the United States where they became enthusiastic propagators of Pestalozzian methods.

Children, an attempt to give Directions to Mothers how to instruct their own Children (1801), Help for Teaching, Spelling, and Reading (1801), together with six manuals relating to the teaching of number and parental guides issued as Pestalozzi's Elementary Books (1803).

In 1805, Pestalozzi reestablished himself at Yverdon, near Neuchatel, where he remained for the next twenty years. Yverdon developed as a place of pilgrimage for the foremost educators of the day, including Robert Owen, Dr. Charles Mayo, Maria Edgeworth, Lord Brougham, and Andrew Bell of England, Friedrich Froebel, Carl Ritter, and Johann Friedrich Herbart of Germany. In its reform mood after 1806, the Prussian Government itself sent 17 teachers to Yverdon for a period of three years to study Pestalozzian methods.

By 1825 the school closed and Pestalozzi returned to Neuhof, where, before his death in 1827, he wrote Swan's Song, and My Fortunes as Superintendent of my Educational Establishments at Burgdorf and Yverdon.

Throughout his career Pestalozzi stressed the paramount importance of recognition by the teacher of what he termed "Anschauung," the gradual unfolding of the developmental processes of the child. The stages of intellectual development could be materially assisted by the exposure of the student to 'realia,' i.e. actual physical objects or, where these proved unattainable, diagrams and illustrations, so as to supplement mere verbal description. In this way the child could be taught to observe accurately and to extend his/her powers of speech by careful reporting. A planned learning environment providing for intellectual, moral, aesthetic, and physical development was essential, and it was upon his practical demonstrations as a classroom schoolteacher that Pestalozzi's fame rests as a pioneer educator.

Friedrich Froebel (1782-1852) visited Yverdon
in 1808 and was much impressed by the atmosphere of
the Institute. Following a varied career, he opened
a school, first at Griesheim (1816) and then at
Keilhau (1818). He was a very sensitive and intro-
spective personality, greatly influenced by the
Romantic idealism of his day. His specific interests
came to lie in the education of younger children
and in 1826 he published The Education of Man, a
work which summarized his ideas and theories of
education. By no means an easily-read book by
reason of its involved symbolism, it remains his
most influential written contribution to education.
In it he expressed the view that the child from the
earliest years should be exposed to the concept of
a divinely-ordained universe within which he/she,
as a participating member of a spiritual community,
formed an integral part. Like Rousseau and
Pestalozzi, Froebel subscribed to the doctrine that
children were innately good, and even divine, and
it was for the teacher to provide the environment
and opportunities for the unfolding of their best
qualities and creative potentialities.

In 1831, Froebel was accorded opportunity to
put his theories into practice when the Swiss government offered him the position as director of an
orphanage at Burgdorf, where he remained for six
years. He returned to Blankenburg, Germany, in 1837
and it was here that he founded and named the first
"kindergarten" (children's garden). He experimented
with two types of play materials:

a) gifts, with fixed symmetrical form, such
   as spheres, cubes, cones, cylinders, linear
   rods and small blocks, all of which illustrated the perfection, harmony, and beauty
   of the physical world;

b) occupations, consisting of malleable
   materials, such as clay, sandpaper, and

cardboard, which a child was free to manipulate in whatever way it pleased.[5]

In 1843, Froebel published his Mother and Play Songs, a book comprising stories, games, and verses to assist parents and teachers to further relate the child's innate sense of unity and harmony with that of the external world. As an unrepentent romantic, Froebel had no objection to exposing the child to the fantasy world of fairy tales and make-believe, an approach for which, long after his death, he was strongly criticized by the other notable pioneer of pre-school education, Maria Montessori (1870-1952), who held that, in the first place, a child should not be taught anything which, at a later date, it would have to unlearn; and secondly, there was ample material in the wide world of nature and science to arouse the wonder and curiosity of children.

Conservative reaction to the European "Revolutions" of the year 1848 led to the suppression of Froebel's kindergarten by the Prussian Government (since he had long been suspected of entertaining radical political viewpoints) so that in 1852 he died a disappointed and frustrated teacher. But his efforts were not in vain. The Prussian Government itself reversed its decision in 1861, while, in the meantime, his innovative ideas had spread to the United States. Among the politically-liberal

----

5. In 1876 the American Centennial Exposition was held at Philadelphia, and among the exhibits was a display of Froebel's 'gifts' and 'occupations', a set of which Mrs. Anna Lloyd-Jones Wright purchased for her son, Frank, aged 6 years. It is an interesting speculation as to how far these play materials contributed to the awakening of the creative and imaginative abilities of the future architect, Frank Lloyd Wright.

Germans who had voluntarily exiled themselves after 1848 was Mrs. Carl Schurz[6] who had seen Froebel's school in action, and it was she who, in 1855, sponsored the first kindergarten in the United States at Watertown, Wisconsin. It was a German-language school. In 1860, Elizabeth Peabody (sister-in-law of Horace Mann) founded the first English-medium kindergarten in Boston, and the first kindergarten-teacher training school in 1868. In 1893 she published her <u>Lectures in the Training Schools for Kindergartners</u>. William Torey Harris, Superintendent of Schools for St. Louis, Missouri, was, in 1873, instrumental in being the first to incorporate the kindergarten as an integral part of the public schools system.

Another famed nineteenth century German educator was Johann Friedrich Herbart (1776-1841), born in Oldenburg. A gifted student, greatly influenced initially by Fichte as a student at Jena University, and, later, by Pestalozzi, following upon a visit to the latter's Institute at Yverdon, he succeeded to the chair of philosophy vacated by Immanuel Kant at the University of Konigsberg and taught there from 1809 until 1833. Herbart's attention became focused upon the science and art of teaching, and uppermost among his assertions was the imperative need for the teacher to be a person of high moral character. Adequate training was necessary, whereby the future pedagogue could be made aware of the most appropriate manner of lesson presentation. According to Herbart, all learning involved the acquisition of knowledge patterns which permitted facts and ideas to be more easily assimilated, and

----

6. She was the wife of Carl Schurz, who became editor of a German newspaper at St. Louis, was elected U.S. Senator in 1870, and later served as Secretary of the Interior under President Hayes.

it was in furtherance of the foregoing principle that he urged adoption of his five (initially four) formal lesson steps: Preparation, Presentation, Association, Generalization, and Application.

Herbart's theory of the "apperceptive mass" found wide acceptance in Western Europe as well as in the United States, where his proponents included Stanley Hall, Charles de Garmo, Frank and Charles McMurray, and John Dewey.[7]

During the latter half of the nineteenth century elementary school teachers in Prussia labored under difficult conditions due to the vacillating policies of the government. Since teachers were considered to be activists in political reform at the very time when union of the German-speaking peoples was within range of being accomplished, the Prussian government imposed a system of stricter supervision by the Church authorities of school curricula and activities.

However, following his success in achieving a politically unified German Empire by 1871, Bismarck embarked upon a "Kulturkampf" (a battle of culture) against the Catholic Church, which he regarded as a divisive dimension impairing the cohesion of a homogeneous German State. In furtherance of his campaign, Bismarck was instrumental in the passage of a series of decrees (1872-5) designed to reduce the amount of Church control and supervision in the German schools. The decrees prohibited all religious orders from partaking in educational activities, and expressly expelled the Jesuit Order

----

7. In 1892 his disciples organized the National Herbartian Society, renamed later (1902) the National Society for the Scientific Study of Education.

from Germany.[8]

To Bismarck's dismay, German Protestants objected to his anti-clerical measures as much as did the German Catholics, to the degree that there resulted an unanticipated increase in representation by the (predominantly Catholic) Center Party in the German Government election of 1877. Quick to recognize his error, Bismarck immediately rescinded what were considered to be the most objectionable of his decrees, although Church involvement in education was not restored.

In the domain of secondary education, opinion was becoming widespread that the existing limited course offerings of the Gymnasia and Realschulen were not providing an adequate response to the growing needs of an industrial Germany. Even Kaiser Wilhelm II entered into the controversy and initiated an educational conference in 1890 which was expected to respond to the dual goals of: a) a greater focus upon science and practical subjects, and b) more specific attention to German language and modern German history so as to promote a sense of citizenship reflecting the emergence of the new German nation-state.

The net result was that by the end of the century there had evolved no fewer than six types of secondary schools, three offering <u>nine years</u> of schooling:

    1) the Gymnasium (with Latin and Greek)
    2) the Realgymnasium (with Latin)
and 3) the Oberrealschule (with neither Latin nor Greek, but with modern languages and more science courses);

---

8. Suppressed in 1772 by Pope Clement XIV, the Jesuit Order had been revived in 1814 by Pope Pius VII.

and three corresponding-type schools offering six
years of schooling:

    4) the Progymnasium
    5) the Realprogymnasium
and 6) the Realschule.

Finally, in the year 1900, all nine-year
schools were accorded equal privilege of admission
to all faculties (except theology) of the universities.

The political turmoil which had accompanied
the French Revolution and its afternath of the
Napoleonic invasions of central and eastern Europe,
led to the closure of a number of the mediaeval
German universities, including those of Bamberg,
Cologne, Duisburg, Erfurt, Mainz, and Salzburg;
even Wittenberg, made famous by Luther and
Melanchthon, failed to survive as a separate
institution and was absorbed into Halle in 1815.
Few of the foregoing universities were missed
since in the first place they had, over the centuries, gradually crystallized into academic
fossils; and, secondly, they were to be replaced
during the nineteenth century by a trio of vigorous,
progressive foundations today recognized as con-
stituting a landmark in the development of higher
education; these were the universities of Berlin
(1809), Bonn (1818), and Munich (reorganized during the early decades of the century). Characteristic of all three was (a) the focus upon research
as an essential component of the university milieu;
(b) the concentration, in terms of curriculum,
upon the physical and social sciences at the
expense of theology; and (c) the insistence upon
recognition of the indispensable need for academic

study untrammelled by petty, parochial, political
irrelevancies.[9]

- - - - - - - - - - - - - - - - - - - -

9. Their success attracted world-wide attention,
    and, in the United States, the first institution
    specifically modeled upon the foregoing prin-
    ciples was that of Johns Hopkins University at
    Baltimore (1876), fortunate to have had at its
    helm, Daniel Coit Gilman, President for the
    initial twenty-five years of its existence.

CHINA

The most outstanding feature of Chinese history has been the retention of a well-defined political territory over a period extending for more than two thousand years. The country was initially united as a nation-state by Shi Huang Ti (the first Emperor) in 221 B.C. and despite centuries of disruption, revolt, and invasion, China in the nineteenth and twentieth centuries A.D. has emerged as a homogeneous political unit, virtually identical to that of the original empire. Moreover, over the same period of time, even though many dialects still exist, the Chinese (written) language has been the universal official and national medium of communication throughout the country and, since possession and use of a common language has been by far the most significant component contributory to the development of a political state, it is evident that, in the case of China, the emergence of a national identity has been greatly accelerated by the felicitous combination of both territorial and cultural factors. In addition, unity has been furthered by the absence of that religious dissension and heresy, so characteristic of the Western World during the Christian era. In place of religion(s) based upon belief and ritual, with major focus upon existence in a world hereafter, the Chinese adopted a cluster of ethical codes demanding appropriate social behavior and action in the world here-and-now.

Confucius (551-479 B.C.), or K'ung-Fu-Tzu, laid emphasis upon a stable society based on law and order, wherein the prevailing class-structured hierarchy should be preserved in the best interests of all. Fundamental to the development of such a desirable goal was an educational system designed to develop altruistic leaders, who were to serve as models of behavior for the society at large, and whose function it would also be to formulate basic ceremonial procedures which would allow for participation by ruled and rulers alike.

Mencius, (ca. 372-319 B.C.) also stressed the need for a durable basis for society, but he progressed one vital stage further when he propounded his theory of the fundamental right of the subjects of any state to rebel against an unjust ruler. This standpoint, later formalized into John Locke's contract theory of government, was expanded still further by Montesquieu of France, and was incorporated into the Declaration of Independence of the American colonists, as well into similar pronouncements by the proponents of subsequent revolutions in France and Latin America.

Lao Tzu, presumed to be an older contemporary of Confucius, expounded yet a third philosophy which advocated complete freedom for the individual from all political and social restraints, since these were imposed by men and governments, whereas the ultimate objective of existence should be the ideal attainment of Tao: The Way of achieving ultimate Harmony with the Universe. In essence, this represents the twentieth century Existentialist viewpoint, wherein the individual, following extensive exercise in introspection, would emerge as a purified personality capable of ascertaining decisions best benefitting both himself, his neighbors, and society.

For obvious reasons, it was the Confucian ethic which came to prevail in Chinese history. Formally adopted by the Earlier Han Dynasty (202 B.C.-A.D.9) there was also instituted an examination system designed to ensure an educated bureaucracy for the management of the extensive empire. The examination, based upon knowledge of the Confucian classics, provided a formalized, institutional method of the selection of candidates, commencing at the local (hsien) administrative level, and progressing

competitively upwards through the prefecture, (the
diploma of the Budding Talent, Hsiu-Tsai), the
province, (the diploma of the Elevated Man, Chu-Jen),
and the capital city, (the diploma of the Advanced
Scholar, Chin-Shih), the final phase being the
Imperial Palace Examination, success in which qualified candidates for appointment at the Han-Lin
Academy, the apex of higher learning institutions
within the empire.

The foregoing elaborate system represented,
possibly, the nearest approach in practice to the
attainment on earth of Plato's ideal of the
"Philosopher King(s)." But its narrowly specified
curriculum which simply demanded accurate and precise regurgitation without deviation of the very
words of the Master eliminated any approach
involving question, inquiry, or discussion relating
to the feasibility and applicability of the traditional concepts and ideas. It was a system
designed to perpetuate the hierarchical status quo,
even though the hierarchy itself was assumed (in
theory) to be one of talent and not one of prescrip-
tion. Students identified as being capable of
memory-mastery of the Confucian classics were
taught by individual scholars at the local district
level or in small schools in the larger towns and
cities.

In the course of centuries, a few changes
occurred in the examination format, including the
requirement of what came to be known as the Eight-
Legged Essay, which simply mandated that responses
in composition be submitted according to specific
rules relating to content, style, and symmetry.

During, and subsequent to the sixteenth century, contact with Europeans increased as the
Jesuit Order, founded in 1539. became militantly
active in all parts of the globe. Francis Xavier
died within sight of the Chinese mainland in 1552.

while Matteo Ricci (1552-1610), arriving in 1582, much impressed the Chinese by his knowledge of Western science, mathematics, and astronomy. The Portuguese obtained trading concessions at Macao (1557), but contact with Europe remained sporadic especially after 1715 when most missionaries were expelled by the Manchus.

China's isolation was abruptly terminated by the military action of Great Britain known as the Opium War (1839-42), which resulted in the British acquisition of Hong Kong as well as in the repeal by China of her anti-Christian decrees. Robert Morrison of the London Missionary Society was the first Protestant to arrive in China (1807), but not until 1845 was the first (American) mission school established (in Shanghai). The founding of the China Inland Mission by Hudson Taylor of England in 1866 greatly accelerated the pace of missionary activity in China.

A trend began of educating talented Chinese students abroad, mainly in the United States but also in Britain, France, and Japan (after the Meiji Restoration of 1868). Upon their return home many of these students, discontented with Manchu domination, became actively engaged in revolutionary activities designed to overthrow the regime.[1]

----

1. The story of Sun Yat-Sen, (1867-1925) "Father of the Chinese Republic" is typical of many students of this period. His father, a poor farmer living near Macao, was converted to Christianity and Sun Yat-Sen attended mission schools in Hawaii. In 1891 he enrolled as a student in the newly-founded medical college of Hong Kong of which in 1894 he was its first graduate. He became involved in a secret revolutionary society and was obliged to flee abroad in 1895 to escape execution. He remained overseas for fifteen years, returning eventually in 1911 to become the provisional president of the new Chinese Republic.

Within China the conservative imperial regime was very slow to respond to the impact of the political and economic encroachment by the Western nations. In 1862, a foreign language school for diplomatic personnel was opened at Peking; in 1866 a maritime technical school was established at Fukien; and in 1881 China's first naval academy was founded at Tientsin. In direct contrast to this lethargic and listless response was the eager adoption of Western concepts and technology by China' near neighbor, Japan, likewise forced out of isolation by the arrival of a U.S. naval force under Commodore Perry in 1853. Following modernization of her army and navy Japan shocked China by provoking a war against her in 1894-5. The defeated Chinese were obliged to cede Formosa and Korea, and the humiliation forced recognition of the need for reforms. In 1898, the Manchu Emperor Kuang-Hsu attempted to put into effect some measures designed to place China more securely on the path to progress. They included the establishment of many new schools incorporating the teaching of both Eastern and Western subjects, revision of the traditional civil service examination, and the founding of the Imperial University (later the National University at Peking). His efforts were aborted by the intervention of the formidable Dowager Empress Tz'u Hsi (1835-1908), who proceeded to foment Chinese opposition to all foreign influences, action which culminated in the Boxer Rebellion of 1900. This futile demonstration resulted in still further Western domination, and the Manchu Empress was faced with no option but to submit to reform.

In 1905, the Confucian-based civil service examination system was finally abolished. Despite its formal rigidity, it had served China well for two millenia, but it was its lack of compromise to global changes wrought by the Industrial Revolution of the West which finally led to its demise. Between 1905-10 it is estimated that at least

35,000 new state schools were founded, with an over-all enrollment of approximately 900,000 students.

The reforms came too late. Revolution broke out on the 10th of October, 1911, at Wu-Han on the middle Yang'tse River. The defection of the army left the Manchu Dynasty defenseless, and within three months, the new Republic of China was proclaimed (February 12, 1912).

JAPAN

The Japanese have often been referred to as
the Romans of the East, for a variety of reasons
including one which surfaced only during the past
century, when a seemingly irrepressible and inex-
haustible fund of energy directed the nation's
activities towards the fulfillment of an insatiable
drive towards imperial domination of the entire
region of the Far East.

In terms of culture, just as the Romans had,
initially, found no impediment or difficulty in
accepting appropriate components of more advanced
Greek learning, so the Japanese readily assimilated,
at a very early stage of their national development, the religion, language, and literature of
the more civilized Chinese. In time, all were modified to bring them into accord with the particular
and essential ethos of Japanese society. Buddhism,
for example, exported from India to China, became
in the latter country merely a thin veneer upon
deep-rooted Confucian philosophy and practice,
whereas, in Japan, it emerged as a major religious
faith, albeit supplemented by the uniquely chauvin-
ist tenets of Shintoism, and complemented by the
ethical admonitions of Confucius and his disciples,
(whose classical writings were basic studies in
Japan well into the nineteenth century). Likewise,
having imported the Chinese language, the Japanese
not only developed the written Kanji script (with
less than 2,000 ideographs as opposed to over
30,000 in Chinese), but also created two sylla-
baries (Katakana and Hiragana, respectively), each
consisting of 48 signs and each representing a
separate syllable, a system which very readily
made possible the adoption of foreign words. Moreover, for the purpose of the more native comprehension of the Confucian classics there was
further evolved a tortuous brand of the Japanese

256

language (used only in reading Chinese), far removed from the normal conversational dialect,
(which itself has eliminated all the tonal compli-
cations of spoken Chinese).

To the Japanese, history began on February 11,
660 B.C., a date celebrated annually as National
Founding Day (Kigensetsu).[1] The Emperor was revered
as a direct descendant of the Sun God, a fiction
maintained until after defeat in World War Two,
when relegation of the former status of the Emperor
made him a mere ineffectual political figurehead.

Historically, and in reference to developments
in education, there is some indication of the existence of schools and colleges as early as the seventh
century A.D., when the Royal Court appears to have
functioned as an educational focus with a clientele
drawn exclusively from the progeny of the noble
classes. During the course of the next millenium,
there developed in Japan a highly structured feudal society, consisting of four classes ranked, in
descending order of priority, as warriors, (Samurai),
peasants, artisans, and merchants.

The first schools in Japan were those presumably established for the sons of the nobility during the reign of the Emperor Tenchi (662-671 A.D.),
when a college (daigaku) was also founded. Basic
to curriculum studies was the tripartite division
of the Confucian classics: Daikyo (the Great
Classics, including the Spring and Autumn Annals);
Chukyo, (the Middle Classics, including Ceremonies
and Rituals) and Shokyo (the Little Classics, including the Classic of Documents and the Classic
of Changes).[2]

Attention was also given to calligraphy, law,
----
1. The legendary founding date of Rome was 753 B.C.

2. Tokiomi Kaigo: Japanese Education, p. 9.

mathematics, astrology, medicine, and court eti-
quette. For the remaining classes of society, it
can be assumed that appropriate instruction was
informally provided at home or during the course
of work activities.

A significant event occurred in the history of
Japan when, in 1600, following a period of considerable internal conflict, Tokugawa Ieyasu
proved victorious over his opponents. Receiving
from the Royal Court the title of Shogun, (Supreme
Commander), an acknowledgement of temporal authority,
Ieyasu transferred his home to Edo (Tokyo), which
was developed as the political capital. The
Tokugawa family henceforward emerged as the formidable dynasty which dominated the affairs of the
state until the Meiji Restoration of 1868. The
dynasty derived its wealth by control over almost
one fifth of the agricultural output of the country,
while most of the remaining lands were held by
feudal lords (daimyos), functioning as vassals to
the Shogun.³

Tokugawa Ieyasu (1542-1616) and his immediate
successors had great interest in the Confucian
classics and they gave official patronage to
Japanese scholars to encourage them in their studies
In 1630 a Confucian academy, the Shoheiko, was
established at Edo, and this served as a model for
subsequently-founded institutions. The Shoguns
expressed concern for the need of the rulers and
governors (the Samurai or warrior class) to be
competent in Bun (learning) and Bu (military arts).

----
3.   In order to ensure obeissance, the wives and
     children of each daimyo were obliged to reside
     at Edo, and the daimyo himself had to spend six
     months of each year there also. Eventually,
     this regulation was gradually relaxed, although
     as late as the 1860's, each daimyo was expected
     to spend approximately three months of every
     three years at Edo.

The military arts included archery, swordsmanship, and horseriding, and demanded individual instruction, normally provided by senior members of the clan. On the other hand, the process of learning was best conducted in schools, and although not unduly emphasized, it was considered appropriate for Samurai to be literate, moreso after warfare as a way of life had vanished by reason of the more stable and settled order of society established and maintained by the Tokugawa dynasty. The primary purpose of Confucian studies was not the acquisition of scholarship, but rather the development of moral character with stress upon family loyalty and filial piety, and a knowledge of the basic principles of human relationships and methods of government.

More formally, there existed two types of Samurai educational institutions: the Bakufu and Han schools, respectively. The Bakufu schools were specialized academies under the direct control of the Tokugawa Shogunate, and they eventually numbered twenty-one, each offering a different specialty. The first and most important was the Shoheiko, the leading institution of orthodox (Chu Hsi) Confucianism, and established by Hayashi Razan, a favored scholar of the early Shoguns. Examples of later foundation were the schools of Oriental Medicine (1765), Japanese Literature (1793), Occidental Literature (1856), and Occidental Military Science (1856).

Japan, outside the personally directed Shogunate domains, was divided into almost 300 feudal districts, or han, within which schools (Hanko) were established for Samurai boys. The curriculum was modeled upon that of the Shoheiko, placing emphasis upon Confucian studies, together with such 'practical' subjects as medicine, military science, and astronomy. It is recorded that attendance was often stipulated according to family rank, the older sons of the wealthier Samurai families being required to be present on 15 days each month, while at the lower end of the scale, junior sons of the least wealthy families attended for only 8 days.[4]

In addition to the foregoing officially supported Samurai schools, there also existed a wide range of private academies (Shijuku) mostly situated in the cities. They were much less restricted in curricular content and teaching method than were the official schools, and "Western studies" were characteristically taught. Since talented students of the commoner (non-Samurai) class were often permitted to attend, the Shijuku are accredited with the introduction of a merit system, adopted later by government schools following the Meiji Restoration.[5] Furthermore, being less orthodox, many of the Shijuku emerged as foci of doctrines and viewpoints contrary to the welfare of the Shogunate, and they contributed measurably to the opposing factions which eventually summoned sufficient strength to effect its overthrow.

Children of commoners attended the terakoya. This type of school is presumed to have originated as a Buddhist institution (tera = temple), but it gradually became independent of priests, although its name was retained. Its function was to equip future village headmen with a modicum of literacy so that they could interpret official documents to their clan members. The basic skills of reading, writing, and number were taught, the texts generally in use being the simpler Confucian classics such as the Four Books and the Classic of Filial Piety, which communicated 'correct' moral precepts. The teachers were often the village headmen themselves, or Samurai without employment, and since fees were

----

4. Passin, H.: Society and Education in Japan, p. 20.

5. Examinations were introduced in 1794 into the Bakufu (and later into the hanko), and they followed closely the Chinese model of assessing subsequent official promotion according to examination grades.

seldom charged, they were dependent upon gifts in kind from grateful parents. Students graduating from the terakoya could proceed to the gogaku, another private institution which provided somewhat more advanced learning.

Feudal Japan evolved a well-structured apprenticeship system. Merchants and craftsmen would receive young boys at age ten into the family, where they would remain and receive appropriate training until they reached the age of twenty, when they would be fully qualified members of the respective occupational fraternity. Conclusion of training was usually accompanied by a formal ceremony of "graduation."

The Tokugawa dynasty had decreed isolation from all foreign contact with the exception of the annual visit by a Dutch vessel to an island off Nagasaki. Over the years, appreciable knowledge of Western science percolated into the country, and "Dutch (Western) learning" in time became acceptable, so long as it was confined to practical matters such as medicine, navigation, shipbuilding, surveying, and military tactics.6

The continued prestige enjoyed by Chinese learning (Gakumon) at, what was considered to be, the expense of the native culture, gave rise to the Kokugaku movement, which stressed the study of the Japanese heritage of religion and literature. Its proponents succeeded, in 1792, in obtaining the introduction of courses relating to ancient Japanese literature into the hanko schools, and one year later, a special school of Japanese
----
6. The translation of a Dutch textbook on anatomy in 1771 is considered as the beginning of serious "Dutch learning." The medium of instruction in Japan's first advanced School of medicine (opened in 1840) was Dutch. (R.P. Dore: Education in Tokugawa Japan, pp. 160-1).

studies, the Wagaku Kodansho, was established. As Western learning gained increasing prominence during the nineteenth century Kokugaku adherents came to direct their resentment more against European studies, an approach also shared by Gakumon intellectuals, to such effect that, in 1839, their collective effort resulted in the imprisonment of certain "Dutch" scholars.7

The foregoing synopsis of Japanese education prior to events accompanying the demise of the Tokugawa dynasty, clearly illustrates the fact that the country possessed a coherent, unified, and well-structured educational system by 1868. It is this situation which permitted the creation of a central and national education plan which was within measurable reach of full implementation, albeit not without the painful on-going processes of normal administrative parturition. The literacy rate itself was comparable to that of most Western states of the period, and was certainly far beyond that of most Asian, African, and Latin American states even a century later. Following the visits of Commodore Perry and his U.S. naval squadron in 1853 and 1854, the Japanese ruling class was quick to recognize the inevitability of political and social change if the country was to be spared further humiliation. It was for this reason that during the 1860's the Shogunate dispatched missions and students abroad and invited foreign technical experts and language teachers to Japan.

In 1868 the Shogun, fifteenth in line, voluntarily surrendered his powers to the Emperor thus initiating the so-called Meiji Restoration. In the same year, the Emperor made public his Charter Oath (in which he stated that "knowledge was to be sought throughout the world"), a School Commission was established, and to it was delegated the
----
7.   The major impact of the Kokugaku movement came
     after the Meiji Restoration of 1868:   vide infra.

responsibility of preparing plans for a comprehensive school system. In 1871, a Ministry of Education was set up, and one year later it issued the Gakusei, the Fundamental Code of Education, with its succinct objective that "There shall,in the future, be no community with an illiterate family, or a family with an illiterate person." In the meantime, the prestigious Iwakura Mission had left Japan in 1871 for an eighteen-month tour of observational duty in Europe and the United States for the purpose of eliciting the specific components of education adaptable to the changing structure of Japanese society. Best known of the Commission members was Tanaka Fujimaro, (later appointed as Deputy Minister of Education), who published no fewer than fifteen volumes summarizing the conclusions of members of the extensive tour. Of major import was the eventual decision to accept the educational system of France as the administrative model for Japan, resulting in a scheme for the division of the country into eight university districts, each with a university (whose chancellor was to serve as the superintendent of the entire school district). Each university district was to be subdivided into 32 middle (secondary) school districts each of which, in turn, was to be subdivided into 210 primary school districts.8 While the foregoing ideal plan was subsequently considerably modifed in the light of experience, the highly administrative centralized system proposed was put into operation and persisted until 1945.

For a full decade following the Meiji Restoration, Japan was enamoured of Western educational ideals. In 1873, David Murray of Rutgers University was appointed as Ministry of Education advisor in curriculum and methods. He remained in Japan until 1878 and he was instrumental in the establishment of co-educational schools, of

----
8. In 1871 feudalism was abolished and the almost 300 feudal domains disappeared.

teacher-training institutions, as well as of vocational schools (based on the model of the U.S. land-grant colleges). Japanese translations of both American and European textbooks were made widely available during this period.

However, towards the close of the 1870-80 decade, a reaction to dominant Western learning (Yogaku) had set in as a result of the propaganda of Kokugaku proponents. The Emperor himself intervened in the controversy and in 1879 there was issued the Kyogaku Taishi (The Great Principles of Education), which declared that a return to Confucian principles was in accordance with Japanese traditions. In 1880, Tanaka Fujimaro was forced to resign, and the primacy of moral (Shushin), as opposed to academic, education was given priority as made public in the Memorandum for Elementary School Teachers of June 1, 1881, Article One:

> In order to guide people, make them good, give them wide knowledge, and to do this wisely, teachers must particularly stress moral education to their pupils.
>
> Loyalty to the Imperial House, love of country, filial piety towards parents, respect for superiors, faith in friends, charity towards inferiors, and respect for oneself, contribute the Great Path of human morality. The teacher must himself be a model of these virtues in his daily life, and must endeavor to stimulate his pupils along the path of virtue.[9]

The overall consequence was a much more nationalistic approach in education, culminating in the appointment of Arinori Mori as Minister of

----

9. Passin. op. cit. p. 85.

Education in 1885. In 1886, Tokyo University[10] was redesignated as the "Imperial University" to stress its function not merely in terms of the pursuit of higher learning and research, but also in terms of its objectives as expressed in the national interest.

Mori considerably strengthened the central control[11] of the Ministry of Education by imposing standardized courses, lessons, and textbooks upon the schools. Students in teacher-training institutions were housed in dormitories and were subjected to quasi-military discipline, best exemplified in the case of the Tokyo Higher Normal School where Colonel Yamakawa, an officer on active service, was appointed director. Emphasis in the Normal Schools was placed upon character education rather than learning, with stress upon the three virtues of "Dignity, Friendship, and Obedience."[12]

Despite his efforts, Mori was assassinated in

----

10. The University had initially been founded in 1868 by the fusion of three institutions of higher learning: the Shoheiko, the Medical School, and the Kaisei-jo (School of Foreign Learning).

11. Mori had been to Germany in 1882-3, an experience which led him to state: "What is to be done is not for the sake of the pupils, but for the sake of the country."

12. Mori had visited the United States in 1867, and had been deeply impressed by his experiences at the Swedenborgian Community at Salem, New York, organized by Thomas Lake Harris, who had formulated these identical virtues as an appropriate slogan for his utopian settlement. (Passin op. cit. pp. 90-91).

1889 for apparent "disrespect for the Emperor."
During the course of the same year there was initi-
ated the practice of sending a portrait of the
Emperor to every school in the nation, along with,
one year later, a copy of the Imperial Rescript on
Education, part of which read:

> Ye, Our Subjects.... pursue learning and
> cultivate arts, and thereby develop intel-
> lectual faculties and perfect moral powers;
> furthermore, advance public good and pro-
> mote common interests; always respect the
> Constitution and observe the Laws. Should
> emergency arise, offer yourselves coura-
> geously to the State, and thus guard and
> maintain the prosperity of Our Imperial
> Throne coeval with heaven and earth.

By 1900, the basic structure of Japanese education until 1945 had been determined as follows:

> Elementary Education: a minimum of four
> tuition-free years of instruction, with
> specific provisions detailed by the Min-
> istry of Education.[13]

> Secondary Education: incorporating Middle
> Schools as well as Girls High Schools,[14]
> again with specific provisions detailed by
> the Ministry.

> Vocational Education: Rapid expansion of
> facilities occurred after 1890 following
> upon adequate training of Japanese, as
> opposed to foreign, instructors. A two-
> tier system emerged--the Semmongakko, a

---

13. In 1908 elementary education was expanded to 6
     years of compulsory instruction.

14. The Higher Girls' School Law of 1899 stipulated
     that at least one such institution should be
     established in each prefecture.

lower technical school, and the Koto-Semmongakko, a higher technical school, from which engineers, accountants, and even doctors and dentists could receive qualification. In addition, many private industrial and commercial companies provided their own well-integrated instructional training.

University Education: only two universities existed in 1900: Tokyo Imperial University (1877) and Kyoto Imperial University (1897). The Ministry of Education had succeeded in delegating the burden of financing both elementary and secondary school education upon local districts, but had reserved for itself the responsibility of developing higher education. An appreciable part of the Ministry's budget until almost the turn of the century had been applied to the overseas training of competent Japanese instructors, but thereafter, new universities were established at Tohoku (1907), Kyushu (1910), and Hokkaido (1918).

An efficient general and technical education system affiliated with intensive indoctrination in national patriotism combined to achieve victory in two wars, first against China (1894-5) and then Russia (1904-5), and these twin components remained characteristic of Japanese education until the close of the Second World War.

BIBLIOGRAPHY

General Readings

Archer, M.S. Social Origins of Educational Systems.
    Beverly Hills: Sage Publications, 1979.
Arles, Philippe. Centuries of Childhood. New York:
    Vintage Books, 1962.
Atkinson, Carroll and Eugene T. Maleska. The Story
    of Education. Philadelphia: Chilton Company,
    1962.
Baskin, Wade. Classics in Education. New York:
    The Philosophical Library, 1966.
Beck, R. A Social History of Education. Englewood
    Cliffs, N.J.: Prentice-Hall, Inc., 1965.
Binder, Frederick M. Education in the History of
    Western Civilization. New York: Macmillan,
    1970.
Blake, Raymond J. A History of Education Through
    Time Lines. Palo Alto, Cal.: The National
    Press, 1962.
Bowen, James. A History of Western Education.
    London: Methuen, 1972.
Boyd, William. The History of Western Education.
    London: A and C Black, Ltd., 1972.
Brubacher, J.S. History of the Problems of Education.
    New York: McGraw-Hill, 1966.
Burridge, Trevor D. What Happened in Education.
    Boston: Allyn and Bacon, 1970.
Butts, R.F. A Cultural History of Western Education.
    New York: McGraw-Hill, 1955.
Butts, R.F. The Education of the West. New York:
    McGraw-Hill, 1973.
Cleverley, J. and D.C. Phillips. From Locke to
    Spock. Melbourne, Australia: Melbourne Univer-
    sity Press, 1976.
Cole, Luella. A History of Education: Socrates to
    Montessori. New York: Rinehart and Winston,
    1962.

Cole, P.R. History of Education Thought. Westport,
    Conn.: Greenwood Press, 1972.
Crary, Ryland W. and Louis A. Petrone. Foundations
    of Modern Education. New York: Alfred A.
    Knopf, Inc., 1971.
Cubberley, E.P. The History of Education. Boston:
    Houghton Mifflin, 1922.
Curti, Merle. The Social Ideas of American Educators.
    Totowa, N.J.: Littlefield, Adams and Co., 1968.
Curtis, S.J. and M.E.A. Boultwood. A Short History
    of Educational Ideas. London: University
    Tutorial Press, 1953.
Davidson, Thomas. A History of Education. New York:
    Charles Scribner's Sons, 1900.
Duggan, S.P.H. A Student's Textbook in the History
    of Education. New York: Appleton-Century-
    Crofts, Inc., 1948
Eby, Frederick, and Charles F. Arrowood. The History
    and Philosophy of Education, Ancient and Medieval
    New York: Prentice-Hall, 1940.
Fisher, Robert T. Classical Utopian Theories of
    Education. New Haven, Conn.: College and Uni-
    versity Press, 1963.
Frost, S.E. The Essentials of the History of Educa-
    tion. Great Neck, N.Y.: Barron Educational
    Series, 1965.
Frost, S.E. Historical and Philosophical Foundations
    of Western Education. Columbus, Ohio: Charles
    E. Merrill, 1966.
Gillett, Marjorie. A History of Education Thought
    and Practice. Toronto: McGraw-Hill, 1966.
Gillett, Marjorie. Readings in the History of
    Education. New York: McGraw-Hill, 1969.
Good, H.G. and James D. Teller. A History of West-
    ern Education. New York: Macmillan, 1969.
Goodsell, W. American Education, Its Men, Ideas,
    and Institutions. New York: Arno Press, 1969.
Graves, Frank P. Great Educators of Three Centuries.
    New York: Macmillan, 1912.
Graves, Frank P. A History of Education before the
    Middle Ages. New York: Macmillan, 1923.

Gutek, G.L. A History of the Western Educational
    Experience. New York: Random House, 1972.
Hart, Joseph K. Democracy in Education. New York:
    The Century Company, 1918.
Hillesheim, James W. and B.J. Baron. Education
    Theories of European Origin. Lawrence, Kansas:
    University of Kansas, 1975.
Jarman, T.L. Landmarks in the History of Education.
    London: John Murray, 1963.
Jupo, Frank. The Story of the Three R's. Englewood
    Cliffs, N.J.: Prentice-Hall, 1970.
Kandel, I.L. History of Secondary Education.
    Boston: Houghton Mifflin, 1930.
Kane, W.S.J. A History of Education. Chicago:
    Loyola University Press, 1938.
Kneller, George F. Foundations of Education. New
    York: John Wiley and Sons, 1963.
Knight, Edgar W. Twenty Centuries of Education.
    Boston: Ginn and Company, 1940.
Lawrence, E.S. The Origins and Growth of Modern
    Education. Baltimore: Penguin Books, Inc.,
    1970.
Lucus, C.J. Our Western Educational Heritage. New
    York: Macmillan, 1972.
McCormick, Patrick J. History of Education.
    Washington, D.C.: Catholic Education Press,
    1915.
McLendon, J.C. Social Foundations of Education.
    New York: Macmillan, 1966.
Martz, Velorus and Henry Lester Smith. An Intro-
    duction to Education. New York: Charles
    Scribner's Sons, 1941.
Mayer, Frederick. Foundations of Education.
    Columbus, Ohio: Charles E. Merrill, 1963.
Mayer, Frederick. Great Ideas of Education. New
    Haven, Conn.: College and University Press,
    1966.
Mayer, Frederick. A History of Educational Thought.
    Columbus, Ohio: Charles E. Merrill, 1973.
Medlin, William K. The History of Educational Ideas
    in the West. New York: Center for Applied
    Research in Education, 1964.

Mehl, Bernard. Classic Educational Ideas. Columbus,
    Ohio: Charles E. Merrill, 1972.
Melvin, A. Gordon. Education, A History. New York:
    The John Day Co., 1946.
Messenger, J. Franklin. An Interpretive History of
    Education. New York: Thomas Crowell, 1931.
Meyer, Adolphe E. An Educational History of the
    Western World. New York: McGraw-Hill, 1965.
Meyer, Adolphe E. Grandmasters of Educational
    Thought. New York: McGraw-Hill, 1975.
Miller, R. Perspectives on Educational Change.
    New York: Appleton-Century-Crofts, 1967.
Moehlman, Arthur H. Comparative Education. New
    York: Dryden Press, 1957.
Moehlman, Arthur H. Comparative Educational Systems.
    New York: The Center for Applied Research in
    Education, 1963.
Mulhern, J. A History of Education. New York:
    Ronald Press Company, 1959.
Myers, Edward D. Education in the Perspective of
    History. New York: Harper, 1960.
Nakosteen, Mehdi. The History and Philosophy of
    Education. New York: Ronald Press Co., 1965.
Nash, Paul (ed.). History and Education. New York:
    Random House, 1970.
Nash, Paul (et al.). The Educated Man: Studies in
    the History of Educational Thought. New York:
    John Wiley and Sons, 1965.
Ornstein, Allan C. An Introduction to the Founda-
    tions of Education. Chicago: Rand McNally,
    1977.
Ozman, H. and S. Carver. Philosophical Foundations
    of Education. Columbus, Ohio: Charles E.
    Merrill, 1976.
Pollard, Hugh M. Pioneers of Popular Education.
    Cambridge, Mass.: Harvard University Press,
    1957.
Pounds, Ralph. The Development of Education in
    Western Culture. New York: Appleton-Century-
    Crofts, 1968.
Power, E.J. Evolution of Educational Doctrine.
    New York: Appleton-Century-Crofts, 1969.

Power, E.J. Main Currents in the History of Education. New York: McGraw-Hill, 1970.
Price, K. Education and Philosophical Thought. Boston: Allyn and Bacon, 1967.
Quick, R.H. Educational Reformers. London: Longmans Green, 1902.
Reisner, Edward H. Historical Foundations of Modern Education. New York: Macmillan, 1927.
Rusk, R.R. Doctrines of the Great Educators. New York: Macmillan, 1979.
Ryan, Patrick J. Historical Foundations of Public Education. Dubuque, Iowa: W.C. Brown, 1968.
Simmons, George C. (ed.). Education and Western Civilization. Arlington, Va.: College Readings Inc., 1972.
Stock, Phyllis. Better than Rubies: A History of Women and Education. New York: Putnam, 1978.
Sylvester, D.W. Educational Documents, A.D. 800-1816. London: Methuen, 1970.
Thomas, R. Murray. Comparing Theories of Child Development. Belmont, Calif.: Wadsworth Publishing Co., 1979.
Thut, I.N. The Story of Education: Philosophical and Historical Foundations. New York: McGraw-Hill, 1957.
Thut, I.N. and Don Adams. Foundations in Education. New York: McGraw-Hill, 1964.
Ulich, R. The Education of Nations. Cambridge, Mass.: Harvard University Press, 1967.
Ulich, R. Education in Western Culture. New York: Harcourt, Brace, and World, Inc., 1965.
Ulich, R. History of Educational Thought. New York: American Book Co., 1968.
Ulich, R. Three Thousand Years of Educational Wisdom. Cambridge, Mass.: Harvard University Press, 1965.
Wilds, Elmer H. and K.V. Lottich. The Foundations of Modern Education. New York: Holt, Rinehart, and Winston, 1970.
Wise, J.E. The History of Education. New York: Sheed and Ward, 1964.
Wodehouse, Helen. The History of Education. London: Edward Arnold and Co., 1929.

CHAPTER ONE

GREEK EDUCATION

Adamson, J.E. The Theory of Education in Plato's
     Republic. New York: Macmillan, 1903.
Barrow, Robin. Plato and Education. Boston:
     Routledge and Kegan Paul, 1976.
Barrow, Robin. Plato, Utilitarianism, and Education.
     Boston: Routledge and Kegan Paul, 1975.
Beck, F.A.G. Greek Education, 450-350 B.C. London:
     Methuen, 1964.
Bolgar, R.R. The Classical Heritage and Its Benefi-
     ciaries. Cambridge, England: University Press,
     1954.
Bosanquet, Bernard. The Education of the Young in
     the Republic of Plato. Cambridge, Mass.: The
     University Press, 1908.
Bowra, Cecil M. The Greek Experience. New York:
     New American Library, 1958.
Burnet, J. Aristotle on Education. New York:
     Cambridge University Press, 1967.
Castle, E.B. Ancient Education and Today. Middlesex,
     England: Penguin Books, Ltd., 1961.
Clark, M.L. Higher Education in the Ancient World.
     Albuquerque: University of New Mexico Press,
     1971.
Crossman, R.H.S. Plato Today. New York: Oxford
     University Press, 1939.
Davidson, Thomas. Education of the Greek People.
     New York: D. Appleton-Century Co., 1904.
Dickenson, G. Lowes. The Greek View of Life. New
     York: Doubleday, Page, and Co., 1927.
Dobson, J.F. Ancient Education. New York: Longmans
     Green, 1963.
Driver, J. Greek Education. Cambridge, England,
     Cambridge University Press, 1912.
Farrington, Benjamin. Greek Science: Its Meaning
     for Us. Baltimore: Penguin Books, 1944.
Freeman, K.L. Schools of Hellas from 600 to 300 B.C.
     London: Macmillan, 1912.
Hollister, C.W. Roots of the Western Tradition.
     New York: John Wiley, 1977.
Jaeger, Werner. Paideia: The Ideals of Greek Cul-
     ture. (G. Highet, trans.). New York: Oxford
     University Press, 1943.

Laurie, S.S. Historical Survey of Pre-Christian
    Education. New York: Longmans Green, 1907.
Livingstone, Richard. Plato and Modern Education.
    London: Cambridge University Press, 1944.
Lodge, R.C. Plato's Theory of Education. Boston:
    Kegan Paul, 1947.
Lynch, J.P. Aristotle's School: A Study of a Greek
    Educational Institution. Berkeley, Calif.:
    University of California Press, 1972.
Marrou, H.I. A History of Education in Antiquity.
    New York: Sheed and Ward, 1956.
Mayer, Frederick. (ed.). Bases of Ancient Education:
    Great Ideas of Education. New Haven, Conn.:
    College and University Press, 1966.
Moberley, Walter. Plato's Conception of Education
    and Its Meaning Today. New York: Oxford Univer-
    sity Press, 1944.
Nettleship, R.L. The Theory of Education in the
    Republic of Plato. New York: Teachers' College
    Press, 1968.
Parry, Hugh. Ideals of Education: Spartan Warrior
    and Athenian All-Round Man. New York: St.
    Martin's Press, 1969.
Smith, William A. Ancient Education. New York:
    Philosophical Library, 1955.
Winn, Cyril and Maurice Jacks. Aristotle and his
    Relevance Today. London: Methuen, 1967.

CHAPTER TWO

ROMAN EDUCATION

Bonner, S.F. Education in Ancient Rome. London:
    Methuen, 1977.
Butler, H.E. Quintilian. Cambridge, Mass.: Harvard
    University Press, 1963.
Clarke, M.L. Higher Education in the Ancient World.
    Albuquerque: University of New Mexico Press,
    1971.

274

Cole, P.R. Later Roman Education. New York:
    Teachers' College, Bureau of Publications, 1909.
Dobson, J.F. Ancient Education and its Meaning to
    Us. New York: Longmans Green, 1932.
Grant, Michael. The Climax of Rome. Boston: Little,
    Brown, 1968.
Gwynn, Aubrey O. Roman Education from Cicero to
    Quintilian. New York: Oxford University Press,
    1926.
Kennedy, George. Quintilian. New York: Twayne Pub-
    lications, Inc., 1969.
Marrou, H.I. A History of Education in Antiquity.
    New York: Sheed and Ward, 1956.
Smail, W.M. Quintilian on Education. New York:
    Teachers' College Press, Columbia University,
    1966.
Smith, William A. Ancient Education. New York:
    Philosophical Library, 1955.
Wheelock, F.M. Quintilian as Educator. New York:
    Twayne Publications, Inc., 1974.
Wilkins, A.S. Roman Education. New York: Cambridge
    University Press, 1921.

CHAPTER THREE

EARLY CHRISTIAN EDUCATION

Benson, Clarence H. History of Christian Education.
    Chicago: Moody Press, 1943.
Drane, Augusta T. Christian Schools and Scholars.
    New York: Macmillan, 1948.
Duckett, Eleanor S. Anglo-Saxon Saints and Scholars.
    New York: Macmillan, 1948.
Duckett, Eleanor S. Alcuin, Friend of Charlemagne.
    New York: Macmillan, 1951.
Gaskoin, C.J. Alcuin, His Life and His Work. New
    York: Russell and Russell, 1966.
Graham, H. The Early Irish Monastic Schools.
    Dublin: Talbot Press, 1923.
Graves, F.P. A History of Education during the Mid-
    dle Ages. New York: Macmillan, 1919.

Hatch, Edwin. The Influence of Greek Ideas on
    Christianity. New York: Harper, 1957.
Healy, J. Ancient Schools and Scholars: Schoolmen
    of Ireland. London: B & O, 1908.
Jaeger, Werner W. Early Christianity and Greek
    Paideia. Cambridge, Mass.: Harvard University
    Press, 1961.
Kevane, E. Augustine the Educator: A Study in the
    Fundamentals of Christian Formation. Westmin-
    ster, Md.: Newman Press, 1964.
Knowles, D.D. Saints and Scholars. Cambridge,
    England: Cambridge University Press, 1962.
Marique, Pierre. History of Christian Education.
    New York: Fordham University Press, 1924.
Mullinger, J.B. The Schools of Charles the Great.
    New York: Stechert, 1911.
Nakosteen, M. History of Islamic Origins of Western
    Civilization A.D. 800-1350. Boulder: University
    of Colorado Press, 1964.
Russell, J.B. Mediaeval Civilization. New York:
    John Wiley, 1968.
Taylor, Marvin J. An Introduction to Christian
    Education. New York: Abingdon Press, 1966.
Thompson, Alexander H. Bede: His Life, Times, and
    Writings. New York: Russell and Russell, 1966.
Wallach, Luitpold. Alcuin and Charlemagne. Cornell
    University Press, 1959.
West. A.F. Alcuin and the Rise of Christian Schools.
    New York: Charles Scribner's Sons, 1903.

CHAPTER FOUR

THE RISE OF THE UNIVERSITIES

Afnan, Soheil M. Avicenna: His Life and Works.
    London: Allen and Unwin, 1958.
Berrigan, J.R., Jr. Mediaeval Intellectual History,
    a Primer. Lawrence, Kansas: Coronado Press,
    1974.
Bokser, Ben Zion. The Legacy of Maimonides. New
    York: The Philosophical Library, 1950.

Cannon, William Ragdale, History of Christianity
in the Middle Ages. New York: Abingdon Press,
1960.
Cobban, A.B. The Mediaeval Universities: Their
Development and Organization. London: Methuen,
1975.
Compayre, Gabriel. Abelard and the Origin and Early
History of Universities. New York: Charles
Scribner's Sons, 1907.
Copleston, F.C. Aquinas. Middlesex, England: Pen-
guin Books, 1955.
Copleston, F.C. A History of Mediaeval Philosophy.
London: Methuen, 1972.
Crane, Leif. Peter Abelard. New York: Harcourt,
Brace, and World Inc., 1964.
Daly, Lowrie J. The Mediaeval University. New York:
Sheed and Ward, 1961.
Dodge, Bayard. Muslim Education in Mediaeval Times.
Washington, D.C.: The Middle East Institute,
1962.
Donohue, S.J. St. Thomas Aquinas and Education.
New York: Random House, 1968.
Federbush, Simon. Maimonides. New York: World
Jewish Congress, 1956.
Haskins, C.H. The Rise of the Universities. Ithaca,
New York: Cornell University Press, 1957.
Laurie, S.S. The Rise and Early Constitutions of
Universities. New York: D. Appleton, 1891.
Lawson, John. Mediaeval Education. London:
Routledge and Kegan Paul, 1968.
Leff, Gordon. Paris and Oxford Universities in the
Thirteenth and Fourteenth Centuries. New York:
John Wiley, 1968.
Lloyd, Roger. Peter Abelard: The Orthodox Rebel.
London: Latimer House, 1947.
Luscombe, D.E. The School of Peter Abelard. New
York: Cambridge University Press, 1969.
Marler, C.C. Philosophy and Schooling. Boston:
Allyn and Bacon, 1975.
Nakosteen, Mehdi. History of Islamic Origins of
Western Education, A.D. 800-1350. Boulder:
University of Colorado Press, 1964.

Rait, R.S. Life in the Mediaeval University.
   Cambridge, England: University Press, 1918.
Rashdall, Hastings. The Universities of Europe in
   the Middle Ages. London: Lowe and Brydone,
   1936.
Russell, J.B. Mediaeval Civilization. New York:
   John Wiley, 1968.
Schachner, Nathan. The Mediaeval Universities.
   London: Allen and Unwin, 1938.
Sikes, J.A. Peter Abelard. New York: Russell and
   Russell, 1965.
Thatcher, Oliver J. and Ferdinand Schwill. Europe
   in the Middle Ages. New York: Charles
   Scribner's Sons, 1897.
Tibawi, A.L. Islamic Education. London: Luzac and
   Co., 1972.
Waddell, Helen. Peter Abelard. New York: Henry
   Holt and Co., 1933.
Waddell, Helen. The Wandering Scholars. London:
   Constable, 1927.
Walsh, James J. The Thirteenth Greatest of Centuries.
   New York: Catholic Summer School Press, 1929.
Weinberg, J.R. A Short History of Mediaeval
   Philosophy. Princeton, N.J.: Princeton Univer-
   sity Press, 1964.
Wieruszowski, Helene. The Mediaeval University.
   Princeton, N.J.: Van Nostrand, 1966.
Zacour, Norman. An Introduction to Mediaeval Insti-
   tutions. New York: St. Martin's Press, 1976.

CHAPTER FIVE

THE RENAISSANCE

Allen, P.S. The Age of Erasmus. London: Oxford
   University Press, 1914.
Born, K.L. (ed.). The Education of a Christian
   Prince by Erasmus. New York: Columbia Univer-
   sity Press, 1936.

Burckhardt, J. The Civilization of the Renaissance in Italy. (S.A.C. Middlemore, trans.) London: George H. Harrop, 1929.

Charleton, K. Education in Renaissance England. London: Routledge and Kegan Paul, 1965.

Dannenfeldt, K.H. The Renaissance: Mediaeval or Modern? Boston: D.C. Heath, 1959.

Faulkner, J.A. Erasmus: The Scholar. Cincinnati: Jennings and Graham, 1907.

Hyma, Albert. Erasmus and the Humanists. New York: Crofts, 1930.

Hyma, Albert. The Youth of Erasmus. Ann Arbor: University of Michigan Press, 1930.

Laurie, S.S. Studies in the History of Educational Opinion from the Renaissance. New York: Humanities Press, 1968.

McMahon, C.P. Education in Fifteenth Century England. New York: Greenwood Press, 1968.

Phillips, M.M. Erasmus and the Northern Renaissance. London: Hodder and Stoughton, 1949.

Ryan, Lawrence V. Roger Ascham. Stanford: Stanford University Press, 1963.

Sowards, J. Kelley. Desiderius Erasmus. Boston: Twayne Publishers, 1975.

Smith, P. Erasmus. New York: Harper and Brothers, 1923.

Symonds, John A. The Renaissance in England. New York: Scribner, 1907.

Watson, Foster. Vives on Education. New York: Putnam, 1913.

Woodward, W.H. Desiderius Erasmus Concerning the Aim and Method of Education. New York: Teachers' College, Columbia University, 1964.

Woodward, W.H. Studies in Education during the Age of the Renaissance, 1400-1600. New York: Russell and Russell, 1965.

Woodward, W.H. Vittorino da Feltre and other Humanist Educators. New York: Teachers' College, Columbia University, 1963.

Zweig, Stefan. Erasmus of Rotterdam. New York: Viking Press, 1934.

CHAPTER SIX

THE REFORMATION

Adamson, J.W. The Educational Writings of John
    Locke. London: Longmans Green, 1912.
Adamson, J.W. Pioneers of Modern Education in the
    Seventeenth Century. New York: Teachers'
    College Press, 1972.
Anderson, Charles S. The Reformation, Then and Now.
    Minneapolis: Augsburg Publishing House, 1966.
Axtell, J.L. The Educational Writings of John Locke.
    Cambridge, England: University Press, 1968.
Bainton, Roland H. Here I Stand - A Life of Martin
    Luther. New York: Abingdon Press, 1950.
Barnard, H.C. The Little Schools of Port Royal.
    Cambridge, England: Cambridge University Press,
    1913.
Battersby, W.J. De La Salle, A Pioneer of Modern
    Education. London: Longmans, 1949.
Boase, A.M. The Fortunes of Montaigne. New York:
    Octagon Books, 1970.
Bruce, G.M. Luther as an Educator. Minneapolis:
    Augsburg Publishing House, 1928.
Cadet, Felix. Port Royal Education. London: S.
    Sonnenschein and Co., 1898.
Cranston, Maurice. Locke. London: Longmans Green,
    1961.
Dampier, W.C. A Shorter History of Science. New
    York: Meridian Books, 1947.
Debus, Allen G. Science and Education in the
    Seventeenth Century. New York: American Else-
    vier, Inc., 1970.
De La Fontainerie, F. The Conduct of the Schools
    of Jean Baptiste. New York: McGraw-Hill,
    1935.
Dempsey, Martin. Jean Baptiste de la Salle.
    Milwaukee, Wisc.: Bruce Publishing Co., 1940.
Dobinson, C.H. (ed.). Comenius and Contemporary
    Education. Paris: Unesco Institute for
    Education, 1970.

Donnelly, Francis P. *Principles of Jesuit Education in Practice*. New York: P.J. Kennedy and Sons, 1934.

Donohue, J.W. *Jesuit Education*. New York: Fordham University Press, 1963.

Eby, Frederick. *Early Protestant Educators*. New York: McGraw-Hill, 1931.

Eiseley, Loren. *Francis Bacon and the Modern Dilemma*. Lincoln: University of Nebraska Press, 1962.

Farrell, Allan P. *The Jesuit Code of Liberal Education*. Milwaukee: Bruce Publishing Co., 1938.

Farrington, Benjamin. *Francis Bacon, Philosopher of Industrial Sciences*. New York: Henry Schumen, 1949.

Farrington, Benjamin. *The Philosophy of Francis Bacon*. Chicago: University of Chicago Press, 1964.

Fisher, Robert T. *Classical Utopian Theories of Education*. New York: Bookman Associates, 1963.

Fitzpatrick, Edward A. *St. Ignatius and the Ratio Studiorum*. New York: McGraw-Hill, 1933.

Fosdick, Harry E. *Great Voices of the Reformation*. New York: Macmillan, 1973.

Frame, D.M. *Montaigne's "Essais": A Study*. Englewood Cliffs, N.J.: Prentice-Hall, 1969.

Gay, Peter. *John Locke on Education*. New York: Teachers College, Columbia University, 1964.

Greaves, R.L. *The Puritan Revolution and Educational Thought: Background for Reform*. New Brunswick, N.J.: Rutgers University Press, 1969.

Harbison, E. Harris. *The Christian Scholar in the Age of Reformation*. New York: Charles Scribner's Sons, 1966.

Hexter, J.H. *More's Utopia*. Princeton University Press, 1952.

Hogrefe, Pearl. *The Sir Thomas More Circle*. Urbana: University of Illinois, 1959.

Keatinge, M.W. *Comenius*. New York: McGraw-Hill, 1931.

Keatinge, M.W. *The Great Didactic of John Amos Comenius*. London: Russell and Russell, 1967.

Lawson, J. Mediaeval Education and the Reformation. London: Routledge and Kegan Paul, 1967.
Leach, A.F. English Schools at the Reformation. Westminster: Constable, 1896.
Lindsay, T.M. Luther and the German Reformation. New York: Charles Scribner's Sons, 1900.
McGucken, William S. The Jesuits and Education. New York: Bruce Publishing Co., 1932.
McNeil, John T. The History and Character of Calvinism. New York: Oxford University Press, 1954.
Masso, Gildo. The Place of Education in Utopias. New York: Teachers College, Columbia University, 1927.
Monroe, Will S. Comenius and the Beginnings of Educational Reform. New York: Charles Scribner's Sons, 1912.
Mulder, J.R. The Temple of the Mind. New York: Pegasus, 1969.
Nef, John. Industry and Government in France and England, A.D. 1540-1640. New York: American Philosophical Society, 1940.
Painter, F.V.N. Luther on Education. St. Louis, Mo.: Concordia Publishing House, 1928.
Piaget, Jean. John Amos Comenius on Education. New York: Teachers College Press, Columbia Univ. 1968.
Pichard, James W. Philip Melanchthon, The Protestant Preceptor of Germany. New York: G.P. Putnam's Sons, 1898.
Reisner, Edward (ed.) Early Protestant Educators. New York: McGraw-Hill, 1931.
Reynolds, E.E. Sir Thomas More. London: Longmans, Green, 1965.
Rossi, Paolo. Francis Bacon: From Magic to Science. (trans. Sacha Rakinovitch). Chicago: University of Chicago Press, 1968.
Sadler, J.E. J.A. Comenius and the Concept of Universal Education. New York: Barnes and Noble, 1966.
Spinka, Matthew. John Amos Comenius: That Incomparable Moravian. Chicago. University of Chicago Press, 1943.

Strauss, Gerald. Luther's House of Learning.
    Baltimore: Johns Hopkins University Press,
    1978.
Townsend, Allen W. A Short Life of Luther.
    Philadelphia: Fortress Press, 1967.
Turnbull, G.H. Samuel Hartlib, A Sketch of his
    Life. London: Oxford University Press, 1920.
Turnbull, G.H. Hartlib, Dury, and Comenius.
    Liverpool: University Press of Liverpool,
    1947.
Walker, Williston. John Calvin. New York: G.P.
    Putnam's Sons, 1898.
Watson, F. Beginnings of the Teaching of Modern
    Subjects in England. London: Pitman, 1909.
Watson, F. Vives and the Renaissance Education of
    Women. New York: Longmans Green, 1912.
Watson, F. Louis Vives: El Gran Valenciano.
    Oxford: Oxford University Press, 1942.
Young, R.F. Comenius in England. Oxford: Oxford
    University Press, 1932.

CHAPTER SEVEN

THE AMERICAN COLONIES

Bayles, E.E. and Bruce L. Hood. Growth of American
    Educational Thought and Practice. New York:
    Harper and Row, 1966.
Best, J.H. Benjamin Franklin on Education. New
    York: Teachers College, Columbia University,
    1962.
Best, J.H. and Robert T. Sidwell. The American
    Legacy of Learning. New York: J.P. Lippincott,
    1967.
Butts, R. Freeman. The American Tradition in
    Religion and Culture. Boston: Beacon Press,
    1950.

Calhoun, Daniel (ed.). The Educating of Americans:
A Documentary History. New York: Houghton
Mifflin, 1969.
Callahan, Raymond E. An Introduction to Education
in American Society. New York: Alfred A.
Knopf, 1960.
Carter, James G. Letters on the Free Schools of New
England. New York: Arno Press, 1969.
Cohen, Sol. Education in the United States: A
Documentary History. New York: Random House,
1974.
Cremin, Lawrence A. American Education: The Colonial
Experience, 1607-1783. New York: Harper and
Row, 1970.
Cremin, Lawrence A. Traditions of American Education.
New York: Basic Books, 1977.
Crow, Lester D. and Alice Crow. Introduction to
Education. New York: American Book Co., 1947.
Cubberley, Ellwood P. The History of Education.
Cambridge: Houghton Mifflin, 1948.
Cubberley, Ellwood P. Readings in Public Education
in the United States. Boston: Houghton Mifflin,
1970.
Edwards, Newton and Herman C. Richey. The School in
the American Social Order. Boston: Houghton
Mifflin, 1963.
Fisher, Sydney G. The Quaker Colonies. New York:
United States Publishers Assoc. Inc., 1919.
Fleming, Sanford. Children and Puritanism. New
Haven, Conn.: Yale University Press, 1933.
French, William M. America's Educational Tradition:
An Interpretive History. Boston: D.C. Heath,
1964.
Furnas, J.C. The Americans: A Social History of the
United States, 1587-1914. New York: Putnam,
1969.
Glubok, Shirley. Home and Child Life in Colonial
Days. London: Macmillan, 1969.
Good, Harry G. and James D. Teller. A History of
American Education. New York: Macmillan,
1973.
Griffin, Edward. Jonathan Edwards. Minneapolis:
University of Minnesota Press, 1971.

Gross, Carl H. and Charles C. Chandler. The History
    of American Education. Boston: D.C. Heath,
    1964.
Gross, Richard E. (ed.). Heritage of American
    Education. Boston: Allyn and Bacon, 1962.
Hanson, Allen O. Liberalism and American Education
    in the Eighteenth Century. New York: Octagon,
    1965.
Hillesheim, James W. and George D. Merrill. Theory
    and Practice in the History of American Educa-
    tion: A Book of Readings. Washington, D.C.:
    University Press of America, 1980.
Hillway, Tyrus. American Education. Boston:
    Houghton Mifflin, 1964.
Hughes, J.M. Education in America. New York:
    Harper and Row, 1965.
Judd, Charles H. The American Education System.
    Boston: Riverside Press, 1940.
Katz, Michael B. Colonial America. Boston: Little,
    Brown and Co., 1971.
Katz, Michael B. Education in American History:
    Readings on the Social Issues. New York:
    Praeger, 1973.
Ketcham, Ralph. From Colony to Country: The Revolu-
    tion in American Thought, 1750-1820. New York:
    Macmillan, 1974.
Kilpatrick, W.H. The Dutch Schools of New Netherland
    and Colonial New York. Washington, D.C.:
    Government Printing Office, 1912.
Loeper, John J. Going to School in 1776. Toronto:
    McClelland and Stewart, 1973.
Mason, Robert E. Educational Ideas in an American
    Society. University of Pittsburgh, Allyn and
    Bacon, 1960.
Mayer, Frederick. American Ideas and Education.
    Columbus, Ohio: Charles E. Merrill, 1964.
Monroe, Paul. Founding of the American Public
    School System. New York: Macmillan, 1940.
Morison, Samuel Eliot. The Intellectual Life of
    Colonial New England. Ithaca, N.Y.: Cornell
    University Press, 1960.

Noble, Stewart. A History of American Education.
    Westport, Conn.: Greenwood Press, 1970.
Noll, J.W. and S.P. Kelly. Foundations of Education
    in America. New York: Harper and Row, 1970.
Perkinson, H.J. Two Hundred Years of American Edu-
    cational Thought. New York: David McKay, 1976.
Potter, R.E. The Stream of American Education.
    New York: American Book Co., 1967.
Power, Edward. Education for American Democracy.
    New York: McGraw-Hill, 1965.
Pulliam, John D. History of Education in America.
    Columbus, Ohio: Charles E. Merrill, 1968.
Ragan, W.B. and George Henderson. Foundations of
    American Education. New York: Harper and Row,
    1970.
Reinhardt, Emma. American Education. New York:
    Harper, 1960.
Rippa, S. Alexander. Education in a Free Society,
    An American History. New York: David McKay,
    1971.
Rippa, S. Alexander (ed.). Educational Ideas in
    America, A Documentary History. New York:
    David McKay, 1969.
Russell, J.D. and Charles H. Judd. The American
    Educational System. Boston: Houghton Mifflin,
    1940.
Ryan, P.J. Historical Foundations of Public Educa-
    tion in America. Dubuque, Iowa: W.C. Brown
    Co., 1965.
Seybolt, Robert Francis. The Public School of
    Colonial Boston, 1635-1775. New York: Arno
    Press, 1969.
Sloane, Eric. The Little Red Schoolhouse. New
    York: Doubleday, 1972.
Slosson, Edwin E. The American Spirit in Education.
    New Haven: Yale University Press, 1921.
Small, W.H. Early New England Schools. Boston:
    Ginn, 1914.
Smith, Wilson. Theories in Education in Early
    America, 1655-1819. Bobbs-Merrill Co., Inc.,
    1973.

Thayer, V.T. Formative Ideas in American Education.
    New York: Dodd, Mead, 1969.
Thayer, V.T. The Role of the School in American
    Society. New York: Dodd, Mead, 1960.
Tyack, David B. Turning Points in American Educa-
    tional History. Toronto: Blaisdell, 1967.
Vassar, Rena L. Society History of American
    Education. Chicago: Rand McNally, 1965.
Vaughn, Alden T. America before the Revolution,
    1725-1775. Englewood Cliffs, N.J.: Prentice-
    Hall, 1967.
Vincent, W.A.L. The Grammar Schools: Their Con-
    tinuing Tradition, 1660-1714. London: Cox
    and Wyman, 1969.
Welter, Rush. Popular Education and Democratic
    Thought in America. New York: Columbia Uni-
    versity Press, 1962.
Wertenbaker, T.J. The Founding of American Civil-
    ization: The Middle Colonies. New York:
    Cooper Square Publishers Inc., 1963.
Woudy, Thomas. The Educational Views of Benjamin
    Franklin. New York: McGraw-Hill, 1931.
Wright, Louis B. The Cultural Life of the American
    Colonies, 1607-1763. New York: Harper and
    Row, 1962.
Wynn, Richard, et al. American Education. New
    York: McGraw Hill, 1977.

CHAPTER EIGHT

THE ENLIGHTENMENT

Aaron, Richard. John Locke. Oxford: Clarendon
    Press, 1971.
Adamson, J. (ed.). The Educational Writings of
    John Locke. Cambridge: University Press,
    1922.
Archer, R.L. Rousseau on Education. London:
    Edward Arnold, 1928
Axtell, J. The Educational Writings of John Locke.
    Cambridge: University Press, 1968.

Blanchard, W.R. Rousseau and the Spirit of Revolt.
    Ann Arbor: University of Michigan Press, 1967.
Bloom, Allan. Jean-Jacques Rousseau. New York:
    Basic Books, 1979.
Boyd, W. The Educational Theory of Jean-Jacques
    Rousseau. New York: Russell and Russell,
    1963.
Brauer, G.C. The Education of a Gentleman. New
    York: Bookman Associates, 1959.
Compayre, Gabriel. Jean Jacques Rousseau and Educa-
    tion from Nature. (trans. R.P. Jago) New York:
    Burt Franklin, 1971.
Cranston, Maurice. John Locke: A Biography. New
    York: Macmillan, 1957.
Davidson, T. Rousseau and Education according to
    Nature. New York: Charles Scribner's Sons,
    1971.
Doobs, A. Educational and Social Movements, 1700-
    1850. New York: A.M. Kelley, 1969.
Dobinson, C.H. Jean-Jacques Rousseau: His Thought
    and its Relevance Today. London: Methuen,
    1969.
Eliot, Charles W. (ed.). English Philosophers of
    the Seventeenth and Eighteenth Centuries.
    New York: Collier, 1938.
Garforth, F. (ed.). John Locke: Some Thoughts
    Concerning Education. New York: Barron's
    Educational Series, 1964.
Green, R.G. Jean Jacques Rousseau: A Critical
    Study of his Life and Writings. Cambridge,
    Mass.: Harvard University Press, 1956.
Huizinga, J.H. The Making of a Saint: The Tragi-
    Comedy of Jean-Jacques Rousseau. London:
    Hamilton, 1976.
Huizinga, J.H. Rousseau, The Self-Made Saint.
    New York: Grossman, 1976.
Jeffreys, M.V.C. John Locke: Prophet of Common
    Sense. London: Methuen, 1967.
Morley, John. Rousseau and his Era. London:
    Macmillan, 1923.

Morley, John. Voltaire and Rousseau. London:
    Macmillan, 1910.
Patterson, Sylvia W. Rousseau's Emile and Early
    Children's Literature. Metuchen, New Jersey:
    Scarecrow Press, 1971.
Plattner, Marc F. Rousseau's State of Nature: An
    Interpretation of the Discourse of Inequality.
    Dekalb, Ill.: University of Illinois Press,
    1979.
Roche, Kennedy F. Rousseau, Stoic and Romantic.
    London: Methuen, 1974.
Sahakian, M.L. John Locke. New York: Twayne
    Publishers, Inc., 1975.
Sahakian, M.L. and W.S. Rousseau as Educator.
    New York: Twayne Publishers, Inc., 1974.
Spurlin, Paul Merrill. Rousseau in America, 1760-
    1809. Alabama: University of Alabama Press,
    1969.
Winwar, Frances. Jean Jacques Rousseau, Conscience
    of an Era. New York: Random House, 1961.
Yolton, John W. John Locke and Education. New
    York: Random House, 1971.

CHAPTER NINE

THE NINETEENTH CENTURY

a) The United States

(see also the general works relating to American
education listed under Colonial_America)

Addams, Jane. Twenty Years at Hull House. New
    York: Macmillan, 1930.
Addams, Jane. The Second Twenty Years at Hull
    House. New York: Macmillan, 1930.
Anderson, G.L. Land Grant Universities and the
    Continuing Challenge. Lansing, Mich.:
    Michigan State University Press, 1976.

Arrowood, Charles F. Thomas Jefferson and Education in a Republic. New York: McGraw-Hill, 1930.
Bailyn, Bernard. Education in the Forming of American Society. New York: Random House, 1960.
Baylor, Ruth M. Elizabeth Palmer Peabody: Kindergarten Pioneer. Philadelphia: University of Pennsylvania Press, 1965.
Brickman, W.W. Educational Systems in the United States. New York: The Center for Applied Research in Education, Inc., 1964.
Briggs, Asa (ed.). The Nineteenth Century. New York: McGraw-Hill, 1970.
Brown, E.E. The Making of Our Middle Schools. New York: Longmans Green, 1905.
Brubacher, John S. Henry Barnard on Education. New York: McGraw-Hill, 1931.
Brubacher, John S. and R. Willis. Higher Education in Transition. New York: Harper and Row, 1958.
Brunner, Henry S. Land Grant Colleges and Universities, 1862-1962. Washington, D.C.: Government Printing Office, 1962.
Bullock, Henry A. A History of Negro Education in the South. Cambridge, Mass.: Harvard University Press, 1967.
Burstall, S.A. The Education of Girls in the United States. London: Sonnenschein, 1894.
Butts, R. Freeman. The American Tradition in Religion and Education. Boston: Beacon Press, 1960.
Butts, R. Freeman and Lawrence Cremin. A History of Education in American Culture. New York: Holt, Rinehart and Winston, 1953.
Caldwell, O.W. and S.A. Courtis. Then and Now in Education, 1845-1923. New York: World Book Co., 1924.
Chambliss, J.J. (ed.). Enlightenment and Social Progress: Education in the Nineteenth Century. Minneapolis: Burgess Publishing Co., 1971.

290

Church, Robert L. and Michael W. Sedlak. Education in the United States. New York: The Free Press, 1976.

Clift, Virgil A. (et al.). Negro Education in America. New York: Harper, 1962.

Cohen, Sol. Education in the United States: A Documentary History. New York: Random House, 1974.

Compayre, Gabriel. Horace Mann and the Public School in the United States. New York: Thomas Y. Crowell, 1907.

Conant, James B. Thomas Jefferson and the Development of American Public Education. Berkeley: University of California Press, 1962.

Cremin, Lawrence A. The American Common School. New York: Teachers College, Columbia University, 1951.

Cremin, Lawrence A. The Genius of American Education. New York: Random House, 1966.

Cremin, Lawrence A. The Republic and the School. New York: Teachers College, Columbia University, 1957.

Cubberley, Ellwood P. Changing Conceptions of Education. Boston: Houghton Mifflin, 1909.

Cubberley, Ellwood P. Public Education in the United States. Boston: Houghton Mifflin, 1947.

Culver, Raymond. Horace Mann and Religion in the Massachusetts Public Schools. New York: Arno Press, 1969.

Curti, Merle. The Social Ideas of American Educators. Totowa, N.J.: Littlefield, Adams, 1959.

Danforth, Eddy, Jr. College for Our Land and Time: The Land Grant Idea in American Education. New York: Harper, 1956.

Davis, R.B. Intellectual Life in Jefferson's Virginia, 1790-1830. Chapel Hill, N.C.: University of North Carolina Press, 1964.

Dearborn, Ned Harland. The Oswego Movement in American Education. New York: Teachers College, Columbia University, 1925.

291

Dexter, E.G. A History of Education in the United
    States. New York: Macmillan, 1904.
De Young, C.A. American Education. New York:
    McGraw-Hill, 1960.
Dillingham, C.T. Life and Works of Horace Mann.
    Boston: Lee and Shepard, 1925.
Downs, Robert B. Horace Mann, Champion of Public
    Schools. New York: Twayne Publishers, 1974.
Drake, W.E. The American School in Transition.
    Englewood Cliffs, N.J.: Prentice Hall, 1955.
Eddy, E.D. Colleges for Our Land and Time. New
    York: Harper, 1956.
Edwards, Newton and Herman G. Richey. The School
    in the American Social Order. Boston:
    Houghton Mifflin, 1947.
Fenner, M.S. and E.C. Fishburn. Pioneer American
    Educators. Washington, D.C.: National Educa-
    tion Association, 1954.
Filler, Louis. Horace Mann on the Crisis of
    Education. Yellow Springs, Ohio: Antioch
    Press, 1965.
Flexner, Abraham. Universities, American, English,
    German. New York: Oxford University Press,
    1930.
Good, H.G. A History of American Education. New
    York: Macmillan, 1962.
Gutek, Gerald L. An Historical Introduction to
    American Education. New York: Crowell, 1970.
Gutek, Gerald L. Joseph Neef: The Americanization
    of Pestalozzianism. Alabama: University of
    Alabama Press, 1978.
Harlan, Louis R. Booker T. Washington: The Making
    of a Black Leader. New York: Oxford Press,
    1972.
Harper, Charles R. A Century of Public Teacher
    Teacher Education. Washington, D.C.:
    National Education Association, 1939.
Healey, Robert M. Jefferson on Religion in Public
    Education. New Haven: Yale University Press,
    1962.
Heffron, Ida Casson. Francis Wayland Parker, A
    Biography. Los Angeles: Ivan Deach, Jr.,
    1934.

292

Henderson, John C. Thomas Jefferson's Views on
   Public Education. New York: Putnam, 1890.
Heslop, Robert D. Thomas Jefferson and Education.
   New York: Random House, 1969.
Hinsdale, B.A. Horace Mann and the Common School
   Revival in the United States. New York:
   Charles Scribner's Sons, 1913.
Hollis, Andrew P. The Contribution of the Oswego
   Normal School. Boston: D.C. Heath, 1898.
Honeywell, Roy J. The Educational Work of Thomas
   Jefferson. Cambridge, Mass: Harvard Univer-
   sity Press, 1931.
Hubbell, George Allen. Life of Horace Mann.
   Philadelphia: Fell Co., 1910.
Jackson, Sidney L. America's Struggle for Free
   Schools. Washington, D.C.: American Council
   on Public Affairs, 1942.
Katz, Michael B. The Irony of Early School Reform:
   Educational Innovation in Mid-Nineteenth
   Century Massachusetts. Cambridge, Mass:
   Harvard University Press, 1968.
Ketcham, Ralph. From Colony to Country: The
   Revolution in American Thought, 1750-1820.
   New York: Macmillan, 1974.
Kilpatrick, William H. Froebel's Kindergarten
   Principles Critically Examined. New York:
   Macmillan, 1916.
Kilpatrick, William H. The Montessori System
   Examined. Boston: Houghton Mifflin, 1914.
Knight, Edgar W. Education in the United States.
   New York: Ginn, 1941.
Krug, Edward A. The Shaping of the American High
   School. New York: Harper and Row, 1964.
Lee, Gordon C. Crusade Against Ignorance: Thomas
   Jefferson on Education. New York: Teachers
   College, Columbia University, 1961.
Matthews, B.J. Booker T. Washington: Education
   Inter-Racial Interpreter. London: S.C.M.
   Press, 1949.
McCluskey, Neil. Public Schools and Moral Education.
   New York: Columbia University Press, 1958.

McMaster, J.B. A School History of the United
    States. Chicago: American Book Co., 1897.
Messerli, Jonathan. Horace Mann, A Biography.
    New York: Alfred A. Knopf, 1972.
Monroe, Paul. The Founding of the American Public
    School System. New York: Macmillan, 1940.
Nevins, Allan. The State Universities and Democracy.
    Urbana: University of Illinois Press, 1962.
Padover, Saul K. Democracy by Thomas Jefferson.
    New York: Appleton-Century Co., 1939.
Parker, S. The History of Modern Elementary Educa-
    tion. New York: Ginn, 1912.
Perkinson, Henry J. The Imperfect Panacea: American
    Faith in Education, 1865-1965. New York:
    Random House, 1968.
Peterson, Merrill D. The Jefferson Image in the
    American Mind. New York: Oxford University
    Press, 1960.
Pruette, Loraine. G. Stanley Hall, A Biography of
    a Mind. New York: D. Appleton and Company,
    1926.
Randels, G.B. The Doctrines of Herbart in the
    United States. Philadelphia: University of
    Pennsylvania Press, 1909.
Reisner, E.H. The Evolution of the Common School.
    New York: Macmillan, 1930.
Ross, E.D. Democracy's College. New York: Arno
    Press, 1969.
Ross, E.D. The Kindergarten Crusade: The Estab-
    lishment of Preschool Education in the United
    States. Athens, Ohio: Ohio University Press,
    1976.
Rudolph, Frederick. The American College and
    University: A History. New York: Knopf,
    1962.
Rudolph, Frederick. Essays on Education in the
    Early Republic. Cambridge, Mass.: Harvard
    University Press, 1965.
Rugg, Harold. Culture and Education in America.
    Cambridge: Houghton Mifflin, 1940.

Russell, J.D. and C.H. Judd. The American Educational System. Cambridge: Houghton Mifflin, 1940.
Sizer, Theodore R. The Age of the Academics. New York: Teachers College, Columbia University, 1962.
Snyder, Agnes. Dauntless Women in Childhood Education. Washington, D.C.: Association for Childhood Education International, 1972.
Spencer, Samuel R. Jr. Booker T. Washington and the Negro's Place in American Life. Boston: Little, Brown, 1955.
Spodek, Bernard. Teaching in the Early Years. Englewood Cliffs, N.J.: Prentice Hall, 1972.
Standing, E.M. Maria Montessori: Her Life and Work. New York: Mentor Omega Books, 1962.
Strickland, C.E. and Charles Burgess. Stanley Hall: Health, Growth, and Heredity. New York: Teachers College, Columbia University, 1965.
Taylor, H.C. The Educational Significance of the Early Federal Land Ordinances. New York: Arno Press, 1969.
Thornbrough, Emma Lou. Booker T. Washington. Englewood Cliffs, N.J.: Prentice Hall, 1969.
Thursfield, Richard. Henry Barnard's Journal of Education. Baltimore: The John Hopkins Press, 1946.
Thwing, Charles F. A History of Higher Education in America. New York: Appleton, 1906.
Ulich, R. The Education of Nations. Cambridge: Harvard University Press, 1962.
Vanderwalker, N.C. The Kindergarten in American Education. New York: Macmillan, 1908.
Weber, Evelyn. The Kindergarten: Its Encounter with Education Thought in America. New York: Teachers College, Columbia University, 1969.
Williams, E.I.F. Horace Mann, Educational Statesman. New York: Macmillan, 1936.
Woody, Thomas. A History of Women's Education in the United States. Lancaster, Pa.: Science Press, 1929.

b)   England and Wales

Adamson, J.W. English Education, 1789-1902. New
   York: Cambridge University Press, 1964.
Archer, R.L. Secondary Education in the Nineteenth
   Century. Cambridge, England: Cambridge Univer-
   sity Press, 1921.
Armytage, W.H.G. Four Hundred Years of English
   Education. Cambridge, England: University
   Press, 1970.
Armytage, W.H.G. The German Influence on English
   Education. London: Routledge and Kegan, Paul,
   1969.
Balfour, G. Education Systems of Great Britain and
   Ireland. Oxford: Clarendon Press, 1903.
Barnard, H.C. A Short History of English Education
   from 1760. London: University of London Press,
   1961.
Baron, G. Society, Schools, and Progress in England.
   London: Pergamon Press, 1965.
Binns, H.B. A Century of Education, 1808-1908:
   History of the British and Foreign School
   Society. London: J.M. Dent, 1908.
Birchenough, C. History of Elementary Education in
   England and Wales. London: University Tutorial
   Press, 1930.
Clarke, I.C. Maria Edgeworth. London: Hutchinson,
   1949.
Cole, G.H.C. The Life of Robert Owen. New York:
   Macmillan, 1930.
Connell, W.F. The Educational Thought and Influence
   of Matthew Arnold. London: Routledge and
   Kegan Paul, 1950.
Compayre, Gabriel. Herbert Spencer and Scientific
   Education. New York: Thomas Y. Crowell, 1907.
Curtis, S.J. History of Education in Great Britain.
   Westport, Conn.: Greenwood Press, 1971.
De Montmorency, J.E.G. The Progress of Education
   in England. London: Knight and Co., 1904.

Evans, K.D. The Development and Structure of the
    English Educational System. London: University
    of London Press, 1975.
Findlay, J.J. Arnold of Rugby. Cambridge, England:
    University Press, 1897.
Fitch, J. Thomas and Matthew Arnold. New York:
    Charles Scribner's Sons, 1897.
Flexner, Abraham. Universities - American, English,
    German. New York: Oxford University Press,
    1930.
Garforth, F.D. (ed.). John Stuart Mill on Education.
    New York: Teachers College, Columbia Univer-
    sity, 1971.
Harrison, J.F. Quest for the New Moral World: Robert
    Owen and the Owenites in Britain and America.
    New York: Scribner, 1969.
Honey, J.R. de Symons. Tom Brown's Universe.
    London: Millington, 1977.
How, F.H. Six Great Schoolmasters. London:
    Methuen, 1904.
Hudson, J.W. The History of Adult Education. New
    York: A.M. Kelley, 1969.
Hurt, J. Education in Evolution (1800-70). London:
    Hart-Davis, 1971.
Hutchins, B.L. and A.A. Harrison. A History of
    Factory Legislation. London: University
    Press, 1902.
Jones, D.K. The Making of the Education System,
    1851-81. London: Routledge and Kegan Paul,
    1977.
Judges, A.V. Pioneers of English Education.
    Bridgeport, Conn.: Faber and Faber, 1952.
Kazamias, Andreas M. Herbert Spencer on Education.
    New York: Teachers College, Columbia Univer-
    sity, 1966.
McCann P. (ed.). Popular Education and Socializa-
    tion in the Nineteenth Century. London:
    Methuen, 1977.
Mack, Edward C. Public Schools and British Opinion,
    1780-1860. New York: Columbia University
    Press, 1939.

Mack, Edward C. Public Schools and British Opinion
    Since 1860. New York: Columbia University
    Press, 1941.
Musgrave, P.W. Society and Education in England
    Since 1800. London: Methuen, 1968.
Nash, Paul. Culture and The State: Matthew Arnold
    and Continental Education. New York: Teachers
    College, Columbia University, 1966.
Parkin, G.R. Edward Thring. London: Macmillan,
    1900.
Podmore, Frank. Robert Owen. New York: Augustus
    M. Kelley, Publisher, 1968.
Raikes, E. Dorothea Beale of Cheltenham. London:
    Constable, 1908.
Rogers, J. Old Public Schools of England. London:
    Batsford, 1938.
Saffin, N.W. Science, Religion, and Education in
    Britain, 1804-1904. Kilmore, Victoria:
    Lowden, 1973.
Salmon, D. Joseph Lancaster. London: Longmans
    Green, 1904.
Scott-James, R.A. (ed.). Education in Britain:
    Yesterday, Today, Tomorrow. London: Friedrich
    Muller, 1945.
Silver, H.C. English Education and the Radicals,
    1780-1850. London: Routledge and Kegan Paul,
    1975.
Silver, Harold. Robert Owen on Education. Cam-
    bridge, England: Cambridge University Press,
    1969.
Simon, B. and I. Bradley. The Victorian Public
    School. Dublin: Gill and Macmillan, 1975.
Smith, Frank. History of English Elementary Educa-
    tion, 1760-1902. New York: Kelley Publishers,
    1970.
Sturt, M. The Education of the People: A History
    of Primary Education in England and Wales dur-
    ing the Nineteenth Century. London:
    Routledge and Kegan Paul, 1967.
Sutherland, G. Elementary Education in the Nine-
    teenth Century. Oxford: Oxford University
    Press, 1973.

Walcott, F.G. The Origins of Culture and Anarchy:
    Matthew Arnold and Popular Education in England.
    Toronto: University of Toronto Press, 1970.
Wardle, David. English Popular Education, 1780-1970.
    Cambridge, England: Cambridge University Press,
    1970.
Webster, F.A.M. Our Great Public Schools. London:
    Ward, Lock, 1937.
Weinberg, Ian. The English Public School. New York:
    Atherton Press, 1966.

                    c) France

Anderson, R.D. Education in France, 1848-70.
    Oxford: Clarendon Press, 1975.
Barnard, H.C. Education and the French Revolution.
    Cambridge, England: University Press, 1969.
Barnard, H.C. The French Tradition in Education.
    Cambridge: University Press, 1922.
Buisson, F. and F.E. Farrington. French Education
    Ideals. New York: World Book Co., 1919.
Clifford-Vaughan, M. Social Conflict and Educa-
    tional Change in England and France, 1789-1848.
    Cambridge, England: University Press, 1971.
Farrington, F.E. French Secondary Schools. London:
    Longmans, Green, 1910.
Farrington, F.E. The Public Primary School System
    of France. New York: Teachers College,
    Columbia University, 1906.
Gershoy, Leo. The French Revolution and Napoleon.
    New York: Appleton-Century-Crofts, 1933.
Halls, W.D. Society, Schools, and Progress in France.
    Oxford: Pergamon Press, 1965.
Kandel, Isaac. The Reform of Secondary Education
    in France. New York: Teachers College Press,
    Columbia University, 1924.
Moody, J.N. French Education since Napoleon.
    Syracuse: Syracuse University Press, 1978

Reisner, E.H. Nationalism and Education since 1789.
    New York: Macmillan, 1922.
Ulich, Robert. The Education of Nations: A Com-
    parison in Historical Perspectives. Cambridge,
    Mass.: Harvard University Press, 1967.

                    d) Germany

Adams, J. The Herbartian Psychology Applied to
    Education. Boston: Heath, 1907.
Alexander, Thomas. The Prussian Elementary Schools.
    New York: Macmillan, 1919.
Anderson, Lewis F. Pestalozzi. New York: Mcgraw-
    Hill, 1931.
Bigler, Rudolf. Pestalozzi in Burgdorf. (trans.
    Klara S. Ingold) Logan, Utah: Utah University
    Press, 1972.
Bolton, F.E. The Secondary School System of Germany.
    New York: D. Appleton-Century Co., 1905.
Bowen, H. Courthope. Froebel and Education through
    Self-Activity. New York: Charles Scribner's
    Sons, 1909.
Cole, P.R. Herbart and Froebel: An Attempt at
    Synthesis. New York: Columbia University
    Press, 1907.
Compayre, Gabriel. Pestalozzi and Elementary Educa-
    tion. (trans. R.P. Jago) New York: Thomas Y.
    Crowell, 1907.
DeGarmo, Charles. Herbart and the Herbartians.
    New York: Charles Scribner's Sons, 1895.
Dunkel, Harold B. Herbart and Education. New York:
    Random House, 1969.
Dunkel, Harold. Herbart and Herbartianism.
    Chicago: University of Chicago Press, 1970.
Felkin, H.E. and E. Herbart's Science of Education.
    Boston: D.C. Heath, 1902.
Fletcher, S.S. and J. Welton. Froebel's Chief
    Writings on Education. Longman's Green, 1972.

                        300

Flexner, Abraham. Universities - American, English, German. New York: Oxford University Press, 1930.

Green, J.A. The Educational Ideas of Pestalozzi. New York: Greenwood Press, 1969.

Gutek, Gerald L. Pestalozzi and Education. New York: Random House, 1968.

Heafford, M.R. Pestalozzi: His Thought and its Relevance Today. London: Methuen, 1967.

Kilpatrick, W.H. Froebel's Kindergarten Principles Critically Examined. New York: Macmillan, 1916.

Kilpatrick, W.H. Heinrich Pestalozzi: The Education of Man. New York: Philosophical Library, 1951.

Krusi, Hermann. Pestalozzi, His Life, Work and Influence. New York: American Book Co., 1903.

Lawrence, Evelyn (ed.). Froebel and English Education. New York: Schocken Books, 1969.

Lilley, Irene M. Friedrich Froebel. London: Cambridge University Press, 1967.

Lilley, Irene M. Froebel: Writings. Cambridge: University Printing House, 1967.

Monroe, W. History of the Pestalozzian Movement. Syracuse, N.Y.: C.S. Bardeen, 1907.

Paulsen, Friedrich. German Education, Past and Present. New York: Charles Scribner's Sons, 1908.

Paulsen, Friedrich. German Universities and University Study. New York: Charles Scribner's Sons, 1906.

Pinloche, A. Pestalozzi and the Foundation of the Modern Elementary School. New York: Scribner, 1901.

Reisner, E.H. Nationalism and Education since 1789. New York: Macmillan, 1922.

Russell, J.E. German Higher Schools. London: Longmans Green, 1907.

Silber, Kate. Pestalozzi: The Man and his Work. New York: Schocken Books, 1973.

Snider, D.J. The Life of Friedrich Froebel. Chicago: Sigma Publishing Co., 1900.

Sweet, Paul R. Wilhelm von Humboldt, A Biography.
    Columbus: Ohio State University Press, 1978.
Walch, Mary R. Pestalozzi and the Pestalozzian
    Theory of Education. Washington: Catholic
    University Press, 1952.
Waltz, J.A. German Influence in American Education
    and Culture. Philadelphia: Carl Schurz
    Publishers, 1936.
Ulich, Robert. The Education of Nations: A Compar-
    ison in Historical Perspectives. Cambridge,
    Mass.: Harvard University Press, 1967.

                    e) China

Biggerstaff, K. The Earliest Modern Government
    Schools in China. Ithaca, N.Y.: Cornell
    University Press, 1961.
Ch'ai C. and Ch'ai W. Confucianism. New York:
    Barron's Education Series, 1973.
Creel, H. Confucius: The Man and the Myth. New
    York: John Day, 1949.
Galt, H.S. A History of Chinese Educational
    Institutions. London: Probsthain, 1951.
Ho, Ping-Ti. The Ladder of Success in Imperial
    China. New York: Columbia University Press,
    1962.
Menzel, J.M. (ed.). The Chinese Civil Service:
    Career Open to Talent. Boston: D.C. Heath,
    1963.
Nivison, D.S. and A.F. Wright. Confucianism in
    Action. Stanford, Cal.: Stanford University
    Press, 1959.
Smith, D. Confucius. New York: Charles Scribner's
    Sons, 1973.
Wu-chi, L. Confucius: His Life and his Time. New
    York: Philosophical Library, 1955.

f) Japan

Adams, D. Education and Modernization in Asia.
    Reading, Mass.: Addison-Wesley, 1970.
Bellah, R. Tokugawa Religion. New York: Free
    Press of Glencoe, 1957.
Dore, R.P. Education in Tokugawa Japan. Berkeley,
    University of California Press, 1965.
Kaigo, Tokiomi. Japanese Education. Tokyo:
    Society for International Cultural Relations,
    1965.
Keenleyside, H. and A.F. Thomas. History of Japanese
    Education. Tokyo: Hokuseido, 1937.
Kikuchi, Dairoku. Japanese Education. London: John
    Murray, 1909.
Passin, H. Society and Education in Japan. New York:
    Teachers College, Columbia University, 1966.
Young, Michael. The Rise of the Meritocracy.
    London: Penguin Books, 1961.

INDEX

A

Aachen, 45
Abelard, Peter, 57, 58,
  64
Aberdeen University, 66,
  172
Aberystwyth, University
  College of, 222f
Abiturienten Examen, 182,
  238
Academie Française, 117f
Academy (Athens), 10
Academy (England), 165,
  166
Academy (Franklin's),
  156-7
Adams, John, 192
Aelius Donatus, 39
Aeneid (Virgil), 29
Aesop's Fables, 97f
Agricola, Rudolf
  (Huysman), 80f
Alaric, 41
Albert the Great, 113
Albigensian heresy, 54,
  86, 113
Alcuin, 44, 45
Alexander the Great, 5
Alexander VI, Pope, 78,
  97f
Alexandria, 1, 35, 37
Al-Kowarizmi, 55f
Ambrose, Bishop, 40
Amish, 100f
Anabaptists, 100f, 164f
Andreae Johann Valentin,
  125
Angers University, 65

Anne (of Bohemia), 89
Anne, Queen (England),
  167f
Anne Boleyn, 93
Anselm, 58
Anthony, Saint, 37
Antioch, 35, 37
Aphrodite, 3f
Apollo, 3
Aquaviva, Claudius, 115
Aquinas, St. Thomas, 59
  60f, 113
Arianism, 35
Aristotle, 5, 17-20, 40,
  56f
Arnauld, Antoine, 118
Arnold, Matthew, 219
Arnold, Thomas, 218,
  219, 221f
Ars Minor (Donatus), 39
Ascham, Roger, 85
Athanasius, Saint, 37
Athens, 1, 2, 4, 7-20
Augsburg, (Treaty of),
  92
Augustine (of Canterbury),
  43
Augustine, Saint, 38,
  39f, 40, 44
Augustinian Friars, 54
Augustus, Emperor, 23
Averroes, 56
Avicenna, 62
Avignon, 65, 70, 88, 91,
  92

Boyce, Lord, 220f
Bradford, William, 130
Brahe, Tycho, 119, 120
Bramante, 75f
Brazenose College,
    (Oxford), 111
Brethren of the Common
    Life, 80
Brinsley, John, 112, 113
British and Foreign
    Schools Society, 211f,
    213
Brougham, Lord, 242
Brown College, 147f
Bruno, Saint, 53f
Bryn Mawr College, 203
Bude, Guillaume, 85
Bugenhagen, Johannes, 99
Burgdorf, 241, 243
Byzantine Empire, 33, 35,
    61

C

Cabot, John, 128
Cabral, 128
Cadoc, Saint, 42
Calliope, 13f
Calvin, John, 100-102,
    143, 144, 164f
Cambridge, (Mass.), 148f
    149
Cambridge Press, (Mass.)
    149
Cambridge University,
    (England), 61f, 65, 66,
    111, 121, 140, 146,
    159f, 215, 221, 222,223
Campanella, Tommaso, 124
Canterbury, 43
Capet (House of), 91
Capet, Hugh, 56

Cardiff University College,
    222f
Carmelites, 54
Carter, James, 197
Carthage, 22, 25, 26, 27
Carthage, (Council of),
    38
Carthusians, 53
Cartier, Jacques, 129
Cassianus, John, 37
Cassino, Monte, 59
Cassiodorus, 39, 40
Castiglione, Baldassare,
    75f, 78
Catechetical schools, 37
Catechumenical schools,
    37
Catherine of Aragon, 93,
    124f
Catherine the Great, 185-6
Cato, 26
Ceuta, 128
Chaeronea, (Battle of), 5
Charitable Trusts Act
    (England), 218
Charlemagne, 34, 35, 44,
    45, 47, 236
Charles I (England), 94,
    107, 158, 159
Charles II (England),
    158, 164, 165f, 174
Charles IV (Holy Roman
    Emperor), 92
Charles V (Spain), 70, 98
Charles VIII (France), 69,
    90
Charles X (France), 230
Charles Martel, 51
Charles, Rev. Thomas, 209
Charterhouse School, 216
Chartres University, 65
Cheever, Ezekiel, 148

307

308

La Salle, 173, 181
Lateran Council, (1179), 63
Latin Grammar (Lily), 149
Leibnitz, 121
Leipzig University, 180f, 183
Leo III, Pope, 34, 35
Leo X, Pope, 93f, 96
Leonard and Gertrude (Pestalozzi), 239, 240
Leonardo da Vinci, 75f
Leontium Pilatus, 73f
Lerins, 37
Letter to the Burgo-masters (Luther) 97
Leuctra (Battle of), 4
Liege, 65
Lincoln, 41
Livius Andronicus, 26
Livy, 29
Locke, John, 159, 166-172
Logic (Aristotle), 20
Loi Guizot, 230
Loi Falloux, 231
Lollards, 89
Lombard, Peter, 58
Lomonosov, Michael, 185
London Company, 130
London Missionary Society, 253
Lords of the Congregation (Scotland) 103
Lotharingia, 33
Louis VII, 65
Louis IX, 49f
Louis XIV, 91f, 160
Louis XV, 160
Louis XVI, 160
Louis of Bavaria, 92
Louis Philippe, 230

Louvain, 118
Lowe, Robert, 214
Loyola, Ignatius, 114
Ludus Literarius (Brinsley), 112
Luther, Martin, 86, 90, 92, 96, 97
Lyceum, 20
Lydia, 4

M

Machiavelli, 78, 84
Magyars, 34
Maimonides, 58f
Mainz University, 248
Makin, B., 111
Malherbi, 72f
Manhattan, 133
Mann, Horace, 197, 245
Marathon (Battle of), 4
Marlborough School, 218
Marriage of Philology and Mercury (Capella) 39
Mars, 3f
Marshall, (Chief Justice) John, 195
Martiannus Capella, 39
Martin, Saint, 37
Mary (Queen of England), 93, 103
Mary (Queen of Scots), 103
Maryland, 132
Massachusetts Bay Colony 130f, 131, 143-147
Massilia (Marseilles), 2, 25, 37
Materia Medica (Galen), 30

313

Naxos, 25
Nazareth Hall Academy, 142
Neapolis (Naples), 25
Neef, Joseph, 241f
Nestorius, 37
Neuhof, 238, 242
New Amsterdam, 133, 151
New Atlantis (Bacon), 123, 125
Newcastle Commission, 214
New Discovery of the Old Art of Teaching (Hoole), 110, 149f
New England Association of Colleges and Preparatory Schools, 205
New England Primer, 150
New Hampshire, 131, 147f
New Harmony, 212
New Haven, 131, 147f, 148
New Heloise (Rousseau), 176, 178
New Jersey, 133
Newnham Hall (Oxford), 222
Newton, Isaac, 120, 121
New York (State), 133, 141f, 194
New York, University of, 194
Nicaea, Council of, 35f
Niccolo III (d'Este), 75f
Nicholas III, Pope, 72
Nicole, Pierre, 118
Norbert, Saint, 53f
Norman Conquest, 91
North Carolina, 132, 191
North Carolina, University of, 194
Northwest Territory Ordinances, 192

Novum Organum (Bacon), 122
Nursia, 37

O

Oberlin College, 203
Odes (Horace), 29
Odyssey, (Homer), 26
Oglethorpe, James, 132, 142
Old Deluder Satan Act 145, 146
Olympic Games, 3, 18
On Manners and Laws of a Well-Ordered School (Comenius), 108
On the Duty of sending Children to School (Luther), 98
On the Education of a Christian Woman (Vives), 85
On the Education of a Prince (Bude), 85
On the Education of Children (Montaigne), 85
On the Liberal Education of Boys from the Beginning (Erasmus), 82
On the Manners of a Gentleman and on Liberal Studies (Vergario), 74
On Pedantry (Montaigne), 85
On the Right Method of Instruction (Erasmus), 82
On the Right Method of Instruction for Girls (Vives), 85

315

Oratory of Jesus (Oratorians), 117, 174, 224
Orbis Sensualium Pictus (Comenius), 108
Origen, 37, 38
Origenes (Cato), 27
Orleans University, 65
Ostrogoths, 24, 32, 40
Oswego, 199
Otto II (Germany), 56
Otto III (Germany), 56
Owen, Robert, 211, 212, 242
Oxford University, 61f, 65, 66, 111, 113, 140, 159f, 215, 221, 222

P

Pachomius, 37
Padarn, Saint, 42
Padua, University of, 63, 74f, 76, 113
Paestum, 25f
Palaestra, 10
Papal Index, 115f
Papal Schism, 70
Paris, University of, 47, 63, 65, 79f, 113, 118f
Parker, F.W., 199
Pascal, 118
Pastorius, Francis, 148f
Patrick, Saint, 42
Paul IV, Pope, 115f
Pavia, 62
Payment by Results, 214, 215
Peabody, Elizabeth, 200, 245
Peasants' Revolt, 88, 97

Peisistratus, 7
Peking University, 254
Pelagius, 42
Pell, John, 111f
Peloponnesian Wars, 4
Penn, William, 133, 152
Pennsylvania, 133, 134, 141f, 142, 148f, 152, 153, 191
Pennsylvania, University of, 157f
Pepin, Donation of, 34
Perry, Commodore, 262
Persia, 4
Persian Empire, 33
Pestalozzi, 238-242
Peter the Great, 185
Peterhouse College (Cambridge), 66
Petrarch, 50f, 72
Philanthropinum, 184
Philbrick, John, 198
Philip of Macedonia, 5
Philip II (Spain), 129f
Philip (Augustus) II (France), 51, 64
Philip IV (France), 70, 88, 91
Phillips Andover Academy, 157f
Phillips Exeter Academy, 157f
Pietists, 180, 182
Pilgrims, 130
Pius VII, Pope, 116f, 228, 247f
Plataea, (Battle of), 4
Plato, 9-17, 40, 252
Pliny, 29
Politics (Aristotle), 20
Polyhymnia, 13f

316

Pompey, 23f
Poor Law (England), 140
Port Royal, Little Schools
  of, 117, 118, 119
Portia, 63f
Positions (Mulcaster), 85
Praemonstratensians, 53
Prague University, 66
Presbyterian Church of
  Scotland, 172
Presbyterians, 142, 164
Prince, The (Machiavelli),
  78, 84f
Princeton College, 153
Principles of Christian
  Religion (Calvin), 100
Priscian, 39
Public Schools Act
  (England), 218
Punic Wars, 25
Puritans, 131, 143-150, 164
Pythian Games, 3

Q

Quadrivium, 39
Quakers, 133, 134, 151,
  164, 165f
Queen's College (Rutgers),
  151
Queen's University
  (Ireland), 223
Quesnay, François, 162
Quincy (Mass.), 199
Quintilian, 27-30, 74,
  76, 77f
Quiroga, Vasco de, 137

R

Rabelais, 85, 124
Racine, 161

Radcliffe College, 203
Raikes, Robert, 209
Raleigh, Sir Walter, 129
Raphael, 75f
Ratke, W., 104
Ratio Studiorum, 115
Ravenna, 62
Raymond (Bishop), 56f
Razan, Hayashi, 259
Recorde, Robert, 120
Reform Act (England),
  213
Reformed Librarie Keeper,
  The, (Dury), 110
Reformed School, The,
  (Dury), 110
Reims, 65
Repton College, 112f
Republic, The, (Plato),
  10
Revised Code (England),
  214
Rhode Island, 131, 147f
Ribot, Alexander, 234
Ricci, Matteo, 253
Richard II (England), 89
Richelieu, 121
Ritter, Carl, 242
Roanoke, 129
Robert II (France), 86
Robinson Crusoe (Defoe),
  177
Rolfe, John, 130
Rome, 22-31, 32, 34, 37,
  41
Rome, Council of, 45
Roscellinus, 58
Roses, Wars of The, 92
Rousseau, 162, 175-180
Royal Commission on
  Secondary Education
  (England), 220

317

Spener, Jacob, 180
Spens Report (England),
  220f
Speyer, Diet of, 98
Spiritual Milk for
  American Babes (Cotton),
  150
Stanz, 240
Statute of Artificers,
  (England), 140
Stevinus, Simon, 120
Stifel, Michael, 120
Stiles, Ezra, 193
Stockholm Academy, 174
Stonyhurst School, 112f
Sturm, Johann, 99, 101
Summa Theologica (Aquinas),
  59
Sun Yat-Sen, 253f
Sunday Schools, 209
Supremacy, Act of
  (England), 93, 95
Synod of Dort, 151

T

Tacitus, 29
Talleyrand, 226
Taylor, Hudson, 253
Tenchi (Emperor), 257
Tennant, William, 153
Terakoya, 260, 261
Terpsichore, 13f
Teutonic Knights, 52
Thalia, 13f
Thebes, 4
Thelema, (Rabelais), 124
Theodoric, 40
Theodosius, 30
Third Republic (France),
  231

Thirty Years War, 94,
  104
Thoughts Concerning
  Education (Locke), 167
Titian, 75f
Tohoku University, 267
Tokugawa Ieyasu, 258
Tokyo University, 265
Toleration Act (England),
  159, 166
Tonbridge School, 112f
Tordesillas, Treaty of,
  128
Torricelli, 120
Toulouse University, 65
Tours, 37, 45
Treatises on Government
  (Locke), 159
Trinity College (Cam-
  bridge), 66f, 111
Trinity College (Dublin),
  222
Trinity College (Oxford),
  111
Trivium, 39
Turks, 49, 70, 73f, 97f,
  98
Tudor Monarchy, 69
Tuskegee College, 203
Twelve Tables, 25, 31
Tyndale, William, 127f
Tz'u Hsi (Empress of
  China), 254

U

Ulpianus, 31
Uniformity, Act of,
  (England), 165
University College,
  London, 65f, 221

University College, Oxford, 66
University of France, 228
University of London, 221
University Tests Act (England), 222f
Uppingham School, 112f
Uppsala Academy, 174
Urania, 13f
Ursulines, 142f
Utopia, (More), 123, 137

V

Valentinian III, 35f
Valladolid University, 66
Valois, House of, 91
Vandals, 24, 32
Vassar College, 203
Venice University, 75
Verdun, Treaty of, 33
Vergerius, 74
Vermont, 191
Verrazano, 129
Vesalius, 120
Vespasian, 30
Victoria University (England), 222
Vienna University, 66, 113
Vikings, 34
Virgil, 29, 72
Virginia, 131, 132, 139, 140, 141, 142
Virginia Company, 139f
Visigoths, 24, 32, 41
Vives, 85
Voltaire, 162
Vulgate, 40

W

Wagaku Kodansho, 262

Waldensian heresy, 87, 113
Waldo, Peter, 87
Wales, University of, 222f
Walpole, Robert, 160f
Ward, Rev. Nathaniel, 144
Wars of the Roses, 69
Washington, George, 192
Watertown, Wisc., 245
Wealth of Nations (Smith), 162
Wearmouth, 43
Wellesley College, 203
Wellington, Duke of, 217f
Welsh Piety (Griffith Jones), 208
Wesley, Charles, 142
Wesley, John, 142
West India Company (Dutch), 133, 151
Westminster School, 112f, 216
Westphalia, Treaty of, 94
Whitbread, Samuel, 210f, 212
Whitby, Synod of, 43
Whitefield, George, 142, 143
Wilfred (Boniface), 44
Wilhelm II, Kaiser, 247
William I (The Conqueror), 51
William of Brabant, 57
William of Champeau, 64
William of Wykeham, 216
William and Mary College, 140f, 149f, 154
Williams, Roger, 131

320

Williamsburg, 140f
Winchester College, 112f,
   216, 217
Winthrop, John, 131
Wishart, George, 102
Wittenberg Church, 86, 96
Wittenberg University, 96,
   97f, 98, 99, 248
Wolsey, Cardinal, 111
Wright, Frank Lloyd, 244f
Wyclif, John, 88, 89,
   127f

X

Xavier, Francis, 114, 252

Y

Yale, Elihu, 147f
Yale College, 154
Yogaku (Western Learning),
   264
York, 41
Yverdun, 242, 243

Z

Zeus, 3f
Zumarraga, Juan de, 137
Zurich, 100
Zwingli, 99, 100, 102